Pragmatics: Teaching Speech Acts

Donna H. Tatsuki and Noël R. Houck

Maria Dantas-Whitney, Sarah Rilling, and Lilia Savova, Series Editors

TESOL Classroom Practice Series

Teachers of English to Speakers of Other Languages, Inc.

Typeset in ITC Galliard and Vag Rounded
by Capitol Communication Systems, Inc., Crofton, Maryland USA
Printed by United Graphics, Inc., Mattoon, Illinois USA
Indexed by Butler Indexing Services, Overland Park, Kansas USA

Teachers of English to Speakers of Other Languages, Inc.
1925 Ballenger Avenue, Suite 550
Alexandria, Virginia 22314 USA
Tel 703-836-0774 • Fax 703-836-6447 • E-mail tesol@tesol.org •
http://www.tesol.org/

Publishing Manager: Carol Edwards
Copy Editor: Kelly Graham
Additional Reader: Terrey Hatcher
Cover Design: Capitol Communication Systems, Inc.

ISBN 9781931185677
Library of Congress Control No. 2010927952

Table of Contents

Part II: Indirect Acts

Part III: Responding Acts

Part IV: Assessment

Dedication

To our loving spouses Shigeo and Michael,
who remind us daily of the importance of pragmatics.

Series Editors' Preface

The TESOL Classroom Practice Series showcases state-of-the-art curricula, materials, tasks, and activities reflecting emerging trends in language education and in the roles of teachers, learners, and the English language itself. The series seeks to build localized theories of language learning and teaching based on students' and teachers' unique experiences in and out of the classroom.

This series captures the dynamics of 21st-century ESOL classrooms. It reflects major shifts in authority from teacher-centered practices to collaborative learner- and learning-centered environments. The series acknowledges the growing number of English speakers globally, celebrates locally relevant curricula and materials, and emphasizes the importance of multilingual and multicultural competencies—a primary goal in teaching English as an international language. Furthermore, the series takes into account contemporary technological developments that provide new opportunities for information exchange and social and transactional communications.

Each volume in the series focuses on a particular communicative skill, learning environment, or instructional goal. Chapters within each volume represent practices in English for general, academic, vocational, and specific purposes. Readers will find examples of carefully researched and tested practices designed for different student populations (from young learners to adults, from beginning to advanced) in diverse settings (from pre-K–12 to college and postgraduate, from local to global, from formal to informal). A variety of methodological choices are also represented, including individual and collaborative tasks and curricular as well as extracurricular projects. Most important, these volumes invite readers into the conversation that considers and so constructs ESOL classroom practices as complex entities. We are indebted to the authors, their colleagues, and their students for being a part of this conversation.

Language teachers have long been aware of the devastating effect of learners' grammatically correct, yet situationally inappropriate spoken or written communication. This volume addresses how to raise learner awareness of pragmatic gaffs through field-tested activities such as e-mail requests, giving advice, making workplace requests, expressing opinions, providing constructive peer-to-peer critical feedback, negotiating refusals, and collaborating activities enabled by an online tool called Talkpoint. Teachers are given vital support in these activities through extensive worksheets, audio files, transcripts, and answer keys.

The chapters in this volume provide information and activities primarily related to the realization of speech acts and the effect of different contexts on their form. The subsequent volume, *Pragmatics: Teaching Natural Conversation*, focuses on the role of formulas in performing speech acts and on the characteristics of longer sequences.

Maria Dantas-Whitney, Western Oregon University
Sarah Rilling, Kent State University
Lilia Savova, Indiana University of Pennsylvania

CHAPTER 1

Pragmatics From Research to Practice: Teaching Speech Acts

Donna H. Tatsuki and Noël R. Houck

Pragmatics: "the study of language from the point of view of users, especially of the choices they make, the constraints they encounter in using language in social interaction, and the effects their use of language has on other participants in the act of communication."
—Crystal, 1985, p. 364

Language teachers have long been aware of the devastating effect of learners' grammatically correct, yet situationally inappropriate spoken or written communication. The study of speech acts, first characterized by Austin (1962) and developed by Searle (1969), offers one resource for addressing some of these instances. However, although native speakers generally have a strong sense of what constitutes appropriate speech for those activities and events in which they participate in their own speech communities, this knowledge is usually unavailable at a conscious level (Kasper, 1997). Even native speakers of a language require information on how to talk about what constitutes appropriate and inappropriate speech acts in different contexts.

Since the 1980s a body of research has accumulated on some of the characteristics of speech acts in a variety of languages, the most well known being the Cross-Cultural Speech Act Realization Project (CCSARP), a comparison of refusals and apologies across cultures (Blum-Kulka, House, & Kasper, 1989). These studies typically focused on linguistic strategies (often categorized in terms of level of directness)—the formulas or grammatical structures used to realize these strategies, the modifiers that can be used to soften or intensify the act or strategy, as well as the sequential management of the act within an ongoing interaction. They have also investigated the effects of social factors such as distance or power relationships between the interlocutors and the degree of imposition or difficulty involved in performing the act. Additional research on interlanguage pragmatics has not only identified strategies that do not conform to the target community norm, but suggested sources of these differences (e.g., effect of the first language [L1], learner proficiency level, learner reluctance to relinquish aspects of L1 identity).

Of primary relevance to English as a second language (ESL) and English as a foreign language (EFL) teachers is the research on effectiveness of different types of pragmatic instruction on second language (L2) learner awareness, comprehension, and production (Alcón Soler, 2005; Bardovi-Harlig, 2001; Jeon & Kaya, 2006; Kasper, 1997; Olshtain & Cohen, 1989; Rose, 2005; Takimoto, 2009). Although this research has profound relevance for language teachers, it is not easily accessible to those who are not deeply involved in the research literature. What is more, outside of dissertations and occasional conference presentations on effective teaching activities, with only a few exceptions (Bardovi-Harlig & Mahan-Taylor, 2003; Houck & Tatsuki, in press; Ishihara & Cohen, 2010; Tatsuki & Nishikawa, 2005; Uso-Juan & Martinez Flor, 2010), connections between the research and pedagogical practice have not been made available in a convenient form for the classroom.

Because native speakers do not have ready access to their own pragmatic competence, most classroom teachers who wish to teach some aspect of pragmatics need access to research results presented succinctly and clearly, with relevant information about how speech acts are performed. They need to know both the strategies and the grammatical forms generally employed, as well as how the social context (relationship to interlocutor, nature of the act) has been found to affect the choice of strategy or form and modifiers. They also need to be aware of variations in appropriateness norms among speech communities in general and in particular situations.

Once teachers are familiar with the strategies and forms generally used by native speakers in a particular community, they need to be able to determine what to teach and what level or type of competence to target with their students. Most importantly, they need access to effective materials and support for implementing the materials. This book attempts to address that need. Each chapter represents a set of field-tested activities, including (a) form-focused instruction on the act or sequence, as well as selected modification strategies; (b) awareness raising of the act and its modifiers; and (c) controlled and guided practice. Each chapter also offers extensive support for the teacher, with explanations of relevant characteristics of the act, along with notes on typical student problems, suggestions on how to implement activities, possible responses, and ideas for adapting the activities for different learner populations. Depending on learner characteristics (e.g., proficiency, need or desire to produce appropriate language), teachers may choose to use only selected awareness raising, identification exercises, or comprehension exercises.

The chapters in this volume provide information and activities primarily related to the realization of speech acts and the effect of different contexts on their forms. The subsequent volume, *Pragmatics: Teaching Natural Conversation*, focuses on the role of formulas in performing speech acts and on the characteristics of longer sequences, along with the interactional acts involved in producing them fluently, coherently, and appropriately, as revealed by conversation analysis research.

Chapter 2, "Misunderstandings: Pragmatic Glitches and Misfires," by Virginia LoCastro, offers a variety of activities including a series of critical incidents to help raise learner awareness of the kinds of pragmatic gaffs that occur between nonnative-English-speaking (NNES) and native-English-speaking (NES) interlocutors. The activities focus on the actual experiences of NNES students in a large university community in the southern part of the United States where mismatches in initiations and responses of nonnative English speakers and native English speakers led to problems in their conversational interactions.

Chapter 3, "It's 8 O'clock in the Morning—Are You Watching Television? Teaching Indirect Requests," by Zohreh R. Eslami and Kent D. McLeod, acknowledges the potential for volatile misunderstandings if learners are unaware of the role of indirectness and mitigation in English requests. To address this possibility, Eslami and McLeod create a series of activities to guide learners to develop awareness of directness levels and the ability to interpret indirect requests. Later activities focus on identifying different types of requests, collecting and analyzing natural data, and practicing request strategies in role-plays.

Chapter 4, "I Want You to Help Me: Learning to Soften English Requests," by Carol Rinnert and Chiaki Iwai, is based on extensive research indicating that some learners may produce more direct requests with fewer softeners due to a misconception of the appropriateness of direct strategies among native English speakers. The sequence of activities suggested by Rinnert and Iwai includes a prelistening activity, a listening activity, and a final self-diagnosis report. Guidelines for teachers include a set of appropriate and inappropriate request formulations based on requests produced by students in Rinnert and Iwai's pilot study, which are intended to help guide teachers in analyzing their own students' requests.

Chapter 5, "Requesting a Letter of Recommendation: Teaching Students to Write E-Mail Requests," by Kumiko Akikawa and Noriko Ishihara, tackles the problem of inappropriate e-mails that can result in denial of students' requests due to the unintentional offense they cause. The activities familiarize students with the cultural norms of e-mail requests, such as appropriate terms of address and discourse components, through awareness-raising analytical tasks and peer-guided discovery, culminating in a cooperative production task. These activities benefit all adult learners who may need to request a recommendation letter or to make some other high-stakes request.

Chapter 6, "Soften Up! Successful Requests in the Workplace," by Lynda Yates and Jacky Springall, focuses on the complex environment of the workplace, which is replete with power differences and requires the use of a variety of deference, rapport-building, and softening strategies. Because requests can be potentially risky even in one's native language, learners in the workplace need support and instruction at both the linguistic and the cultural level. Yates and Springall propose a series of activities that introduce the grammatical forms often used to soften requests and that also encourage cross-cultural comparisons.

Chapter 7, "Teacher, You Should Lose Some Weight: Advice Giving in English," by Noël R. Houck and John Fujimori, takes on students' apparently well-intentioned but sometimes disastrous attempts at advice giving. They begin with a diagnostic activity to discern students' current advice-giving skills and then systematically raise their awareness about and sensitivity to the levels of directness. In the final activities, students practice their newly honed advice-giving skills and consider tips on advice giving in general.

Chapter 8, "Moving Beyond 'In My Opinion': Teaching the Complexities of Expressing Opinion," by Kristin Bouton, Katy Curry, and Lawrence Bouton, notes the importance of developing the ability to recognize and express opinions appropriately. The activities, which were developed for an upper intermediate, nonacademic listening–speaking class, focus on two types of linguistic resources often used in the expression of opinions, but frequently ignored in discussions of opinion giving: (a) negative questions as opinions and (b) selected linguistic resources for softening and intensifying opinions.

Chapter 9, "Teaching Constructive Critical Feedback," by Thi Thuy Minh Nguyen and Helen Basturkmen, addresses the lack of attention to the language used to provide constructive critical feedback. The sequence of activities begins with awareness raising and the identification of feedback strategies, followed by activities designed to develop students' ability to recognize softeners and their sensitivity to directness levels. Students practice softening criticism by selecting appropriate softening markers to modify each turn in an academic writing advisory session. If teachers want to encourage peer editing and other collaborative learning activities, the preparation in this chapter is a must.

Chapter 10, "Indirect Complaints as a Conversational Strategy," by Dana Saito-Stehberger, notes that indirect complaining (grousing or griping) to a sympathetic ear is an integral part of the interactional life of some speech communities. In order to deepen social ties and enhance their ability to get to know others, learners need to become familiar with indirect complaints and their responses. The first activity raises learner awareness through a song by a "complaints choir," which is followed by another listening activity designed to practice recognition and identification skills. The third activity in the sequence focuses on responses with a special emphasis on commiseration, the most frequent response to indirect complaints in most English-speaking contexts. A matching and two guided-practice activities round out the chapter.

Chapter 11, "I'm Sorry—Can I Think About It? The Negotiation of Refusals in Academic and Nonacademic Contexts," by J. César Félix-Brasdefer and Kathleen Bardovi-Harlig, deals with refusals that are negotiated over several turns of an interaction rather than as a single response to an initiating act such as an invitation or an offer. After raising awareness that there are many ways to say "no" in response to a request or suggestion or invitation, learners are given a chance to listen for and identify where the refusal occurs within a negotiation sequence and then to analyze the various strategies employed. The chapter directs the teacher to a website that has a series of refusal situations on video.

Chapter 12, "They Made Me an Invitation I Couldn't Refuse: Teaching Refusal Strategies for Invitations," by Emma Archer, suggests that because even native speakers find refusing invitations tricky to accomplish, learners of English need support and instruction in refusal strategies and in ways of softening them. Archer suggests that the teacher begin by eliciting refusals to an invitation and then perform a visual–kinesthetic demonstration of the effect of a direct refusal by dropping a "breakable" on a hard surface. This is followed up by a discussion of softeners and several activities to develop a range of refusal strategies that employ them. A final discourse completion task offers an opportunity for controlled practice.

Chapter 13, "Online Collaboration for Pragmatic Development—Talkpoint Project," by Emi Yamanaka and Kenneth Fordyce, outlines an innovative series of collaborative activities used online with a Web-based teaching tool called Talkpoint. This is a unique opportunity for learners to have access to authentic and appropriate language examples, which "can then become the object of reflection, analysis, and discussion via direct communication with target language speakers in a partner class" (p. 196). Although the site offers opportunities on a wide range of speech acts and responses, the chapter outlines activities related to refusal situations.

Chapter 14, "Assessing Learners' Pragmatic Ability in the Classroom," by Noriko Ishihara, provides a set of rubrics for assessing learners' pragmatic ability in the target language. The chapter uses research-based information about how speech acts are actually realized to assess both pragmatic production and pragmatic assessment while raising pragmatic awareness. Assessment rubrics range from pure teacher assessments to teacher–learner collaborations to peer- and self-evaluations.

This volume on *Pragmatics: Teaching Speech Acts* makes a significant contribution to materials available to teachers who wish to teach speech acts. A few general comments are in order. It should be kept in mind at all times that pragmatic norms vary greatly not only between English-speaking countries, but within speech communities. Although the contributors have trialed these materials in classrooms around the world, for the most part, the norms represented in this volume are those of North American speech communities.

Furthermore, while the role of this volume is to provide materials for English teachers to raise learners' awareness of the norms of a set of English-speaking communities, we are not suggesting that learners should be required to follow these norms. Once they are aware of how the acts are performed by members of a relevant community, they can choose to adopt the forms or not. In addition, we are also not suggesting that it is solely the nonnative speaker's responsibility to adjust to local speakers' expectations (although see Cohen, 2008, for a persuasive argument for encouraging nonnative speakers to do so). Ideally, through contact with nonnative speakers, native speakers' awareness of different ways of doing things with words will also be raised, leading to beneficial relationships of mutual respect and acceptance.

Donna H. Tatsuki is a professor in the Graduate School for English Language Education and Research at Kobe City University of Foreign Studies in Japan. She is currently researching multiparty talk-in-interaction of Model United Nations simulations and the representations of gender and ethnicity in government approved language textbooks. She has taught in Canada and Japan.

Noël R. Houck is associate professor in the English and Foreign Languages Department at California State Polytechnic University Pomona in the United States. Her research centers on cross-cultural pragmatics and discourse analysis, with a focus on microanalysis of classroom discourse. She has taught and conducted research in Brazil, Mexico, and Japan.

CHAPTER 2

Misunderstandings: Pragmatic Glitches and Misfires

Virginia LoCastro

English as a second language (ESL) learners daily confront feelings of misunderstanding, confusion, and embarrassment as they negotiate university registration procedures, food purchases, leases, and a myriad of other tasks. Many commit to intensive English programs in anticipation of a time when they will be relatively proficient in English grammar and pronunciation. Few are aware of the other dimensions of communicative competence that entail learning and acquiring the local norms for making requests, accepting compliments, and performing many other speech acts.

A number of factors can cause a conversation among native English speakers and nonnative English speakers to dissolve into misunderstanding and stereotyping. The basic idea underlying speech acts is that when we speak, we are actually "acting," that is, carrying out an action. However, a *misfire* (i.e., something said with good intentions that is misunderstood) can result in misunderstanding as well as discomfort for the speaker and the addressee. The speaker or the addressee may be perceived as rude or aloof when each was "acting" based on a different set of rules.

Glitches and misunderstandings often arise from the fact that, even if speaker and listener share the same language, language use is embedded in the contextual framework each speaker brings. For example, if a greeting is made (e.g., "Hi, how are you?"), the speaker expects a response from the addressee (e.g., "Fine, thanks. How're you?"), not silence. Typically, an initiating speech act will be followed by a responding act. Some common examples of initiating–responding acts are offer–acceptance, request–refusal, and introduction–response. Here is an example of an introduction in which a professor introduces herself to a student:

A: Hello, my name is Virginia LoCastro.

B: Nice to meet you. My name is Song, Song Yunkuk.

Speakers can initiate a sequence. For example, a speaker can open a conversation with a greeting and then keep the conversation going by talking about the weather, discussing how the person likes being in a new environment, or inviting the person for coffee at a local café. Here is a sequence that could follow the introduction above:

A: You must be from South Korea. Is the weather as hot in Korea as it is here in Gainesville?

B: Hotter. So I like being here in Florida.

A: That's good. You're a new graduate student here, I understand. What are you interested in specializing in?

B: Well, I'm interested in sociolinguistics. Actually, I wanted to ask you if I could take your introductory course in sociolinguistics without having the prerequisite?

This exchange of talk at a welcoming party for new and continuing students is one example of how a sequence can develop out of a series of initiations and responses. Everyday talk is full of these apparently simple sequences.

However, these instances are embedded with the interlocutors' beliefs and values, which are especially noticeable when they come from different language and cultural backgrounds. For example, a casual, neighborly greeting in China is the equivalent of "Have you eaten yet?" However, just as in American English "Hi, how are you?" does not mean the speaker wants to know details about the addressee's health, the Chinese speaker does not expect information about the addressee's breakfast. A simple, vague response will do. Both cultures have greetings, but the content of the greetings differs.

A more salient cultural difference surfaces with a common speech act that nonnative English speakers comment on in their own accounts of the cultural differences they experience with stereotypically friendly North Americans. It is common for North Americans to end a conversation with a new acquaintance or casual friend by saying "Let's get together for lunch soon" or "We really have to do coffee sometime." The addressee may misinterpret the speaker's intentions, left wondering whether the North American sincerely means to set up time for supper or coffee, or whether the utterance is just a friendly, positive way to end a conversation. Depending on the cultural background of the addressee, the interpretation will vary, as in some countries (e.g., South Africa), dropping by unannounced at an acquaintance's home for coffee is commonplace.

This chapter introduces awareness-raising activities that focus on some of the causes of the glitches or misfires that arise when, for example, a speaker makes a request more directly than expected or uses an unanticipated slang expression. The context, conversational partners, and physical setting, among other features, are important aspects of everyday interactions.

CONTEXT

The situations described in this chapter are based on actual experiences of native-English-speaking (NES) and nonnative-English-speaking (NNES) students in a large university community in the southern part of the United States. Students in an undergraduate course on second language acquisition worked with conversational exchange partners whose first language was not standard English to discuss instances when misfires occurred. The mismatches occurred between the formulation of initiating and responding speech acts by NNES and NES students. The incidents were recounted by the NNES students to their NES partners because they had been misunderstood, or they themselves did not understand what had gone on.

These activities are based on ESL learners' experiences. In addition, they were field tested in graduate classes on teaching ESL in Tokyo (Temple University Japan) and Kobe (Kobe City University of Foreign Studies) with native speakers of English and Japanese, many of them teachers. Students completed the worksheets and provided responses with explanations, as well as critiques. Most of the students found the exercises informative, with some Japanese teachers of English commenting that these were the types of exercises their students needed. Adjustments were made in response to the students' extensive comments.

CURRICULUM, TASKS, MATERIALS 

The following section describes awareness-raising activities for intermediate- and upper-intermediate-level ESL classes. There are three separate but related activities (see Appendix for worksheets and answer keys). The first focuses on responses to a speech act initiated by a native English speaker. The second is composed of contributions to a conversation with responses that are regarded as inappropriate from a native English speaker's point of view. The third activity includes situations in which nonnative English speakers reported that they have difficulty interpreting and responding to the perceived meaning of a speech act by a native English speaker.

Each activity should take about 15–30 minutes, depending on the class size. The teacher can assign these activities together or at different times depending on the syllabus.

Activity 1: Understanding Inappropriate Responses

Instances of misunderstanding are sometimes referred to as *critical moments* (Brislin, Cushner, Cherrie, & Young, 1986), that is, events during which discomfort occurs on some level. Worksheet 1 (see Appendix) is composed of seven critical moments in which a nonnative English speaker is expected to respond to an utterance by a native English speaker. Three possible responses are given. As confirmed by native-English-speaker feedback, one response is definitely inappropriate and the other two range from adequate to most appropriate.

The activity can be carried out in a small-group discussion or, with a large class, in dyads or small groups with 3–4 students. Each participant should receive a copy of the worksheet or have access to shared copies.

Activity 2: Understanding Inappropriate Initiations

Activity 2 presents more real situations in which a nonnative English speaker made a comment or asked a question that was considered offensive by his or her addressee. Students are encouraged to analyze the situation and determine what aspects of the nonnative English speaker's utterance caused offense and why. As with Worksheet 1, Worksheet 2 (see Appendix) should be distributed to students, who can then work alone or in pairs or groups.

Activity 3: Understanding Initiations and Responding Appropriately

Activity 3 also provides instances of real situations in which nonnative English speakers were unable to interpret a native English speaker's talk or were unsure how to respond appropriately. As with the previous exercises, after the teacher distributes Worksheet 3 (see Appendix), students can work alone or in pairs or groups.

Activity 4: Following Up

Pair or group activities need to be brought to a close with follow-up activities that can also serve to solidify learning. Teachers can use a variety of activities. Some possible follow-up activities include the following.

Class Discussion

The teacher has the class come back together and then leads a discussion of each critical moment, eliciting contributions from the learners. This interactive review of the task could be organized by having students answer specific questions or by asking for summaries of each group discussion. The focus is on enabling the learners to understand the underlying cause of the critical moment and to develop their communication strategies so they can avoid similar incidents in their own lives.

Multiple Discussions

After working on the tasks in pairs or groups, the students can switch partners and work with a new group to discuss their answers to the questions. The teacher circulates, facilitating their work. Finally, the teacher brings everyone together for a whole-class review of the task.

Written Response

Writing tasks either can be assigned after the whole-class discussion or can replace the oral review of the tasks. The learners can write about their own experiences, react to the critical moments in the tasks, or make recommendations for handling difficult communicative situations. Their writing can be personal or take a more expository stance. The teacher may need to consider the students' wishes about sharing their more personal writing with their peers.

Outside Activity

For an outside-of-class speaking activity, the learners can interview friends and family members about their own critical moments and then report back to the class through speaking or writing activities.

REFLECTIONS 

This chapter has presented a set of activities designed to raise awareness and to stimulate discussion of how many English speakers use and interpret the intent and the appropriateness of language used to initiate and respond to various speech acts.

The activities can easily be modified for different groups of learners above the preintermediate level by adding a pretask session led by the teacher, simple readings about intercultural communication, or additional awareness-raising activities. More time could also be allowed for the tasks themselves.

Needless to say, pragmatic competence cannot be achieved solely through exposure to these activities. Rather they serve to raise awareness and provide a context for interpreting misunderstandings that may arise inside and outside of class. Teachers need to be aware of the need for great sensitivity in dealing with the content of the tasks because most ESL students can identify with one or more of the instances of misunderstanding presented.

Learners may need to be reminded that those native English speakers who are sensitive to cross-cultural differences will not usually jump to negative conclusions about the learner's intentions and that those native English speakers who respond negatively are missing an opportunity to broaden their awareness of the world beyond their community.

Virginia LoCastro is an associate professor in the linguistics program at the University of Florida in the United States. She has taught English, French, applied linguistics, and linguistics in Japan, Quebec, Mexico, Slovakia, and the United States. She teaches courses and conducts research in second language acquisition, discourse analysis, pragmatics, and intercultural communication.

APPENDIX: WORKSHEETS AND ANSWER KEYS 

Worksheet 1: Detecting Inappropriate Responding Acts

In our everyday activities, we all encounter moments in our communication with others when we realize that something has gone wrong. This can happen to both native and nonnative speakers of a language. These experiences may be "critical," as they can result in communication breakdowns or mistaken impressions about the speaker.

Directions:

- Read through the assigned worksheet and talk with your teacher if you need help in understanding the examples before beginning the task.
- Determine which responses would be considered natural by many native English speakers.
- Determine which response might be considered inappropriate by many native English speakers. Explain why.

Then discuss with classmates the choices given. One response is definitely inappropriate and the other two range from adequate to most appropriate. Provide explanations for the misfires of the possible responses. Then, if possible, suggest other responses and your reasons for them.

1. While in line at a sandwich shop, ordering food, Joe notices that a fellow graduate student, Mario, is not carrying a wallet and does not appear to have any money with him. Joe asks him, "How about if I treat you?" Mario nods his head and says:
   (a) Yes.
   (b) Oh, thank you so much.
   (c) I forgot my wallet. Thank you. It's my treat next time.
2. Marie presents her friend Fatimah with a CD of English music as a gift. Fatimah says:
   (a) Thank you. You shouldn't have done this for me.
   (b) Oh, I don't know what I can give you in return for your kindness.
   (c) Oh, great! I really appreciate your thinking about me.
3. Mark asks a fellow student, Luiz, if he wants to go have lunch after class. Luiz responds by saying:
   (a) I'm afraid I can't today. I've got a lot of work.
   (b) Hmm . . . I have to check with my family.
   (c) I cannot go.
4. Marty asks Ivan, a fellow graduate student, "Do you mind if I borrow your dictionary?" Ivan answers:
   (a) No.
   (b) Of course. Please take it.
   (c) Not at all.

5. When asked if he would like a cup of coffee at a friend's house, Hitoshi responds by saying:
    - (a) Well, I don't really drink coffee—do you have tea?
    - (b) Not right now.
    - (c) I don't drink coffee much.
6. Nita orders a drink at a Starbucks by saying:
    - (a) A caramel frappuccino, please.
    - (b) Could I have a caramel frappuccino?
    - (c) Give me a caramel frappuccino.
7. (a nonverbal response) In a food court, Rex asks if his friend Horst could get him some more salt when he goes to order his own food. Horst says:
    - (a) "OK," and goes off, gets his own food, and brings the salt with him.
    - (b) "So now I'm your personal servant."
    - (c) "Sure," and goes off, comes back with a saltshaker, puts it on the table and leaves to get his own food.

Worksheet 1: Answer Key With Suggested Interpretations

1. (b) or (c) are appropriate answers. (a) would be viewed as too direct and impolite.
2. (a) or (c) is acceptable. (b) implies the responder is only thinking of gifts in terms of reciprocity, a cultural concept that may be transferred from the first language culture.
3. (a) is most appropriate and (b) is adequate. (c) is too directly negative and therefore impolite. (c) would sound a lot better if the speaker preceded the refusal with "Sorry."
4. (a) is too direct and impolite. Both (b) and (c) would be acceptable.
5. (a) is acceptable. (b) may be appropriate with a close friend or family member, where politeness is not mandatory. (c) is rather direct and a bit odd.
6. (a) and (b) are fine. (c) can be a little abrupt, depending on how it is said. Even though some North Americans will order food in a Starbucks or restaurant very directly, not using the word "please" or the phrase "could you," it is much more appropriate to use "please" or be less direct. When in doubt, it is better to err on the side of politeness.
7. (a) is fine. Or if he perceived it as a special favor, the nonnative English speaker could joke, as in (b), "So now I'm your personal servant?" However, joking is very difficult for nonnative English speakers to carry off effectively, so it is not recommended. (c) indicates that the presumed attempt at friendliness on the part of the native English speaker—he was trying to show that he and his nonnative-English-speaking friend were on good terms by asking him to do a favor—was misunderstood by the nonnative English speaker. He seems to have seen it as a task to be completed before he got food for himself. Knowledge and an awareness of the signs of casual, campus friendliness and camaraderie would be useful for him.

Worksheet 2: Explaining Inappropriate Initiating Acts

In this task, you are asked to evaluate the contribution by the nonnative English speaker. Form a pair or a small group with classmates to discuss the critical moments. Try to answer the following questions for each one of the following situations.

(a) Who is involved? What is the context?

(b) What happened? What went wrong?

(c) How could this be avoided in the future?

1. A new nonnative-English-speaking (NNES) teaching assistant opened the first day of class with his students by attempting to make a joke and break the ice. He said to the class, "As you know, my pronunciation is really f***ing bad." [*Note: f***ing* represents a swear word that may be used by in casual conversations between students, but which cannot be used on network television or radio.]

2. While discussing their activities over the last weekend, a NNES male mentioned involving himself in social drinking and then asked the native-English-speaking (NES) female if she drank. When she responded that she was not 21 and chose not to drink very often or in public, he responded, "Are you Christian?"

3. A NNES female greeted people she met on the college campus by asking, "What's your problem?"

4. A NNES male attempted to close a conversation at the end of a conversational exchange meeting that a NES teacher was taping. The setting was outside at a picnic table near a classroom building. The nonnative English speaker suddenly stood up and said, "Let's go."

5. A NES male was attempting to use chopsticks to eat when a piece of food dropped on his plate. His NNES female companion commented, "You use chopsticks very well."

6. (a nonverbal "speech" act) A NNES female, upon being introduced to a native English speaker, ran up to the person and hugged her.

Worksheet 2: Answer Key

1. **Teaching Assistant (TA) Situations**
   (a) A TA and his class on the first day of class
   (b) The TA used a word that is not acceptable when used by teachers in a classroom. Students who use the word in class can be removed from class. The F-word is not permitted on public radio or television and is shocking to North Americans in many situations.
   (c) Teachers need to avoid any potentially offensive language in the classroom. When in doubt, do not say it!

2. **Religion as a Topic**
   (a) Two same-age students who do not know each other very well possibly before class
   (b) One student asked the other about her drinking habits. He then speculated about her religion. Questions about a person's drinking habits (when the other person has not introduced the topic) are usually inappropriate between acquaintances. Questions about someone else's religion are rarely acceptable.

(c) Avoid asking questions about another person's religion, politics, drinking habits, or sexual conduct unless the other person brings them up.

3. Greetings

(a) A nonnative English speaker greeting acquaintances on a college campus

(b) The nonnative English speaker uses an idiomatic greeting that is used with a very limited group of native English speakers. The phrase "What's your problem?" by itself is often used as a criticism.

(c) The speaker could use conventional greetings such as "Hi," "Hey," or "Hey, how's it going?"

4. "Let's Go!"

(a) The nonnative English speaker is probably either assisting the native English speaker with a project or working on his or her conversation. The two are outside at a school, probably during the school day.

(b) The nonnative English speaker signaled a desire to end the session by standing up and saying, "Let's go." Despite native English speakers' apparent casualness about many things, "closings" are very important, negotiated events. Several turns are usually required to close a conversation effectively and appropriately. Most native English speakers would be somewhat shocked by this type of behavior.

(c) The person who needs to leave should mention a reason for needing to end the session. After receiving the response, the person ending the session might want to apologize briefly and then negotiate a closing. For example, the nonnative English speaker might say, "I forgot to tell you—I have an appointment at 3:00 p.m., and I just noticed I need to leave now if I'm going to make it. I'm really sorry."

5. Compliment

(a) A NES adult male and NNES female were involved. This happened during a meal that required use of chopsticks. It seems that the native English speaker is not as adept at using chopsticks as his NNES female friend.

(b) The native English speaker dropped some food, and the nonnative English speaker responded with a compliment on his ability with chopsticks. The compliment called attention to the native English speaker's problem. A compliment on one's ability right after one has had a problem is commonly heard as sarcasm.

(c) In this situation, it is probably best to say nothing or perhaps comment on how slippery the chopsticks are or say something like "I have the same problem with Western style forks."

6. Hugs

(a) Two strangers, who are being introduced

(b) The nonnative English speaker hugged the native English speaker as a greeting. However, native English speakers rarely hug on first acquaintance. In some areas of the English-speaking world and among speakers of a particular social status, certain types of hugs are common among acquaintances. However, this is very rare among strangers.

(c) To avoid such situations, learners should observe what native English speakers do under different circumstances when greeting someone. When in doubt, they might offer their right hand to shake and say "It's nice to meet you."

Worksheet 3: Understanding Initiating Acts and Responding Appropriately

Read the following situations. Working in pairs or groups, first discuss what the problem is in each of the situations, and then give advice about how the nonnative English speaker in the situation should handle the problem. Be ready to present your findings and advice to the whole class.

1. What is meant when a native English speaker:
   (a) Says, "We should get together some time"?
   (b) Responds to a suggestion that a group of people go out for food after an evening class by saying, "I'm good"?
   (c) Tells a story using the present tense, for example, "So, then I go into the store and I see my old boyfriend with his new girlfriend"?
2. What should a speaker say in response?
   (a) When cashiers in supermarkets say, "Hi, how are you doing?"
   (b) When service workers end a transaction by saying, "Thank you. Have a nice day"?

Worksheet 3: Answer Key

1. (a) In this case, knowledge about sequences used to close conversations, which frequently include comments such as "Let's get together again soon," will be helpful. North Americans do not usually expect a follow-up to such a suggestion unless the speaker indicates a specific date. In response to closings such as "We should get together some time," the nonnative English speaker can also end the conversation by learning to say "That'd be nice" or "Sounds good" without intending it to be more than a polite response.

   (b) "I'm good" is an ambiguous colloquial expression. It can mean that the speaker is free and, in this case, wants to go out for supper. On the other hand, confusingly, someone who is satisfied with his or her current situation may also say "I'm good," so the phrase can also function as a refusal. Thus, it can be important to pay special attention to intonation, facial expression, and gesture, as well as context, and in the case of confusion to request clarification. It may not be wise for nonnative English speakers to use slang or colloquialisms. In this case, the nonnative English speaker could say "Sure, I'm free."

   (c) Here, this use of the *historic present* is a strategy on the part of the native English speaker to highlight what most made her angry about the situation she was recounting to her nonnative-English-speaking addressee. The historic present is used in many languages (e.g., French). The nonnative English speaker needs to be aware of this use of the historic present to understand that the speaker is really talking about the past. If confused, the nonnative English speaker could also have asked the native English speaker to explain when the story had taken place. It is always useful to have some strategies to get clarification or confirmation.

2. (a) Many nonnative English speakers come from countries where such greetings and closings do not occur in supermarkets. And in fact, there are regions of the United States where such use of language is rare or uncommon. The nonnative English speaker can learn a phrase to respond appropriately ("Fine, thank you," or, less formally, "Pretty good") while living in an area where this type of friendly talk is common.

   (b) An appropriate response would be "You too."

Requests

CHAPTER 3

It's 8 O'clock in the Morning—Are You Watching Television? Teaching Indirect Requests

Zohreh R. Eslami and Kent D. McLeod

Requests in English are often made using a wide range of subtle linguistic resources. Even speakers in a higher position of authority addressing subordinates often rely on a finely tuned understanding of the scale of directness to indirectness, the supportive moves that precede or follow requests to mitigate the impact, and the linguistic modifiers used to soften the message. If learners are unaware of the function of this indirectness, they may respond only to the form of the utterance and miss the true intent. As a consequence, the potential for misunderstanding by both interlocutors of each other's politeness is high. In response to the need to raise learners' awareness of the role of indirectness and mitigation in English, this chapter provides practical tasks for recognizing levels of directness and the mitigating moves and softeners that are so essential for making appropriate requests in English.

CONTEXT 

The following activities have been used primarily with intermediate English as a second language (ESL) learners in an intensive English program at a major university in the southwestern United States. However, we are confident that they could be successfully tailored to fit the needs of basic, as well as advanced, second language (L2) learners in both an ESL and an English as a foreign language (EFL) context.

According to Blum-Kulka, Danet, and Gherson (1985), a request is a preevent act that expresses a speaker's expectation about some prospective action, verbal or nonverbal, on the part of the hearer. The goals of a request include action (e.g., "Can you open the window?"), goods (e.g., "Can you pass me the salt?"), information (e.g., "Do you know who our teacher is going to be this semester?"), and permission (e.g., "May I leave early?"), and the appropriateness of a particular goal is determined by the social norms of the society in which the speech act is made.

In order to categorize the wide range of request types, Blum-Kulka, House, and Kasper (1989) developed a scale in the Cross Cultural Speech Act Realization Project (CCSARP). The scale is composed of nine subcategories grouped into three broad categories of request strategies depending on the degree of directness. These strategies can be grouped as follows:

1. Direct requests
    - Imperative ("Stop bothering me.")
    - Explicit requesting verb ("I *am asking* you to change your mind.")
    - Hedged requesting verb ("I *must ask* you to move to another table.")
2. Conventionally indirect requests
    - Intention derivable ("You'll have to leave.")
    - Statement of wanting ("*I'd like to* get a ride home with you.")
    - Suggestion formula ("*How about* helping your sister?")
    - Preparatory—using *could you/would you* phrasing in questions: ("*Could you* lend me a couple of dollars?")
3. Nonconventionally indirect requests
    - Strong hint—one that mentions the problem: ("Your room is a mess." [Request to straighten room])
    - Mild hint—one that does not mention the problem or solution explicitly: ("It's already 11 o'clock." [Request for companion to leave])

(adapted from Blum Kulka, House, & Kasper, 1989, pp. 278–280)

These categories are relatively standard. However, the terms "direct request" and "indirect request" can be misleading. Direct requests, as well as indirect intention-derivable and statement-of-wanting requests, can be perceived as orders or as rather pushy requests, depending on the content and context. Furthermore, intention-derivable and statement-of-wanting strategies are sometimes eliminated in discussions of requests (see Rinnert & Iwai, Chapter 4 of this volume).

The supportive moves used to mitigate (or aggravate) the force of a request can be either internal or external to the speech act itself. Internal modifications are part of the request itself and include softening words or phrases such as *please*, *just*, and *only*. External modifications can occur before or after the request. Blum-Kulka, House, and Kasper (1989, pp. 287–288) describe six types of external modifications in the CCSARP:

1. Preparatory ("I'd like to ask you something.")
2. Getting a precommitment ("Could you do me a favor?")
3. Grounder ("*I wasn't feeling good yesterday.* Could I borrow your notes?")
4. Disarmer ("*I know you're tired*, but . . .")
5. Promise of reward ("Can you call the rest of the club members? *I'll do it next time.*")
6. Imposition minimizer ("Would you help me with this problem, but *only if you have the time.*")

Levels of directness and mitigation are employed in rather subtle ways by native English speakers, which makes these linguistic resources ideal candidates for instruction.

CURRICULUM, TASKS, MATERIALS 

The following lesson focuses on developing an appreciation of the different levels of directness and the linguistic resources for expressing them, as well as raising awareness of some of the resources for mitigating requests. The activities illustrate the often subtle manner in which requests can be made.

The goals of this set of activities are to enable learners to distinguish between direct and indirect requests and to develop an initial awareness of softeners and their importance. (For a more detailed discussion of softeners, see Rinnert and Iwai, Chapter 4 of this volume.) This lesson includes activities involving (a) awareness of differences in directness levels, (b) analysis of a request from a movie, (c) practice recognizing different levels of directness, (d) collection of natural requests, (e) analysis of the collected requests, and (f) discussion of softeners and mitigation devices.

Activity 1: Developing Awareness of Directness Levels

The first step in developing learners' awareness of directness levels is activating their prior knowledge by asking them what they know about requesting in general and about requesting in English in particular. Questions such as "How is requesting in English similar to and different from requesting in your first language?" and "How does a higher status person ask a lower status person to do something?" can stimulate a discussion and prod students to think about request forms. Questions such as "How would you ask a younger brother to wash the dishes?" draw students' attention to their relationships with different people to whom they regularly make direct requests. A common result of this elicitation of requests is that most students provide extremely polite forms involving modals (e.g., "Would you please wash the dishes, Hyun Su?") or extremely direct forms using the imperative (e.g., "Wash the dishes, Miguel!") with few examples in between.

Once students begin to contribute examples, teachers can list them on the board. Then learners can examine the list for similarities and differences and comment on any that are found. Students generally note likenesses and variation among the requests such as the use of imperatives, modals, conditionals, softeners (e.g., *please, just, a little*), and external modifications (i.e., preparatory statement, precommitment, grounder, disarmer, promise of reward, and imposition minimizer, examples of which are presented in the previous section).

Activity 2: Interpreting a Request

Once students are aware of the existence of differences in the ways of making requests in English, the teacher can show a short clip from a movie titled *Pleasantville* (Ross, 1998; Scene 15: "A Red Rose," from approximately 36:55–37:22). The teacher may want to distribute Worksheet 1 (see Appendix) and go over the background of the scene before showing the clip. (Teachers who do not have access to the movie can rely solely on the text included in Worksheet 1.)

After watching the clip and answering the questions, students can discuss their answers with the rest of the class. By the end of the discussion, students should realize that the mother was expressing an indirect request for her son to turn off the television and come eat breakfast. The mother in this scene initially seems surprised (perhaps astonished) and concerned to find her teenage son engaged in an activity (watching television) that he normally did not do.

Activity 3: Identifying Different Request Types

At this point students are ready to learn about the wide variation in English requests. They need to begin to recognize that even though many North Americans are considered very direct, requests can sometimes be quite subtle. Worksheet 2 (see Appendix) presents an opportunity for learners to practice categorizing different possible request forms. If students are more advanced or culturally sophisticated, they could label each of the requests on the worksheet according to one of the nine directness level subcategories previously presented. (*Note:* The requests have been placed in the CCSARP format order from the most direct to the most nonconventionally indirect, but it might be more effective to scramble them; see Appendix for the answer key.)

After students complete the form, students can discuss their answers as a class. Teachers can use this opportunity to reinforce the notion that requests can be framed very differently to convey different levels of directness.

Activity 4: Collecting Natural Data

Activity 4 is a homework activity using Worksheet 3 (see Appendix). Students are required to collect naturalistic requests, focusing on the characteristics of the speaker and addressee and the situation (including the degree of imposition) in which the request is made. Teachers may want to go over the terminology on the worksheet before assigning the homework.

In an EFL setting in which students have little or no access to English speakers, students can collect data in their first language (L1). This option can be quite effective, as the translation of the request into English can be especially helpful in cases where there are clear differences or clear similarities between L1 and L2 norms. Alternatively, learners could work with a partner to create examples of direct and indirect requests given various scenarios.

At this point, students may need to be reminded of the importance of recognizing explicit and implicit request forms and the pragmatic variables associated with them. In particular, it can help if the teacher highlights the importance of considering variables such as distance and dominance between the interlocutors, as well as the level of imposition, when assessing the appropriateness of a request.

The last two activities focus on raising learners' awareness of and ability to produce a range of mitigation and softening techniques employed in making requests and their understanding of how these differ according to the interlocutors, situation, setting, distance, dominance, and imposition.

Activity 5: Analyzing Natural Data

Activity 5 requires students to look for patterns between settings and request formulations using the data they collected for their homework. It may be helpful for them to review what was learned from the previous lesson exploring the differences between direct and indirect requests. In this activity, students' attention is drawn to the characteristics or the situations and the speakers of particular requests. They will then consider what kinds of mitigation and softening devices were used. Worksheet 4 (see Appendix) can also be completed on the board or on a transparency as a follow-up to small-group work.

After students have worked through several of their fellow students' worksheets, the teacher may have a group present some of their unordered requests and situations and have class members predict which request matches up with which setting characteristics. The teacher may want to direct learners to any differences in mitigation and softening between males and females and formal or informal situations. Learners could also be asked how they feel about the use and amount of mitigation in the collected requests as a point of comparison with their own cultures.

During this activity, it may be beneficial for the teacher to provide explicit instances that he or she feels are important for learners to become aware of and acquire. As previously discussed in the Context section, some particularly common forms and formulas include:

1. Internal modifications
    - *please, just, um, cool, OK,* and *only*
    - *It would be . . . if you could . . .*
    - *for a moment/for a little while*
    - *I was wondering if . . .*
    - *Would it be possible/all right/OK/etc. . . .*
2. External modifications such as those discussed in the Context section

Activity 6: Practicing in Role-Plays

To provide opportunities to practice mitigation or softening in requests, teachers can make role-play cards with information about the characteristics of the interlocutors, setting, situation, and request (see Activity 6 in the Appendix for an example with a suggested answer).

Students can write down and submit their requests. Time permitting, one or two pairs could perform in front of the whole class followed by a brief discussion of the appropriateness of the request.

REFLECTIONS 

The lessons presented illustrate the oftentimes subtle manner in which requests can be made, the scale of directness to indirectness, and the supportive moves that precede or follow requests in order to mitigate the impact. Additionally, the usefulness of authentic audiovisual input in the improvement of learners' pragmatic awareness and production of requests in both ESL and EFL contexts is clearly evident in these lesson plans.

In particular, these activities can be readily adapted to the needs of basic, as well as advanced, learners of all ages and in both ESL and EFL contexts. Irrespective of the characteristics of the group, the selection of media or examples should reflect an appreciation for their proficiency level, interest, maturity, and environment. For younger learners, for example, the selection of animation or comic books would be a popular choice. For learners in an EFL context, where the availability of authentic materials may be somewhat circumscribed, the translation of native language media could offer excellent opportunities for cross-cultural exploration of requests in the native and target languages.

Of course, one of the challenges of the language used in media is that it may not represent authentic language use. However, with the popularity of reality television shows (e.g., *Survivor*) more genuine sources of language are increasingly available. Furthermore, the level of difficulty of the language used in these programs should match the students' level of language proficiency.

Zohreh R. Eslami is an associate professor of ESL education at Texas A&M University in College Station, Texas. She has a joint appointment with Texas A&M University at Qatar. Her research interests include sociocultural aspects of ESL teaching and assessment, intercultural and developmental pragmatics, English for academic purposes, and ESL teacher education.

Kent D. McLeod is a lecturer in the English Language Institute at Texas A&M University in the United States. His professional interests include culture shock, issues associated with English as an international language, and the use of technology in the classroom. He has taught in the United States and South Korea.

APPENDIX 

Worksheet 1: Video Exercise

You are about to see a short video clip taken from a North American movie about two teenagers, a brother and sister, who are pulled into a 1950s television show. The video clip contains an interaction between a mother and her son. It begins with a teenage boy watching television as his mother enters the room. As soon becomes evident, it is 8:00 a.m. and time for breakfast before heading off to school. The following interaction takes place:

Mother: It's 8 o'clock in the morning. Are you watching television?

Boy: (Gestures toward the television with an exasperated look on his face as if to say, "Of course I am. Isn't it obvious?")

Answer the following questions:

1. How do you interpret the mother's comment and question?
2. How do you feel the mother's comment affects possible interpretations of her question?
3. Did you recognize the mother's question as an indirect request or did you think it was simply a yes or no question?
4. Would this happen in your home? If not, how would your mother have asked you to turn off the television and come to breakfast before heading off to school?

Worksheet 2: Identifying Request Directness Levels

Individually or in small groups, identify the following requests as either direct, indirect, or neither:

1. Turn off the television now! It's time for breakfast.
2. I'm asking you to turn off the television, son.
3. I would like to ask you to turn off the television now and come to breakfast.
4. You have to turn off that television, son.
5. I really wish you'd turn off that television.
6. How about turning off the television now?
7. Son, your breakfast is getting cold. Why don't you come into the kitchen and eat?
8. I don't want you to be late for school, son. Could you turn off the television now?
9. I don't know why I even bother to make breakfast for you.
10. I know that can't be the television I hear.
11. You know how I feel about watching television in the morning.
12. I'm sorry I forgot to make breakfast today.
13. Oh! What's on television?
14. That's my favorite program, son.

Worksheet 2: Answer Key

1. direct; imperative
2. direct; explicit requesting verb
3. direct; hedged requesting verb
4. conventional indirect; intention derivable
5. conventional indirect; statement of wanting
6. conventional indirect; suggestion formula
7. conventional indirect; suggestion formula with external modification
8. conventional indirect; *could you* phrasing in question with external modification
9. nonconventional indirect; strong hint
10. nonconventional indirect; mild hint
11. nonconventional indirect; mild hint
12. neither
13. neither
14. neither

Worksheet 3: Homework—Collecting Requests

Directions:

1. Collect five examples of requests in English. You can listen for requests in your favorite television programs, movies, music, or even in conversations around you. You can also find examples in print media, such as magazines, newspapers, websites, comic books, or books.
2. Identify the characteristics of the request situation. Include the following information:
   - Speaker and addressee—gender, age, and any other relevant information
   - Speaker's social distance—close friend, acquaintance, stranger, etc.
   - Speaker's dominance—superior, equal, subordinate, etc.
   - Degree of imposition involved in the request—high, medium, low
   - Situation—what the speaker and addressee are involved in doing
   - Setting—where the speaker and addressee are
3. Analyze whether the request is direct or indirect.

***Note:* You may want to use the following form to organize your data:**

Request #: ____

Speaker: ____

Addressee: ____

Speaker's social distance: ____________ Speaker's dominance: __________

Imposition: _____________ Situation: __________________________

Setting: __________________________ Directness level: _______________

Worksheet 4: Matching Requests With Situations

Part I: On the sheet below, write down the request and the setting of three of the examples you collected for homework in random order. For example, you might write your first request in slot #1 and the situational characteristics of the first request in slot #3.

	Request	Situation Characteristics
1.	____________________	________________________
		________________________
		________________________
2.	____________________	________________________
		________________________
		________________________
		________________________
3.	____________________	________________________
		________________________
		________________________
		________________________

Part II: With a partner or in a small group, look at each other's requests and try to match up each request with its setting.

1. Explain your rationale for each pair including the following:
   - Describe the specific nature of the request.
   - Make a guess about the characteristics of the interlocutors (in terms of gender, age, occupation) and their relationship.
2. Identify any mitigation and softening techniques and speculate as to why they were used.

Activity 6: Example Role-Play Card

Request:	Ask your teacher to let you turn in your homework a day late.
Speakers:	Teacher and student
Setting:	Classroom after class has finished

Activity 6: Suggested Answer

Student: Excuse me, Dr. McLeod. I've had a family emergency, so I was wondering if it would be OK if I turned in my homework tomorrow.

CHAPTER 4

I Want You to Help Me: Learning to Soften English Requests

Carol Rinnert and Chiaki Iwai

The goal of this chapter is to raise students' awareness about the need for softening (and for indirectness strategies) in requests through listening activities[1] designed to stimulate discussion of what makes a request more or less appropriate, along with opportunities for students to produce requests and evaluate their appropriateness. It is particularly relevant to teachers whose students produce direct requests in English either because they transfer strategies from their first language (L1) or because they assume that English speakers are naturally direct.

Requests represent complex, difficult pragmatic skills (Alcón Soler, 2005; Blum-Kulka, 1987; Brown & Levinson, 1987; Kobayashi & Rinnert, 2003, to name but a few). The instructional approach in this chapter is based on results from our own previous research, as well as research by others (Fukushima, 1990), which has suggested that cross-cultural variation in request realization can cause difficulties for Japanese students of English as a foreign language (EFL). For example, Japanese students tend to produce more direct strategies (Iwai & Rinnert, 2001) and use fewer softeners when making English requests (Iwai & Rinnert, 2002; Nogami, 2005). They also tend to judge such direct strategies as more appropriate than native English speakers do (Kitao, 1990). These judgments correspond with evaluations of Japanese L1 direct requests (e.g., "*hon-o misete,*" "show me the book") as being appropriate among friends, in contrast to English L1 judgments of comparable direct requests as relatively inappropriate in the same situations (Rinnert, 1999). Thus, this chapter highlights the ways that indirect strategies and softeners are selected, even in the most intimate relationships, to fit the magnitude of the imposition that each request involves.

[1] The audio files and transcripts for this chapter are available at http://www.tesolmedia.com/books/pragmatics. The transcripts also appear in Appendix C.

CONTEXT

In response to a lack of resources targeting the politeness requirements of requests among close friends and intimates, we developed and piloted a set of activities designed to raise students' awareness of how indirect and softened requests are used in natural native-English-speaking (NES) interaction. These activities were designed to highlight the fact that on many occasions it is appropriate to make requests in English indirectly and softly, even when speaking with friends and family members.

The original pilot consisted of activities based on four video clips excerpted from two North American television shows and a North American movie, each of which contained a request to an intimate (e.g., son, sister, close friend). The activities were quite effective at raising students' awareness of the need for softeners even in requests to intimates. However, the video clips produced unexpected results. In particular, although the language was naturalistic, it was scripted and thus, as Rose (1997) pointed out is often the case, more stylistically interesting and clever than ordinary everyday requests. This was especially problematic as students who had produced appropriate requests often later rejected them in favor of the request in the video clip.

The activities on which the activities in this chapter are based were piloted on intermediate to advanced students in the international studies faculty of a relatively competitive public university in western Japan. The main goal of this class was for students to learn how to give speeches and ask and answer questions about their speeches. The actual instruction was conducted in two sessions of 45 minutes (about half of the whole class time) in two consecutive weeks.

Participants engaged actively in the tasks in both sessions. Most of the requests the students first wrote in response to high imposition situations were direct formulas or simple, conventionally indirect formulas with little or no softening. These were not appropriate. Once they were aware of the shortcomings of these forms, students showed considerable interest in learning to make indirect, mitigated requests. Some of them expressed admiration for the new request formulations they were exposed to, and a number attempted to use some of what they had learned the first week in a new context the following week.

The activities in this chapter are based on two of the original piloted activities, emphasizing those aspects of the activities that were most effective at raising students' awareness of the importance of softeners and indirectness in effective, appropriate English requests, often even to close friends and relatives.

As mentioned by Eslami and McLeod (Chapter 3 of this volume), requests are commonly categorized into three levels of directness (Blum-Kulka, House, & Kasper, 1989):

1. Direct ("Lend me the book.")
2. Conventionally indirect ("Will you lend me the book?" or "Can I borrow the book?")

3. Nonconventionally indirect—hints: ("Do you have the book?" or "I forgot to bring my book.")

In addition to differing levels of directness, requests at any directness level can be softened in a variety of ways. The Cross-Cultural Speech Act Realization Project (CCSARP) Coding Manual contains a comprehensive list of common ways of softening requests, including syntactic and lexical downgraders and mitigating supportive moves (Blum-Kulka, House, & Kasper, 1989, pp. 281–288). Examples of English softeners include the following:

1. Past-tense marking (e.g., *could you* instead of *can you*, *did you* instead of *do you*)
2. *Please*
3. Hesitation markers (e.g., *um, well*)
4. Preparatory expressions leading up to the request (e.g., *I was wondering, If it isn't too much trouble*)

Appendix A provides a chart that lists the specific subtypes of direct, conventionally indirect, and nonconventionally indirect strategies, each with various degrees of softening, using the softeners listed in the previous paragraph.

CURRICULUM, TASKS, MATERIALS 

The instructional materials consist of a sequence of activities based on short dialogues adapted from dialogues used in television dramas involving requests between siblings or friends. In each case, the speakers are socially close but nevertheless use indirect or mitigated request formulations in natural-sounding ways. The key activities—a prelistening activity, a listening activity, and a final self-diagnosis report—draw students' attention to forms that can make the difference between a friendly, appropriate request and a rude, inappropriate one. A group discussion and a whole-class discussion are also introduced for use after students have completed their analysis of the first three dialogues. In addition, examples of appropriate and inappropriate request formulations based on requests produced by students in the pilot study are provided to help guide teachers in analyzing their own students' requests.

The first set of activities focuses on an interaction between siblings. The weight of the impositions of the requests in these scenes varies from very low (asking a sister to clean up after dinner) to very high (asking a sister to move out and find another place to live).

In the first activity, the learners are invited to produce their own written utterances (prelistening activity) in specific situations. This approach is based on Swain's (1996) output hypothesis, which asserts, as one of the four benefits, the potentially important role of learners' *noticing* during the process of language production.

Activity 1: Prelistening Prompt

The first activity (see Worksheet 1 in Appendix B) presents a description of three similar situations, in which three different requests must be supplied by the students. A blank has been inserted where the request occurs, and students are instructed to fill in what they would consider to be an appropriate request in that situation. The teacher can read the dialogue aloud with a student or ask two students to read it, leaving out the missing request. After the dialogue is performed, students can be asked to write their own request utterances in the space provided on the handout.

The three requests described in Worksheet 1 are all directed to an intimate, the speaker's sister. However, they involve different degrees of imposition. The first is the least imposing, whereas the last has the greatest potential for harming the relationship between the speaker and hearer. The answer key for Worksheet 1 (see Appendix B) provides examples of typical inappropriate student responses to the high imposition request, with a brief explanation.

Activity 2: Group Discussion

It is beneficial to present alternative formulations for the same situation (see Eslami & McLeod, Chapter 3 in this volume, for an example) including both highly appropriate and "dangerous" strategies in terms of potential harm to the social relationship (e.g., *want* statements and direct requests without *please*). After all the students have written in their requests for the three situations (using Worksheet 1), the class can divide into groups with four or five members. Group members will compare their individual responses and decide on the best one, including the reasons for their choices, for each of the three requests. As students discuss their answers with one another, the teacher can distribute the Problem Response Sheet (see Worksheet 2 in Appendix B). Students then can consider how these responses differ from those they are discussing. The Problem Response Sheet contains the same situation descriptions and dialogues, with potentially problematic sample request formulations (direct or unmitigated requests) inserted.

It is important to explain clearly that the sample responses do not, in this case, represent effective strategies. The answer key for Worksheet 2 (see Appendix B) provides possible explanations and answers.

Activity 3: Whole-Class Discussion

At this point the groups can share the results of their discussion with the class, focusing on the formulation they prefer and their reasons. The teacher or students from the different groups can write the top selection from each group on the board. The teacher can comment on such features as directness, indirectness, and particularly on the use of softeners. In addition, he or she can point out those formulas that seem particularly effective or appropriate.

Activity 4: Listening to Requests

In this activity (see Worksheet 3 in Appendix B), students listen to recordings of the three interactions with relatively natural requests. Students work with transcripts of the dialogues (see Appendix C) that include the request formulations used in the audio clips. After playing the audio clips, the teacher can review the actual language used and point out the relevant indirectness and softening employed. This provides an excellent opportunity for students to comment, offer interpretations, and ask any questions that may have come up.

At this point, the teacher may wish to provide an explicit explanation of some of the different strategies or softening devices, making it clear that the form used in the audio is not the only acceptable response. The chart in Appendix A provides a resource for this discussion.

Activity 5: Self-Diagnosis Report

In this activity, using the Self-Diagnosis Report Sheet (see Worksheet 4 in Appendix B), the student writes the first request chosen in Activity 1, then writes the request he or she now thinks is most appropriate after completing the instructional procedures. Finally, the student explains the reasons for these preferences (in English or the L1, if the teacher understands the L1).

When they have completed the self-diagnosis reports, students hand them in to be checked and returned by the teacher in a future class. The teacher may wish to remind students once again that the requests made in the audio are not necessarily better than those they have come up with themselves. Note that despite this warning, students tend to choose the model in the audio. They need to be reassured that if they have produced responses with the appropriate level of indirectness and softening, they are on the right track.

The teacher reads the self-diagnosis reports and writes comments and suggestions on them. This is a chance to provide individualized feedback, as well as correction of students' choice of language and pragmatic strategies, which many learners have been found to favor strongly (see Katayama, 2007a, 2007b).

When the self-diagnosis reports are returned in a later class, the teacher has an excellent opportunity to explain to the whole class any recurring problems with their use of appropriate pragmatic language and to share some of the more interesting alternative formulations that have been reported. It is worth emphasizing again the use of indirect, softened requests in English, even among people who are very close.

A review of the summary of the directness levels and softening strategies for English requests provided in Appendix A can also be helpful at this point. In particular, the teacher may want to reemphasize the inappropriateness of using such formulas as "*I want you to . . .*" and "*I would like you to . . .*" with peers. Formulas such as these may be translated from the L1, in which they represent polite, appropriate strategies (Rinnert, 1999).

Follow-Up Activity

For teachers who would like to recycle the activity with different situations, we have provided Worksheet 5 (see Appendix B), audio files, and transcripts (see Appendix C) that can be played as a listening activity.

Students will most likely come up with a variety of answers, some of which are perfectly appropriate and some of which are problematic. Examples of some problematic responses to Situation 3, given by students, follow:

1. I want you to help my study for the test.
2. I'd like you to help me with study for the test.

Such formulations with *want* statements are generally perceived as highly inappropriate for requests to peers (Rinnert, 1999), because they are often used as "orders" from higher to lower status people, for example, parents to children or teachers to students.

Direct imperatives with *please* are also strange:

3. Please help me study for exams.

Some conventionally indirect forms that sound generally acceptable include the following:

4. Could you help me study for the test?

More indirect formulations that would be particularly effective with a friend include Examples 5 and 6, the second of which sounds particularly natural:

5. I need your help.
6. I could (really) use your help.

The actual request as it occurred in a television drama was rather similar, although it was more indirect and contained much more softening (in italics):

7. *You know*, *maybe* you *could* help *uh*, help me study for the test. (Weiss & Danski, 2003)

Students will likely produce many direct formulations and *want* statements, and there may be some evidence of transfer of knowledge gained from Session 1. When we piloted the materials the following week using a film situation between a father and a son, a number of students used a formula ("*I think it's time*") that had been heavily favored the previous week for the first situation, asking the sister to move out ("I think it's time to think about your future").

One refinement of this activity would be to ask students to write multiple responses, rather than just one, for each situation. We suggest this because what is important in learning pragmatic strategies is not only to know how native English speakers respond in certain situations, but also to consider in how many different ways learners can strategically realize what they want to say and then evaluate for themselves how appropriate their productions are cross-culturally.

Teachers can use activities similar to those used for the first set of situations. In particular, Activity 4 (Listening to Requests) using the audio files and transcript provided (see Appendix C), and a self-diagnosis report, as in Activity 5. In addition, teachers can easily develop their own worksheets using the format provided in Worksheets 3 and 4.

REFLECTIONS 

The activities in this chapter were effective for raising learners' awareness of the need for softeners depending on the degree of imposition, even between intimates. At the same time, experience with the pilot activities revealed how important it can be to note students' lack of confidence regarding their initial responses, even when they are highly appropriate. This suggests a need for finding ways to build their confidence in their own abilities. By focusing on ways in which their L1 norms are similar to the L2 norms (e.g., the widespread use of permission formulations for requests), teachers can encourage students to apply what they know about politeness and appropriateness in their L1 to their L2. For example, Nogami (2006) identified very similar softening strategies and patterns in Japanese and English, and these correspondences could be taught explicitly to Japanese EFL learners. At the same time, it needs to be explained that pragmatic norms are not the same as grammar rules. In particular, whereas grammar is almost always either correct or incorrect, pragmatic formulations are more or less appropriate in a particular context. What should be emphasized in actual instruction is that students can acquire pragmatic awareness and flexibility as they learn to test their hypotheses in actual situations.

The approach presented here could be used with younger and older learners at proficiency levels ranging from intermediate to advanced, as long as the learners have some motivation to communicate in English. Learners' readiness is also a crucial factor for pragmatic instruction. The local instructor is obviously in the best position to decide whether the learners are ready for such instruction, both in terms of their language proficiency and their motivations to learn the language.

The main key to success would be the selection of the request situations. The complexity of the content and the relationships portrayed in the situations needs to match the maturity level and interests of the learners. At the same time, the difficulty of the language has to be carefully checked to ensure that the vocabulary and grammatical structures are not too far beyond the students' current knowledge. One adjustment that might need to be made for younger or lower intermediate proficiency learners would be to simplify or translate the information presented in the transcripts of the audio files (see Appendix C). With those students at lower-intermediate levels, it may be effective in EFL contexts to allow the use of L1 to enable lower-level students to have more substantial group and class discussions comparing the different forms, as well as to give clearer explanations of the reasons for their choices in the final reports. As long as the modified versions fit these criteria, all the activities are simple and straightforward enough for junior and senior high school students to manage.

ACKNOWLEDGMENTS 

This study was supported by an academic research grant from the Japan Society for the Promotion of Science [Grant Code–Scientific Research (C) 19520499]. We would like to express our deep appreciation to the editors for the numerous key contributions they made to this chapter.

Carol Rinnert is a professor at Hiroshima City University in Japan. Her research interests include cross-cultural pragmatics, spoken and written discourse analysis, and the development of academic literacy in L1 and L2, focusing on English and Japanese comparison. She has studied and taught in Idaho and New York in the United States, and in Japan and Yemen.

Chiaki Iwai is a professor at Hiroshima City University in Japan. He is interested in researching and teaching strategic language use among L2 learners, particularly communication strategies and pragmatic strategies for English as an international lingua franca. He has studied and conducted research in Texas, Minnesota, and Hawaii in the United States, and in Japan.

APPENDIX A: STRATEGIES FOR MAKING REQUESTS IN ENGLISH

DIRECT	**Plain/Informal**	**More Polite/Formal**	**Softer, Even More Polite**
	Command form	Add *Please*	Add softeners and/or hesitation markers
	Give me the book.	*Please* give me the book.	*If possible, uh, please* give me the book *for a second*
INDIRECT	**Conventional formulas**	**Past tense/more polite and formal**	**Add softeners and hesitation markers**
Ability	*Can you* give me the book?	*Could you* give me the book?	*Do you think you could perhaps* give me the book?
Possibility/ Permission	*Can I* have the book?	*Could I* have the book?	*Would it be possible* to have the book *for a minute?*
	May I have the book?	*Might I* have the book?	*If it's not too much trouble, might I possibly* have the book?
Willingness	*Will you* give me the book?	*Would you* give me the book?	*Do you think you would maybe* give me the book?
	Do you mind giving . . .?	*Would you mind* giving . . .?	*I was wondering if you would mind* giving me the book?
HINTS			
Feasibility	*Do you have the book?*	*Was it you* who had the book?	*Did you, by any chance, happen* to have the book?
Grounder	*I don't have the book.*	*I forgot* to bring the book.	*Oh, it looks like I may have* forgotten to bring the book.
Vague question	*Do we need the book today?*	*Was it necessary* to bring the book?	*Oh dear, I wonder if* we *might* need the book today.

***Please note the following are not requests when uttered under certain conditions; for example,**

ORDERS (from higher to lower status; required action; no choice but to do it)

Command	*Give me the book (right now).*		*Give* me the book *when it is convenient.*
Desire	*I want you* to give me the book.	*I'd like you* to give me the book.	*When you have time, I'd like you* to give me the book.
Requirement	*You must/have to* give me the book.		*At your convenience, you are required* to give me the book.

Note: This set of strategies includes a subset of the standard strategies set forth in Blum-Kulka, House, and Kasper (1989). For instance, the three indirect strategies listed in this table are separate instances of a single conventionally indirect strategy, which is commonly referred to as a preparatory strategy. The first hint type represents a precondition on a successful request (checking on the feasibility of the request); the second offers a reason for the request (which could be a supportive move if a more direct head request act were expressed, but serves as a hint when no other head act is present); and the third, a vague question, is a less transparent kind of hint (Weizman, 1989). Because they contain elements of the intended request act, they fall somewhere within the conventional category of strong hints.

APPENDIX B: WORKSHEETS AND ANSWER KEYS 

Worksheet 1: Producing Requests

Read the description of the situation below. Then read the dialogue. In all three situations, Sandy [S], her husband Roger, and her sister Jessica [J] are eating dinner together. Jessica has been living with Sandy and Roger for several months. A blank has been inserted where a request occurs. Fill in the blank with an appropriate request for the situation in each of the following:

Situation 1: Jessica always cooks dinner, and Sandy and Roger clean up. However, Sandy just found out that she and Roger need to go out this evening. In this scene, Sandy asks her sister to do the cleaning this evening.

S: Jessica . . .

J: Mm, what?

S: [write a request for Jessica to clean up]

____

Situation 2: Sandy and Roger's babysitter has just called to say that she is sick and can't take care of Sandy and Roger's 3-year-old daughter Annie tomorrow. Sandy knows that Jessica plans to meet a friend tomorrow, but Sandy can't stay home from work, and neither can Roger. In this scene, Sandy asks her sister to stay home and take care of Annie.

S: Jessica . . .

J: Mm, what?

S: [write a request for Jessica to stay home and take care of Annie tomorrow]

____

Situation 3: Roger has never been happy about Jessica staying with them, and Sandy has finally begun to get tired of her sister's inconsiderate behavior. In this scene, Sandy asks her sister to find another place to live.

S: Jessica . . .

J: Mm, what?

S: [write a request for Jessica to find another place to live]

____

Worksheet 1: Answer Key

Following are examples of inappropriate and appropriate requests for Situation 3, grouped according to characteristics that account for their inappropriateness.

Examples 1–8 below would be considered inappropriate in a high imposition request such as Situation 3.

Direct, no softening except *please* (generally inappropriate)

(1) Please move out.
(2) Please get out of my home, and find a home for yourself.
(3) You have to find a place to live by yourself.

Conventionally indirect, no softening except past tense or occasional *please* (generally inappropriate)

(4) Would you get out of my house?
(5) Will you find some other place to live?
(6) Could you please look for a place to live?

Relatively direct, with one softener (generally inappropriate; softeners are in italics)

(7) *I think* you should live by yourself soon.
(8) *I'm sorry but* I want you to leave our house.

Other more indirect and softened strategies were produced by students in the pilot: The following Examples 9–10 are less offensive than Examples 1–8; however, they still seem too abrupt.

Nonconventionally indirect (hints), with little or no softening (generally inappropriate)

(9) It's time to find another place to live.
(10) When will you leave this place? I think it's better for you to live alone.

Examples 11–14 (with some grammatical modifications) were also produced by students. These examples, which rely on hints or suggestion formulas with softening and positive/empathy strategies, would be appropriate for the situation. These are the types of expressions that the activity is designed to make students aware of.

Hints or suggestion formulas, with softening (underlined) or positive/empathy strategies (in italics; generally appropriate). In the following example, the request is double underlined.

(11) Jessica, *I'm so sorry, but* I think we should live separately. (Hint)
(12) *I haven't wanted to say anything . . . but, . . .* how about thinking about looking for another place to live? (Suggestion)
(13) *Jessica, I think it might benefit you to live alone. You should be able to live your own life.* How about looking for a new apartment *together*? (Suggestion)
(14) *You know, you've been living here for long time. I'd like to help* you find a new apartment or something. *Sounds nice, doesn't it?* (Hint)

Worksheet 2: Problem Response Sheet

Read the description of the situation below. Then read the dialogue. In all three situations, Sandy [S], her husband Roger, and her sister Jessica [J] are eating dinner together. Jessica has been living with Sandy and Roger for several months. In each situation S makes a request of her sister using language that that could cause problems with J. Explain what is wrong with S's request and then provide a more appropriate version of the request.

Situation 1: Sandy [S], her husband Roger, and her sister Jessica [J], are eating dinner together. Jessica has been living with Sandy and Roger for several months. Jessica always cooks dinner, and Sandy and Roger clean up. However, Sandy just found out that she and Roger need to go out this evening. In this scene, Sandy asks her sister to do the cleaning this evening.

S: Jessica . . .

J: Mm, what?

S: <u>Please clean up tonight.</u>

____

____

Situation 2: Sandy and Roger's babysitter has just called to say that she is sick and can't take care of Sandy and Roger's 3-year-old daughter Annie tomorrow. Sandy knows that Jessica plans to meet a friend tomorrow, but Sandy can't stay home from work, and neither can Roger. In this scene, Sandy asks her sister to stay home and take care of Annie.

S: Jessica . . .

J: Mm, what?

S: <u>I want you to take care of Annie tomorrow.</u>

____

____

Situation 3: Roger has never been happy about Jessica staying with them, and Sandy has finally begun to get tired of her sister's inconsiderate behavior. In this scene, Sandy asks her sister to find another place to live.

S: Jessica . . .

J: Mm, what?

S: <u>You have to find another place to live because you've been living here too long.</u>

____

____

Worksheet 2: Answer Key

Note: Softeners are indicated by italics.

Situation 1:
Even to a sister, a direct request to clean up alone when this has not been previously negotiated sounds thoughtless and abrupt. A more appropriate request could be:

S: Hey Jessica . . .

J: Mm, what?

S: Roger and I are planning to go out after dinner this evening. *I was wondering* if you *would* mind doing the cleaning up tonight. I*'d* really appreciate it.

(Indirect, softened request with supportive moves: grounder [reason for the request] and expression of appreciation)

Situation 2:
"I want you to . . ." sounds like an order from a parent to a child, or from a teacher to a student, so it would probably be seen, even by a younger sister, as bossy or overbearing. A more appropriate request could be:

S: Jessica . . .

J: Mm, what?

S: The babysitter can't come tomorrow and we can't miss work. *Would it be possible* for you to meet your friend here at home tomorrow, so you *can* take care of Annie?

(Indirect, softened request with supporting grounder and offer of suggestion for compromise)

Situation 3:
Without any softener or offer of options, a strong statement of what Jessica is required to do would undoubtedly make her feel manipulated and angry. A more appropriate option could be:

S: Jessica . . .

J: Mm, what?

S: Have you *started* thinking about where you *might* want to move after this? Today I heard about a great-sounding apartment downtown.

(Hint formulation with softeners and offer of positive alternative)

Worksheet 3: Listening to Requests—Using Audio Transcripts

Listen to the audio clips of the following requests (available at http://www.tesolmedia.com/books/pragmatics). Write the request that Sandy actually made in the blank on the sheet.

Situation 1: Jessica always cooks dinner, and Sandy and Roger clean up. However, Sandy just found out that she and Roger need to go out this evening. In this scene, Sandy asks her sister to do the cleaning this evening.

S: Jessica . . .

J: Mm, what?

S: ____

Situation 2: Sandy and Roger's babysitter has just called to say that she is sick and can't take care of Sandy and Roger's 3-year-old daughter Annie tomorrow. Sandy knows that Jessica plans to meet a friend tomorrow, but Sandy can't stay home from work, and neither can Roger. In this scene, Sandy asks her sister to stay home and take care of Annie.

S: Jessica . . .

J: Mm, what?

S: ____

Situation 3: Roger has never been happy about Jessica staying with them, and Sandy has finally begun to get tired of her sister's inconsiderate behavior. In this scene, Sandy asks her sister to find another place to live.

S: Jessica . . .

J: Mm, what?

S: ____

Worksheet 3: Answer Key

Note: Softeners are indicated by italics.

Situation 1:

S: *Do you think* you *could* clean up tonight? Roger and I have to go out right after dinner. I'll cook and clean up tomorrow.

(Indirect, softened request form with supporting reason and offer to repay the favor)

Situation 2:

S: I know you have plans tomorrow, but *is there any chance* you *could* take care of Annie? The babysitter is sick and we can't miss work.

(Indirect, softened request with supporting moves [a preceding disarmer and following reason])

Situation 3:

S: *I was wondering* if it *wasn't* time for you *to start* thinking about finding a place of your own. I'm sure you'd be happier somewhere you can enjoy your privacy and independence.

(Indirect request with multiple softeners and expression of concern for the welfare of the hearer)

Worksheet 4: Self-Diagnosis Report Sheet

Evaluate your answer to each of the three dinner table situations using the following questions.

(Situation 1) Requesting sister to clean up

A. Your first answer ______________________________

B. The answer you like best now ______________________________

C. Why? ______________________________

____

(Situation 2) Requesting sister to stay home and watch Annie

A. Your first answer ______________________________

B. The answer you like best now ______________________________

C. Why? ______________________________

____

(Situation 3) Requesting sister to move out

A. Your first answer ______________________________

B. The answer you like best now ______________________________

C. Why? ______________________________

____

Worksheet 4: Answer Key

Any answers the students write are acceptable. The teacher can correct any grammatical or word-choice errors and comment on the appropriateness of the original and final choices, as well as the reasons expressed by the student (e.g., if the original request written by the student seems just as good as or better than the final choice, the teacher should point that out). Besides returning the worksheet with feedback, the teacher can look for recurring patterns in the students' responses and share frequently observed points with the whole class.

Worksheet 5: Producing Requests

Read the description of the following situations. Then read the dialogue. In all three situations, Carl (C) and Alex (A) are high school students who know each other from classes they have taken together. They are not close friends, but they often talk before class. A blank has been inserted where a request occurs. Fill in the blank with an appropriate request for each situation. When you are finished, you can listen to the dialogue (available at http://www.tesolmedia.com/books/pragmatics) and compare your answers.

Situation 1: Carl and Alex are both in the classroom waiting for class to begin. Today is a major test, and Carl realizes that he doesn't have anything to write with. Carl asks Alex for a pen.

C: Hey Alex . . .

A: Yeah?

C: [write Carl's request to borrow a pen]

____

Situation 2: Carl and Alex are just leaving school. Alex is rushing, as he has told Carl that he has an appointment after school and he can't be late. To finish his homework, Carl desperately needs to borrow a book that Alex has put away in his backpack.

C: Hey Alex . . .

A: Yeah?

C: [write Carl's request to borrow the book]

____

Situation 3: Carl knows that Alex understands the material in the class. He also knows that Alex is extremely busy outside of class with work and family obligations. A major test is coming up, and Carl needs help. He wants to ask Alex to spend an evening helping him study for the test.

C: Hey Alex . . .

A: Yeah?

C: [write Carl's request for Alex to help him study]

____

Worksheet 5: Answer Key

Note: Softeners are indicated by italics.

Situation 1:
This is a low imposition request between friends, so a short request would be likely, and explicit softeners are unnecessary. However, it would still be most appropriate to ask indirectly or as a hint. For example:

C: Can I borrow a pen? OR Do you have a pen? / Got a pen?

(Indirect request OR hint [questioning feasibility])

Situation 2:
This is a higher imposition request, because Alex is in a hurry and would be delayed by taking the book out of the bag, and he may be planning to use the book himself. Indirect requests with softening and supportive moves would be appropriate. For example:

C: *Do you think* I *could* borrow the book in your bag? I really need it tonight. I'll give it back tomorrow.

(Indirect, softened request with supporting reason and promise to return it)

Situation 3:
This is a high imposition request because it requires substantial time and effort and could interfere with Alex's other responsibilities. Therefore, hints or other indirect forms with softening and supportive moves would be most appropriate.

C: *You know*, *maybe* you *could* help me understand the stuff for the test tomorrow. You really *seem to* know it, and I'm *pretty much* lost.

(Hint: indirect question with softening and reasons [including positive evaluation of the hearer])

APPENDIX C: TRANSCRIPTS 

Activity 4: Listening to Requests

Situation 1:

S: Jessica . . .

J: Mm, what?

S: Do you think you could clean up tonight? Roger and I have to go out right after dinner. I'll cook and clean up tomorrow.

J: OK, sure.

Situation 2:

S: Jessica . . .

J: Mm, what?

S: I know you have plans tomorrow, but is there any chance you could take care of Annie? The babysitter is sick and we can't miss work.

J: Yeah, I guess I can.

Situation 3:

S: Jessica . . .

J: Mm, what?

S: I was wondering if it wasn't time for you to start thinking about finding a place of your own. I'm sure you'd be happier somewhere you can enjoy your privacy and independence.

Follow-Up Activity

Situation 1:

C: Hey Alex . . .

A: Yeah?

C: Got an extra pen I can use?

Situation 2:

C: Hey Alex . . .

A: Yeah?

C: I really need to borrow that book. Can I run with you while you dig it out of your bag?

Situation 3:

C: Hey Alex . . .

A: Yeah?

C: Do you have some time tonight? I could really use your help studying for the test.

CHAPTER 5

Requesting a Letter of Recommendation: Teaching Students to Write E-Mail Requests

Kumiko Akikawa and Noriko Ishihara

E-mail requests from students to professors have become increasingly common in both English as a second language (ESL) and English as a foreign language (EFL) settings. E-mail requests can be less intimidating than face-to-face requests for students who fear losing face in interpersonal negotiation with a professor. Yet students often lack the knowledge and skills for making appropriate requests (e.g., Bloch, 2002). Some ESL learners believe that North American English speakers are always direct and explicit, and this oversimplification sometimes leads to inappropriately straightforward or overly casual requests (Matsuura, 1998; Takahashi, 2005). With inappropriate e-mails, students run the risk of having their request denied or of unintentionally offending professors. This chapter discusses a lesson that attempts to raise students' awareness of the language forms, sociocultural norms, and discourse structure used in e-mail requests to professors. In order to enhance students' *noticing* of pragmatic norms, analysis of discourse is incorporated as a core activity in the lesson plan.

CONTEXT

The lesson is designed for advanced ESL learners, particularly those who are in an academic (or preacademic) context in the United States. Some of the learners may have greater grammatical competence than pragmatic knowledge; some others typically have basic pragmatics but do not have comparable control of the language. Advanced-proficiency students are normally ready to fine-tune their requests through the analysis of discourse and language structures. The lesson described in this chapter is based on 16 pragmatically appropriate e-mail samples, 11 authentic and 5 elicited. The lesson has been pilot-tested with 22 high intermediate to advanced ESL learners. The inductive approach, which is used here to encourage learners' noticing and self-discovery, is intended to help learners become conscious of areas for improvement, and to motivate them to learn pragmatic norms.

Three of the most important social factors involved in requests are hearer status, distance, and degree of imposition of the request (Brown & Levinson, 1987). Although teachers are clearly in a position of power, some university students may have a less formal relationship with their professors. Whereas recommendations are considered part of a professor's responsibilities, they can be time-consuming. Thus, providing ample time for writing a recommendation letter can minimize the degree of imposition involved.

At the discourse level, e-mails to professors usually follow conventions similar to those of a formal letter. The e-mail has a subject line, a salutation/greeting, an opening, a body, a closing, and a signature. Within the body, request strategies for a recommendation may include, albeit not necessarily in this order: (a) apology for short notice, if relevant; (b) request; (c) detailed explanation regarding the application; (d) request for information on the professor's availability to write the letter; and (e) thanks, which can be included in the closing. Figure 1 provides a schematic overview of the structure.

Grammatical forms commonly used in requests of this type are usually somewhat more complex: "I was hoping that you would/might be willing to . . ." and "I was wondering if you would/could/might . . . ."

CURRICULUM, TASKS, MATERIALS 

For effective learning of pragmatics, students will need to notice both the second language (L2) forms and the relevant contextual factors (Schmidt, 2001), as well as the discourse structure of the request. This lesson incorporates various activities designed to explicitly raise students' awareness of the core features of an e-mail request and to solidify their knowledge.

Activity 1: Describing and Understanding Relationships From the Context

To maximize instructional effects, it is essential to accustom students gradually to doing analysis of contextual factors and discourse structure. This set of activities begins with a homework assignment in which students describe their relationship with a professor and analyze the context of their request by completing Worksheets 1 and 2 (see Appendix A). As part of Worksheet 2, students also write a first draft requesting a letter of recommendation and bring it to class. This homework provides an opportunity for students to become aware of aspects of social context that influence the request form.

Subject: Letter of recommendation

To: abc@xyz.edu

Dear (Professor/Prof.) XXX,

— Opening
— Apology for a short notice (if relevant)
— Request
— Explanation
  - Reason for application
  - Job description
  - Due date
  - Who to address the letter to
  - What information should be stressed
— Request for indication of professor's availability
— Thanks (can be in closing)

Closing,

Signature

Figure 1. Basic Structure of an E-Mail Requesting a Letter of Recommendation

Activity 2: Peer-Analysis of Contextual Factors and Language Forms

Critical observations of their peers' and their own e-mail letters raise students' pragmatic awareness and develop analytical skills, while helping them become independent learners in the long run (see Activity 5 for peer evaluation of group work). Using Worksheet 3 (see Appendix A) as a guide, students work in pairs and examine their partner's request e-mails. Although interactive e-mail exchanges are fluid, this serves as a general guideline based on our analysis of authentic e-mail samples. The teacher encourages learners to use this checklist as a guide when revising their first drafts as homework.

Activity 3: Analyzing the Discourse Structure of E-Mail Requests

In this core activity, the teacher uses the sample e-mails provided on Worksheets 4 and 5 (see Appendix A) to direct students' attention to the structure of the discourse and to the contextual factors. With an explicit explanation, the teacher promotes their noticing of the relationship between the two. Students can reflect on what contextual factors likely affect the language use and how the writer's intention is realized in the L2 forms.

The teacher displays the sample e-mails provided on Worksheets 4 and 5 (see

Appendix A) on an overhead projector or distributes them as a handout for analysis. While the teacher explains each request situation, he or she elicits students' analyses of the contextual factors. The analysis can also be facilitated through a visual organizer that shows the basic structure of a request e-mail, such as that previously provided in Figure 1, which can be used as a handout after the students' discussion of the examples. The teacher leads students to inductively discover the structure of a typical request e-mail, helping them to clarify the pragmatic functions of each component. The taxonomy of request strategies listed on the right in Worksheets 4 and 5 (see Appendix A) has been adapted from Blum-Kulka, House, and Kasper (1989) and Blum-Kulka and Olshtain (1984) to accommodate the specificity of the task in this lesson. After students have discussed the structure of the e-mail, they can answer the questions in the worksheet alone or in pairs. The discussion for Part II allows students to consider some of the ways that social factors can affect language in English. Some possible responses are provided in the answer key following the worksheet (see Appendix A).

In the conclusion of this core activity, the teacher encourages students to notice specific language forms; request strategies; and different degrees of directness, formality, and politeness seen in the samples. Then he or she visually organizes the information as in Handout 1 (see Appendix B), which can function as the students' reference point in subsequent activities.

In using these materials, the teacher can draw students' attention to the cultural reasoning behind the L2 pragmatic norms (Richards & Schmidt, 1983). The teacher can ask why the writers commonly use certain structures, request strategies, or language forms, and he or she can encourage students to relate the language use to the underlying values commonly shared in the culture. For instance, highlighting the frequent use of an embedded "if" clause and a subjunctive mood ("I was wondering *if* you *could* . . ."), the teacher can guide students to discover or confirm that showing deference to professors is important in an English-speaking culture that may seem egalitarian and informal in communication style (e.g., "What is an appropriate student-professor relationship like? Why is it appropriate?" "How does the student express formality and informality in the e-mail? Why does the student express informality?" and "How does the student address the professor and why?"). The teacher can also explain that although writing recommendations is usually regarded as part of a professor's responsibilities, showing consideration for the professor and giving him or her enough time can minimize the imposition of the request because it takes a great deal of time and effort to write an informative and personalized letter. These discussions can facilitate students' understanding about how underlying cultural values and beliefs are manifested in pragmatic behavior (see Ishihara, 2007, for examples).

Activity 4: Writing E-Mails to Request a Recommendation Letter

In addition to understanding and analyzing the structure of the e-mail messages, students need to compose such e-mail messages themselves. In the following production-oriented activity, the teacher divides students into small groups of three and provides each group with a description of the request situation in Worksheet 6 (see Appendix A). Each group receives a sheet of paper and writes a request message on it. If available, an overhead projector may be used for students' in-class presentations. Each student plays a role in the group, of either a writer, a facilitator, or a presenter. While monitoring their progress, the teacher encourages each group to explain why they have employed certain language forms or request strategies in the given context.

Activity 5: Reviewing and Responding to Peers' E-Mail Requests

Working in groups, students use the Peer-Evaluation Worksheet (see Worksheet 7 in Appendix A) to critique their peers' e-mail request letters. After presenting their e-mail request, each group receives oral feedback from their peers. Next, the teacher collects the Peer-Evaluation Worksheets and adds his or her feedback in the teacher's column. The follow-up discussion may address the feedback in the worksheets.

Activity 6: Revising E-Mail Request Letters

Students are asked to revise their first draft as homework and turn it in. They are encouraged to incorporate peer and teacher feedback in their second drafts. The following guidelines can be used to assess students' efforts.

- Assess students' pragmatic awareness and understanding of the context by grading homework and observing pair and group work.
- Assess students' pragmatic awareness by examining their peer evaluation.
- Assess the second draft of students' e-mails according to the Teacher's Assessment Rubric (see Handout 2 in Appendix B) with a main focus on the discourse structure and other linguistic features. Comment on how much and where their second draft has improved compared to their first draft. (Also see Ishihara, Chapter 14 this volume, for other evaluative options.)

REFLECTIONS 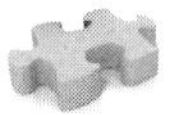

This series of activities has been successful in raising students' awareness of the pragmatics of written requests for recommendations. After instruction, all students were able to express their requests more appropriately, employing common request expressions and appropriate request strategies. This lesson could also benefit professional job candidates and preacademic ESL and EFL students, who may need to request a recommendation letter from a professor or a supervisor by e-mail. It can be adapted to suit beginning to low-intermediate levels by exposing students to abstract pragmatics-related concepts step by step, ensuring multiple levels of scaffolding if necessary.

Learners' motivation may be enhanced by exposing them to multiple e-mail samples so that students can see a variety of forms, discourse patterns, and styles, as well as the diversity in sociocultural norms. Although teachers may have difficulty obtaining many authentic e-mail samples, even a few can facilitate a class discussion about cross-cultural differences (e.g., meaning and conventions associated with recommendation, typical professor-student relationships, teachers' rights and obligations, and appropriate degree of directness and politeness). Alternatively, teachers could encourage a comparison of strategies in students' first and second languages and cultures to address the diversity of pragmatic norms in the target and native language.

Finding a balance between teachers' styles and local educational contexts can be a challenge. Pragmatics-focused instruction and inductive learning and teaching styles may take some time and effort before becoming effective in some settings where grammar-focused instruction and a deductive, teacher-centered style are more valued. If there is considerable administrative pressure to provide grammar-focused instruction, teachers may consider placing more emphasis on the structures of request expressions and vocabulary. With necessary adjustments, the lesson plan above can be adapted to educational settings where most students will be in need of letters of recommendation.

Kumiko Akikawa received her master's in TESOL from American University, Washington, DC. She is currently teaching ESL at Montgomery College in Maryland in the United States. Before coming to the United States, she taught English at Japanese universities. Her research interests include instructional pragmatics, nonnative-English-speaking teachers, and classroom-based research.

*Noriko Ishihara is associate professor in EFL at Hosei University, Japan, and leads language teachers' professional development courses in Japan and in the United States. Her academic interests include pragmatics and identity, and teacher development. She has recently co-authored teachers' resources in instructional pragmatics (*Teaching and Learning Pragmatics, *with Andrew Cohen, Pearson/Longman;* Communication in Context, *with Magara Maeda, Routledge).*

APPENDIX A: WORKSHEETS AND ANSWER KEYS 

Worksheet 1: Identifying Context

Situation:

You are applying to a graduate school in the United States and are preparing application documents. The university requires two letters of recommendation. You have decided to e-mail a professor at your university to request a recommendation letter.

1. To whom are you writing?

   I'm writing to ______________________, *who teaches*
   (name)

   ____________________________________.
   (name of the course)

2. How well do you know the professor? Do you think the professor will recognize you without an explanation of who you are?

   ____

   ____

3. Do you think he or she is willing to help you? How much trouble do you think the request will cause the professor?

   ____

   ____

Worksheet 1: Answer Key

The following are model responses.

1. I'm writing to ___Prof. Kim___, who teaches ___History 01 and 02___.
2. I have known him for one year. He knows me well and I often visit his office to ask questions.
3. He teaches many classes and seems to be very busy. But he is always kind and helps me a lot. So, I'm sure he can help me.

Worksheet 2: Analyzing Context and Responding Appropriately

Directions:

- For the analysis of the context, circle the letter that you think describes your situation most closely.
- Considering social status, distance, and the imposition of the request, what language forms will you use? Give a brief comment in the space under these 3 sections.

	Social status	**Distance**	**Imposition of the request**
Part I: Analysis of the context	The professor's status is a. higher b. lower c. equal than/to yours.	Your relationship with the professor is a. close b. fairly close c. not so close d. not close at all	The request you are making is a. greatly imposing on the professor b. moderately imposing on the professor c. not imposing on the professor too much d. not imposing on the professor at all
Part II: Analysis of language form	(Example) "Because the professor's status is higher than mine, I will use polite forms such as 'I would like to' instead of 'I want to.'"		
Part III: Considering the context you have just analyzed in Parts I and II, write your first draft to your chosen professor requesting a letter of recommendation. Write on a new sheet of paper and bring it to next class.			

Worksheet 2: Answer Key

The following sample is an actual student response. It has not been edited.

	Social status	**Distance**	**Imposition of the request**
Part I: Analysis of the context	The professor's status is (a.) higher b. lower c. equal than/to yours.	Your relationship with the professor is a. close (b.) fairly close c. not so close d. not close at all	The request you are making is a. greatly imposing on the professor b. moderately imposing on the professor (c.) not imposing on the professor too much d. not imposing on the professor at all
Part II: Analysis of language form	*Because the professor's status is higher and he's much older than me, I use polite language such as the expression "I was wondering if you could . . ." This way, it doesn't sound that I take his help for granted. Also, I make sure to thank him for considering the possibility of writing a support letter for me.* *Although I have known him for more than one year, I think it's better to introduce myself so that I can make sure that he knows who I am ("I was in your Introduction to American History course last semester"). Since he is a friendly professor and we are fairly close, I insert a greeting into this e-mail in order to make it sound less businesslike.* *I don't think my request is so imposing because he has more than 2 weeks to write the letter. But since he is always busy, I ask him first if he is willing to do this for me.*		
Part III: First draft	**From:** mtanaka@wsc.edu **To:** jhkim@wsc.edu **Subject:** Letter of recommendation **Date:** Fri, 14 Dec 2007 10:47 --- Professor Kim, I hope you had a nice break and that your semester is off to a good start. I was in your Introduction to American History course last semester and am writing to ask if you have some time to write recommendation letters for me to graduate programs. I've decided to do Master's studies in colonial history after my graduation this year and so far am planning to apply for the University of XXX. They request a letter to be submitted online by December 31 (you can find the form at http://www.xxx.edu/admissions/). Since I took two classes with you, your point of view would be valuable, and I was wondering if you could write a letter on my behalf. I have attached my current resume for your reference. Thank you in advance for your consideration regarding this matter. Sincerely, Mami		

Worksheet 3: Peer-Analysis Checklist

Directions: Work in pairs and familiarize yourself with the basic components of e-mail requests below. Read your partner's e-mail carefully and answer the questions in the list. If the answer is "Yes," put a check mark (✓) in the left column. If "No," put a cross mark (✗) instead. Write down your suggestions below the chart so that your partner can refer to them when revising.

	Does the e-mail have a subject?
	Does the e-mail have a salutation? (e.g., "Dear XXX")
	Can the professor identify your partner easily? (If not, did your partner make an effort to help the professor remember who he or she is?)
	Did your partner make a request politely?
	Did your partner explain the reason why he or she needs a recommendation letter?
	Did your partner tell the professor the deadline?
	Does the e-mail have a closing and/or thanking (e.g., "Sincerely," "Thank you")?
	Did your partner sign at the bottom of the e-mail?

Your suggestions:

____

____

____

____

____

____

____

____

Worksheet 4: Sample E-Mail #1

Situation: The writer in e-mail #1 is a graduate student who is about her professor's age. The student and the professor call each other by their first names. The student has known the professor through three of the professor's courses. The e-mail was written 21 days before the due date.

Part I: Read the following e-mail and then answer the questions below.

Subject: Letter of reference	**Subject**
Cathy,	**Salutation**
I was wondering if you could write me a letter of reference for the teaching positions I am applying for. The first deadline I know of so far is March 3. I hope that 3 weeks notice is enough.	**Request** **Explanation & Reason** **Notifying of the deadline**
I would be honored to have you as a reference as I apply for my first "real" teaching job!	**Thanking ("sweetener")**
Thank you,	**Thanking/closing**
Jen	**Signature**

Part II: Answer the following questions about Jen's e-mail.

1. What kind of language forms does Jen generally use? How appropriate do they sound?
2. How directly or indirectly does Jen make a request? Why?
3. How does the context (i.e., social status, distance, and imposition of the request) affect her language forms?
4. What kinds of information about the recommendation letter are provided? How important are they?
5. What are the strategies for making the request polite and less imposing?

Worksheet 4: Answer Key

1. Jen uses lots of "softeners" in her request e-mail, such as "I was wondering if you could . . ." and "I would be honored to . . . ," which make her request courteous. These language forms sound more polite and are more appropriate than direct statements of want such as: "I want you to write a letter of reference by March 3."
2. Jen's request is clear but indirect. She starts off with her request and keeps her message short with a minimal expression of concern for the professor ("I would be honored to . . ."). This might be partly because Jen is on friendly terms with the professor and might assume that the professor is willing to help her. Perhaps she has already talked about her job application with the professor. The (North American) value of "short and sweet" may also be at work in an attempt not to waste the reader's or writer's time.

3. Although Jen is on friendly terms with the professor and is about the professor's age, she shows her respect to the professor by using polite language consistently. This is because of the professor's relatively higher social status. However, because the professor knows her well and probably Jen assumes that the professor is willing to help her, she comes straight to the point. Also note that the severity of imposition is relatively small in this case. If she were making a request at the last minute, her request would be much more imposing, and then she would probably add a word of apology and even a reasonable excuse.

4. Jen includes information regarding the purpose of the recommendation letter and its due date. This information is crucial for the professor to decide whether or not she can help Jen. In other words, it is important for the professor to know what skills and knowledge of the student she is to assess in the letter, and by when she needs to write it. However, the professor may want more detailed information about the position that Jen is applying for, if Jen has not provided it.

5. Jen uses politeness strategies such as "I was wondering if you could . . ." and "I'd be honored to . . ." Jen is also showing her respect for the professor's time by giving her 3 weeks for writing the letter ("I hope that 3 weeks notice is enough"). This probably minimizes the level of imposition of her request.

Worksheet 5: Sample E-Mail #2

Situation: The writer in e-mail #2 took two courses taught by this professor during the previous semester and has been working as an assistant for the program. The professor knows that the student has planned to apply for a position in the ABC Institute. The e-mail was written more than 60 days before the due date.

Part I: Read the following e-mail and then answer the questions below.

Subject: ABC Institute recommendation	**Subject**
HI Prof. Johnson--	**Salutation**
How are you? Did you survive the first week of class?	**Friendly Greetings**
I was wondering if you would be willing to write a recommendation for me as my professor.	**Request**
I need 3 letters of recommendation: employer, professor, and personal. I figured that since I was in 2 of your classes last semester, you would be familiar with my work. If you're willing to do this, the recommendation can be done online, I will submit your name and e-mail address with my application, and you will receive an e-mail from ABC Institute with a link to the page where you fill out the recommendation form. I believe you have 60 days to complete it once I submit my application. If you prefer to do it on paper, let me know and I will print out the necessary form. And if you are too busy right now or don't want to do this for whatever reason, I will understand and it's not a problem :-)	**Explanation & Reason for the request** **Further explanation** **Showing consideration**
Hope your week went well and that you have a great weekend, and I'm sure I'll see you next week!	**Closing**
Thank you,	**Thanking**
Sarah	**Signature**

Part II: Answer the following questions about Sarah's e-mail.

1. Compared to the distance between Jen and Cathy, how close or distant is Sarah to Prof. Johnson?
2. How imposing is Sarah's request on Prof. Johnson?
3. How directly or indirectly does Sarah make a request? Is the degree of directness greatly different from Jen's e-mail? Is it appropriate?
4. What does Sarah do to make her request more likely to be granted?

Worksheet 5: Answer Key

1. Sarah appears to know the professor well and be on friendly terms with her: She took two courses and has been working closely with the professor in the program office. Sarah's e-mail is friendly and informal (e.g., the use of an exclamation mark and smiley icon, as well as the tone of the opening question, "Did you survive the first week of class?"). However, she still addresses the professor by title and the name ("Prof. Johnson"). Note that Jen uses the professor's first name. Jen also had a stronger expectation of a positive response than Sarah did. Sarah shows her consideration for the professor by leaving some room for her to say no ("if you are too busy right now or don't want to do this for whatever reason, I will understand and it's not a problem :-)").

2. Sarah makes the request well ahead of time, which minimizes the imposition of her request. Since Prof. Johnson has known Sarah through two courses and they work in the program office on a regular basis, it is likely that Prof. Johnson knows Sarah well enough to write an informative letter. Sarah's previously mentioned consideration for the professor also made her request less of an imposition.

3. Sarah's request is also clear but indirect—she explicitly states what she wants Prof. Johnson to do ("I was wondering if you would be willing to write a recommendation for me as my professor") using a considerably softened form. Compared with Jen's e-mail (Sample E-Mail #1), however, Sarah uses different request strategies, which makes her e-mail much longer than Jen's. Sarah inserts friendly greetings before making a request, provides information regarding the procedure for letter submission, shows her consideration and respect for the professor, and closes the message by wishing the professor well. Although the degree of directness of her request does not greatly differ from Jen's request, Sarah's choice of politeness strategies makes her request friendly, pleasant, and less businesslike. Sarah's request is as appropriate as Jen's "short and sweet" request.

4. Requesting the letter well ahead of time is one way to minimize the severity of imposition. This makes the request more likely to be granted. Sarah's friendly but polite tone in her language also makes her request amiable. For example, her consideration and respect for the professor's time and right to say no help minimize the imposition of the request.

Worksheet 6: Production Activity

Directions: Write an e-mail message to request a recommendation letter. Consider the situation described below.

Situation 1:

- You are a college student, Mary Smith.
- You want to ask Professor Jane Lee to write a recommendation letter within 30 days.
- Prof. Lee is a young, energetic, female professor at your college.
- You are fairly close to Prof. Lee. She is always nice to you and willing to help students.

	Social status	Distance	Imposition of the request
Analysis of the context	The professor's status is a. higher b. lower c. equal than/to yours.	Your relationship with the professor is a. close b. fairly close c. not so close d. not close at all	The request you are making is a. greatly imposing on the professor b. moderately imposing on the professor c. not imposing on the professor too much d. not imposing on the professor at all

Situation 2:

- You are a college student, Tom Peterson.
- You want to ask Professor John Miller to write a recommendation letter within 7 days.
- Prof. Miller is a well-known, male, senior professor at your college.
- You are not so close to Prof. Miller even though he knows that you are in his class. He seems to be nice but very busy.

	Social status	Distance	Imposition of the request
Analysis of the context	The professor's status is a. higher b. lower c. equal than/to yours.	Your relationship with this professor is a. close b. fairly close c. not so close d. not close at all	The request you are making is a. greatly imposing on the professor b. moderately imposing on the professor c. not imposing on the professor too much d. not imposing on the professor at all

Worksheet 6: Answer Key

Request Situation 1

	Social status	Distance	Imposition of the request
Analysis of the context	The professor's status is (a.) higher b. lower c. equal than/to yours.	Your relationship with this professor is a. close (b.) fairly close c. not so close d. not close at all	The request you are making is a. greatly imposing on the professor b. moderately imposing on the professor (c.) not imposing on the professor too much d. not imposing on the professor at all

Request Situation 2

	Social status	Distance	Imposition of the request
Analysis of the context	The professor's status is (a.) higher b. lower c. equal than/to yours.	Your relationship with this professor is a. close b. fairly close (c.) not so close d. not close at all	The request you are making is (a.) greatly imposing on the professor b. moderately imposing on the professor c. not imposing on the professor too much d. not imposing on the professor at all

Worksheet 7: Peer-Evaluation Worksheet

Directions: How would most English speakers evaluate the appropriateness of a request e-mail written by ______'s group? Circle one of the symbols (☺; 😐; ☹) that best describes your evaluation. If you think their e-mail has some problems or good points, specify them and make comments under Your Comments. (For example: Why do you think it's a problem/good point? If anything is problematic, what do you suggest instead?) Be ready to explain your evaluations.

		Your Comments	**Teacher's Comments**
How appropriate is their choice of request strategies? **Do they include all the following components? If not, is their choice still appropriate in the context?** • Explanation (e.g., reason for a request, job descriptions, deadline) • Request • Apologizing for the trouble • Showing consideration • Thanking for considering the request	☺ Very much 😐 Somewhat ☹ Inappropriate		
How appropriate is their word choice for the request? ***Note:*** Focus on the main request expression here. For example, how appropriate is "Please write me a recommendation letter"?	☺ Very much 😐 Somewhat ☹ Inappropriate		
How appropriate is the level of formality, politeness, and directness overall? ***Note:*** Given the imposition of the request, distance, and social status, how appropriate is their request tone?	☺ Very much 😐 Somewhat ☹ Inappropriate		
How well organized is their writing? Is their point clear? Is it easy for the reader to follow? ***Note:*** If you organize each component in a logical order (e.g., opening → request / explanation → thanking and closing), it will be easy for the reader to see the point.	☺ Very smooth and clear 😐 Comprehensible ☹ Confusing!		

Worksheet 7: Answer Key

The following sample is an actual student-teacher response. It has not been edited.

		Your Comments	Teacher's Comments
How appropriate is their choice of request strategies? **Do they include all the following components?** **If not, is their choice still appropriate in the context?** • Explanation (e.g., reason for a request, job descriptions, deadline) • Request • Apologizing for the trouble • Showing consideration • Thanking for considering the request	**☺ Very much** 😐 Somewhat ☹ Inappropriate	*They include all the request strategies but "apologizing for the trouble." Because the professor has much time and knows the student well, and because the student thanks the professor politely, we think it's OK not apologizing for the trouble.*	***Your overall analysis is appropriate and well supported by examples. Excellent job!*** ***You have a good point about the expression "I hope I can get your reply soon!" As you have pointed out, it's a little imposing and not very appropriate even if the student is fairly close to the professor. Maybe they could have said "I'm looking forward to hearing from you," instead.***
How appropriate is their word choice for the request? ***Note:*** Focus on the main request expression here. For example, how appropriate is "Please write me a recommendation letter"?	**☺ Very much** 😐 Somewhat ☹ Inappropriate	*They make a polite request "I was wondering if . . ."*	
How appropriate is the level of formality, politeness, and directness overall? ***Note:*** Given the imposition of the request, distance, and social status, how appropriate is their request tone?	☺ Very much **😐 Somewhat** ☹ Inappropriate	*Their request is polite, but "please complete it within 30 days" may not be very polite. Although the student is rather close to the professor, "I hope I can get your reply soon!" may sound a bit imposing.*	
How well organized is their writing? Is their point clear? Is it easy for the reader to follow? ***Note:*** If you organize each component in a logical order (e.g., opening → request / explanation → thanking and closing), it will be easy for the reader to see the point.	**☺ Very smooth and clear** 😐 Comprehensible ☹ Confusing!	*Their point is very clear. They write about the student's future plan first, make request, explain details, and then thank the professor.*	

APPENDIX B: HANDOUTS 

Handout 1: Forms for Making a Polite Request

When you are writing a request e-mail for a recommendation letter, you may consider the following:

- **Language forms**
  - Subjunctive mood
    "would"
    "could"
    "if"
  - Polite request expressions
    "I was wondering if you could . . ."
    "I was hoping you might be willing to . . ."
    "If you could kindly write . . ."
    "If you would be kind enough to write . . ."
- **Politeness strategies**
  - Show consideration for the reader
    "if you are busy"
    "if you feel that this notice is too short"
    "If you feel that you don't know me enough to write a letter of support for me, I understand"
  - Give the professor enough time
  - Tone: "Short and sweet" → efficient
    Longer with greetings and updates → friendly, pleasant, less businesslike

Handout 2: Teacher's Assessment Rubric

4–very appropriate; 3–fairly appropriate; 2–not so appropriate; 1–inappropriate

Strategies of the request (e.g., giving a reason for the request, showing consideration for the professor)	**4 3 2 1**
Level of directness, formality, and politeness in the context	**4 3 2 1**
Grammar, vocabulary, and phrases (e.g., Would you . . .? / I was wondering if . . . / Would it be possible . . .? / a *big* favor / I *just* need . . .)	**4 3 2 1**
Organization of the request discourse	**2 1 0** good fair poor
Total Score	**/ 14**

Teacher's comments:

CHAPTER 6

Soften Up! Successful Requests in the Workplace

Lynda Yates and Jacky Springall

This chapter focuses on helping adult learners of English participate in complex problematic request sequences in the workplace in situations in which power differences exist between the speakers. Requests are potentially risky because we try to get others to do things for us. Requests, whether to peers or to superiors, are challenging in one's native language, and even more so in a foreign language because adults routinely make use of various deference, rapport-building, and softening strategies, which they may transfer from their native language and culture.

For English speakers, the range of available language constructions involves the level of grammar, vocabulary, and supporting information. For example, instead of saying to an assistant "Drop by my office," a native speaker is likely to use the grammatically more elaborate "Can you drop by my office?" The speaker might also try to reduce the size of the imposition of the request with words like *just* or phrases such as *for a moment* and use a past-tense verb form that distances the speaker from the present force of the request such as: "*Could* you *just* drop into my office *for a moment*?" English speakers generally provide a reason for a request and may even anticipate objections the assistant might have in complying with the request, which they may attempt to defuse by showing empathy. In some workplaces, the speaker may also use the assistant's first name to reduce social distance. Thus, he or she might say the following:

> *Louisa, I know it's getting a little late*, but *could* you *just* drop into the office *for a moment* before you go; *the report is back and I just need a bit of advice on where to go next.*

In the above example, the speaker used the following strategies to soften the request: (a) grammar (question form, past form, modals); (b) extra words to minimize the imposition (*just*, *for a moment*); (c) a reason ("the report is back";

"I need advice on where to go next"); and (d) an acknowledgment that she is aware of the imposition involved ("it's getting late").

In situations in which it might be difficult or inconvenient for someone to comply, a speaker may use these and similar devices over several turns, often supporting the request with other moves such as (e) apologies or (f) offers to help solve the problems created by the request. The speaker may prepare for the request using small talk or a compliment or greeting. Once the recipient of the request has agreed to comply, the speaker may offer some sort of service in return or simply say thank you. Sometimes the speaker may need to check that agreement has been reached and that both parties are clear on what will happen. In such complex problematic request situations, a request is not a simple act, but a whole sequence of acts supporting the speaker's requestive intent.

Such events present challenges for adult learners of English who have grown up in a different culture speaking a different language. First, they may have incomplete control of the English grammar and vocabulary that is necessary to manipulate the forms expected in a polite request. Second, and perhaps even more importantly, they may not be aware of what forms are used to soften a request, how often they are used, and in what circumstances. Learners will have a set of conventional strategies in their first language, but these may be very different from those commonly used in English. An obvious example is Japanese, which makes great use of honorifics, that is, a completely different set of words for different levels of politeness. Because politeness is conveyed through the use of these honorifics, Japanese speakers of English may be unsure how to be polite in English, which does not signal politeness in the same way. Similarly, speakers of Russian who are accustomed to a slightly different range of softening strategies, including the use of a variety of diminutives for people and things, and to whom direct requests in the imperative appear perfectly acceptable, may be confused about how to be polite in English. Although the English polite form "can you" exists in Russian, it is used not for this purpose, but only to enquire whether someone has the ability to do something. Therefore, a Russian speaker not only may think that direct imperative forms are routinely appropriate, as they are in Russian, but may also be unaware of the polite requestive function of the most common polite formulas for requests in English.

The unit presented in this chapter provides students with a model for negotiating or making a request in the workplace, a stimulus for a discussion of cross-cultural issues in making requests to supervisors, and the language and strategies they need to soften their requests.

CONTEXT

To find out how native English speakers (in this case Australian English) negotiate complex request tasks in work-related contexts and to determine what adult learners of English from a range of backgrounds might need to learn about how to do this, a series of projects was undertaken (Wigglesworth & Yates, 2007; Yates, in press). Data from the native speakers and adult learners were collected using two different role-plays and analyzed using a framework adapted from Blum-Kulka, House, and Kasper (1989), which was expanded to include softening strategies that also aimed to establish rapport between the speakers. Comparison of these data highlighted the need for instruction and reflection on both the cultural and linguistic aspects of complex requests.

Prototype versions of the materials[1] developed in response to this research were trialed with students who were preparing to enter the workforce and who were studying English in the Adult Migrant English Program (AMEP)—the national program for teaching English to migrants who arrive in Australia without functional English. Depending on their background, eligible migrants are entitled to between 510 and 910 hours of free instruction. The program follows a national curriculum, the Certificates of Spoken and Written English, at three levels from beginner to intermediate. The learners come from a wide variety of learner backgrounds, particularly from Africa, Asia, and the Middle East. Many are refugees and have had little workplace experience in Australia or elsewhere.

Feedback from the trials of earlier versions had suggested that learners found the natural-sounding dialogues extended their skills in ways that were sometimes challenging but very useful.

As discussed in more detail in Yates and Wigglesworth (2005), both teachers and learners appreciated the opportunity to explore the pragmatic areas of interpersonal communication that had appeared rather mysterious to them beforehand. On a cultural level, results of the current trials suggested that learners can benefit from insight into the tenor of the boss-employee relationship and the rights and obligations of both parties in local workplaces (in this case, Australian). The learners tended to approach the event more as a supplicant with a problem that they wanted the employer to fix for them, whereas the native speakers tended to approach the boss more as a colleague and tried to negotiate a solution to any problem that would be caused by compliance with their request through the use of preparators, disarmers, empathetic markers, and consultative devices. In this way, they showed a willingness to take responsibility for the consequences of their request.

---

[1] The dialogue used as the basis for these materials and earlier versions of some of the activities appeared in Unit 5: Negotiating and Making Requests in the Workplace (Springall, J., 2007, *Taking Care—Trainer Guide and DVD/CD Pack*, Melbourne, Australia: AMES). Thanks are due to Adult Migrant Educational Services Victoria for permission to use these.

On a linguistic level, the learners made little use of relatively simple lexical and syntactic devices such as past forms or the word *just* to mitigate their requests, even though, at this level (certificate level III in the national curriculum), they were aware of their existence, at least in other functions. Thus, whereas the native speakers frequently used linguistic devices such as past and continuous forms, hedging and down-toning expressions such as *just*, and embedded requests after phrases such as "I wonder if" to soften the impact of their requests, the learners did so much less often.

In summary, learners needed to know more about cultural issues, including the tenor of workplace interactions, as well as linguistic issues, including the following:

- Conventional indirect request strategies such as "can you give" rather than "give" or suggestory formulas such as "how about giving"
- The use of lexis to soften the force of the request. In particular:
  - — The expression *just* (e.g., I *just* need . . .)
  - — Word choice (e.g., *be able to* rather than *can*)
  - — Empathetic markers (e.g., I *realize* how hard it is)
  - — Interpersonal markers (e.g., I know)
- The use of syntax to soften the force of the request. In particular:
  - — Past and continuous (e.g., I was hoping that/for . . .)
  - — Modals (e.g., Could I . . . ? Would you . . . ?)
  - — Embedding (e.g., I was wondering if . . . Would it be all right if . . . ?)
- The use of preparatory moves, explanations, and offers (Yates, in press). In particular:
  - — Prerequests (e.g., Can I talk to you for a minute?)
  - — Reasons (e.g., My parents are flying down for the weekend.)
  - — Offer (e.g., I'd be happy to work next weekend if that would help. How about if I tried to organize . . .)

CURRICULUM, TASKS, MATERIALS 

The activities in this section are part of an integrated unit on requests in the workplace in which students can practice a range of language skills, including listening and speaking and vocabulary development. The unit outlined in this chapter is set in the workplace context of a residential aged-care facility for senior citizens in Australia, but similar speech act sequences making use of similar strategies and language have been found in data from workplace conversations in a wide range of industrial, professional, and office settings (Holmes & Stubbe,

2003; Riddiford, 2007; Wigglesworth & Yates, 2007). As is common in Australia, this workplace is rather informal, and that aspect is stressed in these exercises. Students need to be made aware that each organization has its own corporate culture regarding formality and informality, and therefore they need to be prepared to adopt the norm of the business in which they are participating. The materials come with an audio file and transcript[2] and are intended to be used in sequence to develop both receptive and productive skills that are useful in a range of contexts.

The recorded dialogue used in the unit was based on native speaker interactions. The basic structure of a typical, successful negotiated request sequence was distilled from native speaker data collected during the projects. The devices and techniques used to mitigate the impact of a request and negotiate a solution were identified and incorporated into rough guidelines for speakers (who were not professional actors) to follow. Thus, the recording used in this chapter, although semi-scripted, is representative of natural speech.

The following activities are sequenced to help develop learners' receptive and productive skills. Activities 1–4 are designed to draw learners' attention to the characteristics of English requests in the workplace. They begin with a dialogue in which an employee makes a complex request to her supervisor, that is, to someone with greater power in the workplace. Her request is complex because it is not obvious that the supervisor is able to comply, so she approaches it with care. The resulting dialogue is used as the basis for the first four activities, which are designed to lead the learners to notice features used by native speakers and to promote reflection on how similar these might be to devices used in other cultures.

Activity 1: Listening to a Request in the Workplace

In the first activity, learners explicitly practice making inferences about people and contexts. These are the types of inferences that often influence assumptions about what people are saying and whether their behavior is appropriate. They then listen to a dialogue between a subordinate and her supervisor in the workplace. As the unit progresses, this dialogue is exploited as input for speaking practice and vocabulary development.

In Activity 1, students look at the picture on Worksheet 1 (see Appendix) and discuss the questions in Part I in pairs. After discussion of the questions, the teacher elicits the students' suggested answers, and then asks them to listen to see if they are right. He or she plays the recording and they discuss the situation as a class. The students then try to answer the questions in Part II. The teacher may play the dialogue again at this point if necessary to resolve any disagreements.

[2] The audio file and transcript are available at http://www.tesolmedia.com/books/pragmatics. The transcript also appears in Worksheet 3 (see Appendix).

Then he or she asks the students to reflect on the questions in Part III in order to raise their awareness of how the participants approach the request situation and what language forms they choose to construct it with. (For suggested answers, see the answer key in the Appendix.)

Activity 2: Raising Awareness of Similarities and Differences in Requests Across Cultures

In Activity 2, the teacher should invite learners to discuss in pairs the reflective questions on Worksheet 2 (see Appendix), which suggest areas in which work-place cultures may differ across cultures. The teacher should then facilitate a class discussion on cross-cultural differences in expectations. Questions 2 and 3 are designed to guide this discussion. There are no right or wrong answers, but some notes reflecting on what might be considered appropriate to many workplaces in Australia are provided in the answer key (see Appendix).

Activity 3: Using Informal Expressions

In this activity, learners' attention is drawn to the kinds of informal words and phrases that are typically used at each stage of the dialogue in many Australian workplaces. After they have listened to the dialogue as suggested in Activities 1 and 2, the students read the transcript in order to concentrate on vocabulary development as indicated in Question 1 on Worksheet 3 (see Appendix). They should not read it before this point so that they concentrate on listening as a skill rather than reading. This activity helps learners to identify, by themselves, vocabu-lary items that are unfamiliar and to use context to guess their meanings before they undertake a guided activity in Question 2, which suggests some possible meanings.

Activity 4: Identifying Stages of a Request Interaction in the Workplace

In Activity 4, learners are guided toward an understanding of how a request speech event is structured. Worksheet 4A (see Appendix) provides students with an opportunity to focus on and identify the different stages in the request: (a) prerequest, (b) request; (c) reason, (d) offer to help resolve the problem that will result from agreeing to the request, and (e) closing. The teacher should play the audio and allow learners to reflect on the stages in the request.

Students should now read the dialogue in Worksheet 4B (see Appendix) in pairs and decide where they think the different stages of the request are. They should then copy into the worksheet table the specific part of the dialogue that corresponds to each stage of the request.

Activity 5: Practicing a Request Interaction

In the next two activities, learners practice producing appropriate moves and language for complex requests. With Activity 5, learners put instances of each of the stages of a request speech event together into a coherent dialogue. The instructions for this activity are given to the students on Worksheet 5 (see Appendix). Teachers can put the students into pairs and ask them to construct a dialogue using the phrases in the table by choosing one phrase from each side. Some choices depend on others, so students should be warned to make sure that the phrases from the two sides match up grammatically, as well as for meaning (see the Appendix for a sample dialogue). Students should then practice the dialogue, if possible without reading directly from the text, so that their dialogue is as natural as possible.

Activity 6: Softening Requests

Activity 6 introduces important grammatical forms that are commonly used to soften requests. Part I of Worksheet 6 (see Appendix) introduces some grammar that is used to soften requests. Students should study these in pairs. The teacher may want to give further examples and answer any questions they may have.

Activity 7: Making Problematic Requests in the Workplace

The final activity broadens the domain of use to help learners understand how request forms might be used in different situations, and to practice selecting the most appropriate form for different types of requests. Teachers can have students look at Worksheet 7 (see Appendix) and discuss the different ways of starting a request and which ones they have heard, which ones they use regularly, and when they might be used. Then, working in pairs, students should attempt the first exercise, which requires ranking the request forms in order of politeness/softness. There is no one right answer to this, because how polite a request is perceived to be depends on the contest in which it is used. In some situations, a request that is too polite for the context may be considered just as inappropriate as a very bold and direct one because it may seem sarcastic or imply that the speaker thinks that his or her interlocutor will not do what they are being asked. As a general guide, though, the longer and more elaborate the softening, the more formal and polite the request, and a request in a question form is usually less demanding than one that simply states what the speaker wants. This would give a ranking similar to the one shown in Figure 1.

REFLECTIONS 

This chapter addressed the particular concerns of learners who make semi-formal requests in the workplace, focusing not only on appropriate request forms, but also on interactional request sequences.

The students for whom the activities were developed were adult migrants whose English was at the low intermediate to intermediate level, who had some previous schooling, and who were preparing to enter the workforce. Some were

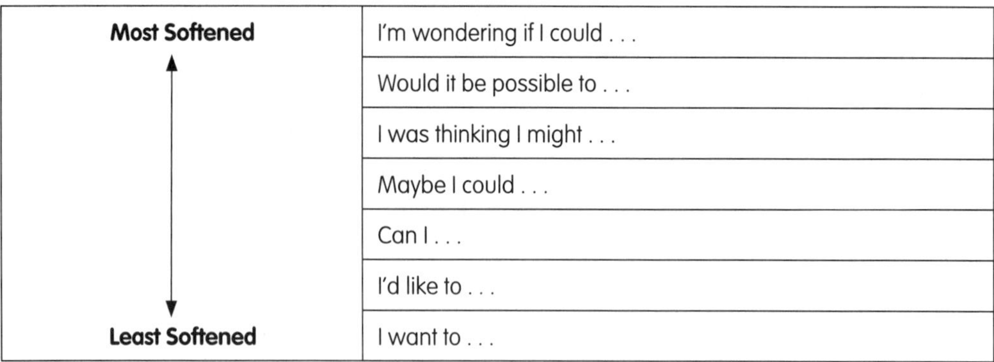

Most Softened	I'm wondering if I could . . .
↑	Would it be possible to . . .
	I was thinking I might . . .
	Maybe I could . . .
	Can I . . .
↓	I'd like to . . .
Least Softened	I want to . . .

Figure 1. Range of Introductions for Softening Requests

also studying for vocational certificates in aged care. However, the material in this unit could easily be adapted through the use of different role-play extensions and model dialogues based on a similar sequence to other contexts and adult learner groups. Teachers can record dialogues set in contexts useful to their learners and devise sets of activities to practice them, using the basic ideas illustrated in the unit above. For example, whereas this unit is aimed at a workplace with many female migrants, slightly different strategies might be used in settings with male employees or with white-collar professionals.

Although the strategies and forms used in the request sequences discussed in this chapter were similar for subordinate–superior, colleague–colleague, or superior–subordinate interaction, this is not always the case, and workplaces differ. This type of informality is quite common in many workplaces in Australia, for example, but less so in other English-speaking environments. Also, males often soften their speech considerably less often and use different forms from those exemplified by the females in this chapter. Thus, it is important to discuss with students the level of linguistic formality and social distance that is common in different workplaces for people of similar status and gender. As there is no easy prescription ahead of time how formal a workplace is likely to be, the aim here is to equip students with the analytical tools they will need to work out for themselves the particular relationships in a particular workplace.

Lynda Yates is associate professor in the Department of Linguistics at Macquarie University in Sydney, Australia. Her research interests include various aspects of adult language learning and use and professional development in TESOL. She has taught in France, Egypt, Armenia, the United Kingdom, and Australia and has been involved with teacher education for more than 20 years.

Jacky Springall has worked in the Adult Migrant English Program in Melbourne, Australia, for many years both as a teacher and in the area of professional develop-

ment. She is currently managing the Employment Pathway Programs for AMES Victoria and is the author of two recent teaching resources (Taking Care *and* Keys to Work: A Teaching Kit) *designed to assist learners preparing for the Australian workplace.*

APPENDIX: WORKSHEETS AND ANSWER KEYS 

Worksheet 1: Listening Activity—Requests in the Workplace

Part I: Understanding Context

1. Look at the picture and answer the following questions:
   - (a) Who are these people?
   - (b) Where are they?
   - (c) What do you think they are talking about?
2. Now listen to the recording (available at http://www.tesolmedia.com/books/pragmatics) and answer these questions again. Were you right?

Part II: Understanding What Happened

1. Why does Naomi need to change her roster?

   ____

   ____

2. Why does this cause a problem for Brenda?

   ____

   ____

Part III: Reflecting on How to Approach the Boss

1. How does Naomi greet Brenda when she goes into her office?

   ____

   ____

2. What do they talk about before Naomi makes her request? Why do you think they do this?

   ____

   ____

Worksheet 1: Answer Key

Part I: The picture shows an employee in an aged-care facility, Naomi, entering the office of her supervisor, Brenda. Naomi is asking Brenda to change the work roster and they are discussing this request.

Part II: Naomi needs to change the roster so that she can be with her parents, who are flying in to visit her over the weekend. This causes a problem for Brenda; because they are very busy, she has already made the work roster, and it is difficult to find people to work at the last minute.

Part III: Naomi uses the informal greeting "Hi," addresses her boss using her first name "Brenda," and asks if she is able to talk at this time—"Hi Brenda, have you got a minute?" They joke about how much paperwork there is and how busy Brenda is. In this way Naomi shows Brenda that she understands the difficulties that Brenda is facing and sympathizes with her. It helps to build solidarity between them.

Worksheet 2: Looking for Similarities and Differences Across Cultures

1. Read the questions below and indicate yes or no.

In your culture would you usually . . .	**Yes**	**No**
• ring up and tell your boss if you are going to be absent?		
• tell your boss if you had a personal problem?		
• call your boss by his or her first name?		
• knock on the door before entering your boss's office?		
• negotiate with your boss for more pay?		
• negotiate with your boss for holiday leave?		

2. Compare your answers with others in the class.

3. Discuss the following questions:
   (a) Are there any differences across different cultures?
   (b) Are there differences across different types of jobs?

Worksheet 2: Answer Key

Note: It is normally expected that employees will telephone their supervisors if they are going to be absent, but how specifically they discuss particular personal problems will vary according to the kind of relationship they have. The tenor of communication in many workplaces in Australia tends to be informal (more so than in other English-speaking countries), so first names are often used, even with those higher in rank. We would recommend knocking on the door of the boss's office before entering, and feel that in many circumstances the timing of holiday leave might be negotiable. Whether or not pay rates can be negotiated will depend on whether there is a general industry or workplace agreement on such issues. There are likely to be differences in views and experiences among speakers from different cultural backgrounds.

Worksheet 3: Informal Expressions in Requests to Colleagues

Talk between colleagues at work is often informal.

1. Read the dialogue below. Underline the expressions that you do not know. Some informal expressions are marked in *italics*. Find them and try to guess what they mean.

Naomi: Hi Brenda, have you got a minute?

Brenda: Yeah, come in . . . sit down, Naomi.

Naomi: (walks in and sits down, looks at stack of paperwork on desk) You look like you've got *a bit of* a fun morning ahead!

Brenda: Yeah my favorite—paperwork! (laughs)

Naomi: Yeah, I've got *a bit* of that to do myself after lunch . . . now Brenda, I was just wondering if I could talk to you about the latest roster you've just put up.

Brenda: Oh don't tell me there's another problem.

Naomi: (sounds apologetic) Yeah, I know . . . it must be a nightmare trying to get all the shifts covered at the moment. (Brenda signals assent.) But um . . . I've got *a bit of a problem*. I just had a call from my mum last night and she and my dad are flying down to Melbourne next weekend. It's the first time they've been able to come down since I moved here and I was really hoping I could have the weekend free.

Brenda: Oh Naomi . . . you know how short staffed we are at the moment . . .

Naomi: Yes, I do . . . I just thought maybe I could swap the following weekend with Carla. I'm happy to *do two in a row*.

Brenda: OK . . . yeah, so . . . that'd be great *if Carla's OK with it*. Actually, she's coming this afternoon to pick up a group certificate so I could ask her then.

Naomi: Oh that would be great, Brenda. Shall I *pop in* when I *knock off* and check if that's OK?

Brenda: Yeah . . . OK . . . *we'll sort something out*.

Naomi: (gets up to leave) That'll be great. Thanks, Brenda.

2. Now match the phrases in the first column with the meanings in the column. The first one has been done for you

Phrase	Meaning
a bit of a problem	Come
short staffed	one after another
Two in a row	finish work
Is OK with that	thinks this is a good arrangement
See what we can sort out	a little difficulty
Pop in	without many people working
knock off	Try to come to an agreement

Note: A "group certificate" is a certificate issued to Australian employees that shows how much they have earned and how much tax they have paid.

Worksheet 3: Answer Key

Question 2

Phrase	Meaning
A bit of a problem	a little difficulty
short staffed	without many people working
Two in a row	one after another
Is OK with that	thinks this is a good arrangement
See what we can sort out	try to come to an agreement
Pop in	come
knock off	finish work

Worksheet 4A: Stages of a Request Interaction—Request to a Boss

In the dialogue, Naomi makes her request in a number of stages. Listen to the dialogue (available at http://www.tesolmedia.com/books/pragmatics) and look at the table below; see what Naomi says in each of the stages. Next to the examples from the transcript of Naomi's speech in the dialogue are notes on the language she used. Note that Naomi and Brenda are interacting in an Australian context.

The following table presents the stages in a request interaction:

Stages	Example	Notes
Greeting	Hi *Brenda* . . . have you got a minute?	In Australia workers often call each other by their first name, even the boss. This practice may vary in other English-speaking countries. "Have you got a minute" makes the interruption seem less important.
Prerequest/ support move	You look like you've got a bit of a fun morning ahead . . . I've got a bit of that (i.e., paperwork) to do myself after lunch. *I was wondering if I could* talk to you about the latest roster you've just put up.	Naomi tries to establish rapport with Brenda by finding some common ground. Naomi prepares Brenda for what is to come. The phrase "*I was wondering if I could*" makes the sentence less direct and the past tense makes it seem less direct and urgent.
The request	*I was really hoping I could* have the weekend free.	The past and continuous forms have been used to make the request less direct in "*I was hoping.*" The word "*really*" is added to make the request stronger.
Reason	I just had a call from my mum last night and she and my dad are flying down to Melbourne next weekend.	Naomi gives a reason but not a lot of details as it's a personal matter.
Offer/ support move	*I just thought maybe I could* swap the following weekend with Carla. I'm happy to do two in a row.	Naomi offers a possible solution to the problem. This shows her willingness to take responsibility for her actions and to make it easier for Brenda.
Closing	That'll be great. Thanks Brenda	Thanks.

Worksheet 4B: Stages of a Request Interaction—Request to a Colleague

1. Look at the dialogue that Sue, one of Naomi's colleagues, had with Brenda, the supervisor, earlier in the week. Look at how Sue stages her request.

   Sue: Hello Brenda . . . could I have a quick word with you please?

   Brenda: Yes, sure . . . come in.

   Sue: Now Brenda, I know we're pretty busy at the moment, but I haven't taken any of my leave yet this year.

   Brenda: Mmm.

   Sue: So, I was wondering if I could take three weeks of my leave now . . . well starting next week when you do the new rosters.

Brenda: Oh Sue . . . I know you have got the leave owing but it's really not a good time right now.

Sue: Yes, I understand that but I'm starting to feel very tired and so I'm making silly mistakes. I really need a break.

Brenda: Oh dear . . . that's no good is it? . . . Do you think you could wait for a couple of weeks . . . then we'll have Jenny back?

Sue: Mmm . . . OK . . . well another two weeks is all right I guess if I know there's some light at the end of the tunnel!

Brenda: OK then Sue . . . if you fill out your leave forms today I'll sign them so we can get them in.

Sue: Good . . . thanks Brenda . . . I'll get them to you by the end of the day.

2. Now put Sue's part of the dialogue into the table below.

Stages	Sue says . . .
Greeting	
Prerequest/support move	
Request	
Reason	
Offer /support move	
Closing	

Worksheet 4B: Answer Key

Stages	Sue says . . .
Greeting	Hello Brenda.
Prerequest/support move	Could I have a quick word with you please? Now Brenda, I know we're pretty busy at the moment, but I haven't taken any of my leave yet this year.
Request	So, I was wondering if I could take three weeks of my leave now.
Reason	. . . but I'm starting to feel very tired and so I'm making silly mistakes. I really need a break.
Offer/support move	Mmm . . . OK . . . well another two weeks is all right I guess if I know there's some light at the end of the tunnel!
Closing	Good . . . thanks Brenda . . . I'll get them to you by the end of the day.

Worksheet 5: Practicing a Request Interaction

1. With a partner, begin a request dialogue by choosing phrases from the table. Partner A chooses a phrase from each of the two boxes in the first row. Partner B chooses responses from the two boxes in the second row. For example:

    Partner A: Hello, Amy. I was wondering if you had a moment.

    Partner B: Yes sure. What can I do for you?

    Partner A: (continues)

    When you have selected your phrases, practice your dialogue with your partner. Notice that these phrases don't include a resolution.

• *Hi Sam* • *Hello Amy* • *Good morning Jenny*	• *Could I have a word with you?* • *Have you got a few minutes?* • *I was wondering if you had a moment*
• *Ah yes* • *Yes sure* • *Yeah*	• *Come in* • *Sit down* • *What can I do for you?*
• *Look I know it's a busy time at the moment* • *Well I realize it's probably not the best time* • *I was just wondering*	• *if I could talk to you about my annual leave?* • *but I wanted to talk to you about my holidays* • *but something urgent has just come up*
• *OK* • *Yes, what did you want to know?* • *Mmm*	
• *I was hoping* • *I was wondering if I could* • *I would like*	• *to take two weeks off now* • *have a few days of my holidays now* • *to have the rest of the month off*
• *Oh dear* • *Well,* • *Right, well*	• *You can't be serious?* • *It's not a good time at the moment* • *We normally prefer staff to plan their leave at the start of the year*
• *Yes I know* • *I realize that* • *Yeah, I appreciate that*	• *but something has come up that I've got to attend to* • *but my husband is having surgery* • *but I've got some family business I've got to deal with*

2. Complete the dialogue with your partner. Try to come to a suitable arrangement. Remember to use offers and support moves.

Worksheet 5: Answer Key

A completed dialogue might look something like the following:

Hi Sam, I was wondering if you had a moment.	
	Yes sure. Come in.
Well . . . I realize it's probably not the best time but something urgent has just come up.	
	Mmm.
I was wondering if I could have a few days of my holidays now.	
	Well, it's not a good time at the moment.

Worksheet 6: Creating Softened Requests

Part I: These grammatical structures can be used to "soften" requests. For example:

- **Past-tense forms**
  For example, I *wanted* to ask you to finish the paperwork tonight.
- **Continuous forms**
  For example, *I was wondering* if you could give me any extra work.
- ***Would like* rather than *want***
  For example, *I would like (I'd like)* some extra help on the shift.

Part II: Using the softening forms above, write requests according to the instructions below.

1. Make requests using the words below and use the **past-tense form** to soften them:

   can / give / box

   (a) ______________________________

   want / talk / about my training

   (b) ______________________________

   wonder if / can leave / early tonight

   (c) ______________________________

2. Make requests using these words and use the **continuous form** to soften them:

   wonder / take a few days off

   (a) ______________________________

   hope / finish at 9:00 p.m.

   (b) ______________________________

3. Make requests using these words and use **would like** to soften them:

   want / take tomorrow off

   (a) ______________________________

   want / start a bit later in the morning

   (b) ______________________________

Worksheet 6: Answer Key for Part II

1. (a) Could you give me the box? (b) I wanted to talk to you about my training. (c) I wondered if I can leave early tonight?
2. (a) I am wondering if I can take a few days off. (b) I am hoping to finish at 9:00 p.m.
3. (a) I would like to take tomorrow off. (b) I would like to start a bit later in the morning.

Worksheet 7: Making a Problematic Request

A variety of strategies are used to ask for something important. Different requests are used in different situations. For example, a speaker would be likely to use softer or more polite requests:

- with people the speaker does not know very well
- with people who are in positions of power
- when the request is for something that is difficult or expensive
- when the speaker expects some resistance

Here are some common ways of starting a request:

Maybe I could . . .
I want to . . .
I'm wondering if I could . . .
Can I . . .
Would it be possible to . . .
I'd like to . . .
I was thinking I might . . .

leave early today

1. Discuss with a partner which of the request forms listed above are the most polite. Put them in order of politeness/softness:

   Most softened ______________________________

   ____

   ____

   ____

   ____

   Least softened ______________________________

2. Discuss with your partner which one you would use to request in the following situations. Why? Would you prepare the ground for each request in some way? If so, how?
   (a) You want your colleague to pass you a chart that is on the desk in front of her.
   (b) You have an interview for a job, but you have not been able to find child care arrangements for that time and would like to change it. You telephone the job agency.
   (c) You want your colleague to swap your Saturday night shift for her Saturday morning shift.
   (d) You want to ask your supervisor if you can have annual leave at a time you know will be very busy at work.
   (e) You want to ask your manager if you can leave early because someone has given you free tickets to a show.

Worksheet 7: Answer Key

1. There is no one right answer to the question posed in this activity. What is most appropriate depends on the specific context.

   Would it be possible to . . .
   I'm wondering if I could . . .
   I was thinking I might . . .
   Maybe I could . . .
   Can I . . .
   I'd like to . . .
   I want to . . .

   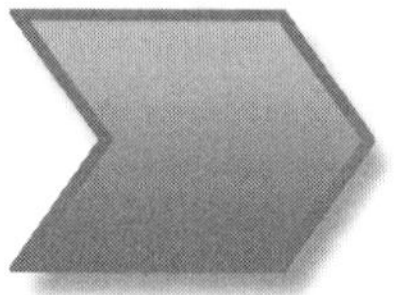

   leave early today

2. The following forms would be appropriate in many Australian workplace contexts:
   (a) Can I have that chart?
   (b) Good morning. I have an interview for . . . tomorrow but I've had a lot of trouble trying to find childcare. I know this is rather short notice, but I was wondering if I could change the time of my appointment.
   (c) I've just been given a couple of free tickets to . . . I was wondering if we could . . .
   (d) I was wondering if I could take some leave next month. I know it is a busy time but . . .
   (e) I'd like to leave a bit early tonight, (if that's OK).

Indirect Acts

CHAPTER 7

Teacher, You Should Lose Some Weight: Advice Giving in English

Noël R. Houck and John Fujimori

Acts such as requests, apologies, refusals, and compliments have been frequently identified as particularly problematic for English as a foreign language (EFL) and English as a second language (ESL) learners at all levels. One less obvious act that is frequently misused by nonnative English speakers is advice giving. This chapter[1] offers a set of activities for raising learners' awareness of the different levels of directness and provides general guidelines on how to offer advice appropriately in many English speech communities.

Advice giving involves telling someone to do something (i.e., perform or not perform some action) that the speaker thinks will benefit the addressee. In this speech act, as opposed to acts of giving permission or ordering, the speaker has no power to oblige or permit the addressee to perform the act, and the speaker believes that the person will not perform the act on his or her own. For example, you might give a coworker the following advice: "*You should go home and rest.* You're really looking sick" (the advice is in italics). Advice giving should not be confused with giving directions, a speech act for which it is perfectly appropriate to use imperatives in English (e.g., "Turn in your paper," "Attach the legs to the table after attaching the drawer," "Go two blocks north, then turn left").

One of the authors, Fujimori, teaches English to native speakers of Japanese in a high-level Japanese high school. His attention was caught by his students'

[1] This chapter is based upon work previously published as "Practical Criteria for Teaching Speech Acts" by J. Fujimori, N. Houck, and the Japanese Association for Language Teaching (JALT), 2004, *The Language Teacher, 28*(5), pp. 3–8. Copyright 2004 by the JALT Board of Directors. Adapted with permission.

apparently well-intentioned advice to their native-English-speaking (NES) teachers, which included the following examples:

1. You should get married.
2. Teacher, you had better buy a better car.

These examples illustrate two types of problems: (a) use of advice in situations in which advice is considered inappropriate (Example 1); and (b) use of inappropriate linguistic forms to express advice, that is, the rather abrupt-sounding forms *should* and *had better* (Examples 1 and 2). In fact, from a student to a teacher, Example 1 is so inappropriate as to sound presumptuous and rather offensive. And inappropriate advice giving does not seem to be restricted to Fujimori's students. Hinkel (1994) cited instances of students advising teachers that they should not smoke so much and telling friends that they should not eat so many sweets.

This chapter compares the different strategies employed by nonnative English speakers and native English speakers in advice giving, targeting in particular the tendency of learners from cultures such as Japan to use offensively direct strategies when speaking English. The activities[2] offer instruction in the identification and production of direct, softened, and indirect advice.

CONTEXT

During the past 8 years, Fujimori has developed a series of activities on advice giving in English. He uses them in a senior-level spoken English class at a top-level high school in Japan. Fujimori regularly revises the activities to accommodate his students' problems. Due to the demands of the curriculum, the activities are presented during three class periods, with a follow-up lesson about 6 months later.

Fujimori regularly evaluates the immediate effectiveness of the activities by checking on his students' controlled production. He has students respond to the same scenarios that he used to assess their initial advice-giving strategies. The results have been dramatic, with student responses displaying a marked change from their preinstruction answers. After instruction the majority of the class give softened or indirect advice to a friend, with 75% of the class producing some form of indirect advice to the teacher.

In addition to Fujimori's final assessment, students have provided informal feedback on their impressions of the lesson. Many have stated that they find the activities illuminating. Specifically, instead of preprogrammed responses, they have to consider the situation and the hearer, and measure their responses accordingly. One student commented that this was the first time that she had learned

[2] The audio file and transcript for this chapter are available at http://www.tesolmedia.com/books/pragmatics. The transcript also appears in Appendix B.

about the appropriateness of her responses. Other students have expressed similar sentiments.

Similar to these students, there may be others who are unaware of the communicative dimensions of advice giving, which, depending on the situation, can perform a number of interactional functions such as establishing/maintaining rapport, flattering, or helping, as well as criticizing, distancing, or dominating (DeCapua & Huber, 1995). Unlike in the students' native cultures, in Anglo-American cultures advice giving is often associated with criticism, especially when it is unsolicited (Mandala, 1999). Thus, Anglo American speakers of English may choose to opt out of giving unsolicited advice or at most use an indirect strategy. On the other hand, in other cultures such as Japan, unsolicited advice is more often used to show "warm interest in the other's well-being" (Masuda, 1989, as cited in Hinkel, 1994, p. 5) and is frequently used in making small talk. Therefore, native speakers of Japanese tend to feel more comfortable administering advice and using direct strategies to do so.

Thus, it is not surprising that these students and other nonnative English speakers may transfer their first language (L1) pragmatic rules into their second language (L2) communicative interactions by offering unsolicited advice when advice would normally be avoided or downplayed in English—without realizing the negative impact their behavior may have (Blum-Kulka, 1983).

Educating such students about appropriate advice-giving behaviors may begin with introducing them to Hinkel's (1994) three directness levels for advice-giving strategies, as follows:

1. Direct: "You should buy a train pass."
2. Softened: "Maybe you should buy a train pass."
3. Indirect: "I bought a train pass last year, and it really made life easier."

Through students' collection of naturally occurring English advice, one of the authors has observed similarities between some advice-giving strategies and some conventionally indirect requests. Thus, formulaic *suggestory* strategies (e.g., "Why don't you"); statements or questions regarding the hearer's ability (e.g., "You could buy a train pass," "Could you buy a train pass?"); or statements of the hearer's want or need, often softened (e.g., "You might want to buy a train pass") often signal advice giving. Other researchers have organized advice-giving phrases into those appropriate for equal status or higher status recipients (Martinez-Flor & Fukuya, 2005).

Even when advice is warranted, nonnative English speakers with many different L1s tend to rely on the forms associated with direct advice or softened advice such as *should* or *had better* (Altman, 1990), as opposed to the indirect advice strategy often favored by native English speakers. In Japan, these forms are taught as the equivalent of a polite Japanese advice-giving form in the junior high and high schools.

CURRICULUM, TASKS, MATERIALS 

Fujimori's students probably did not perceive their advice giving to the Anglo-American teachers as intrusive or impolite. However, because these remarks were having an unrecognized and unfavorable effect on their recipients, Fujimori decided that this particular act was an important one to spend class time on. This prompted him to develop a set of activities based on Hinkel's (1994) three types of advice-giving strategies with the following goals: (a) to determine students' current knowledge of English advice-giving strategies; (b) to raise students' awareness; (c) to build students' knowledge of some of the alternatives available for producing the act (e.g., the ability to recognize direct, softened, and indirect strategies); and (d) to develop students' ability to produce the act appropriately in different situations.

Activity 1: Determining Students' Existing Advice-Giving Skills

To determine whether students would use appropriate advice-giving strategies if they are given sufficient time and are focused on the activity, and whether they would use the same advice-giving strategies with superiors and peers, students can respond to Worksheet 1 (see Appendix A), which provides one advice-giving situation with a peer and two with a superior. Students write what they would say in English in each situation. One alternative to focusing on all three levels is to focus only on contrasting the direct and indirect levels, as this is often the contrast that students need most in order to avoid problems.

Current research indicates that an effective approach to teaching speech act production involves providing explicit instruction on the acts (Tateyama, Kasper, Mui, Tay, & Thananart, 1997) and an opportunity to practice them (Morrow, 1995). The following activities include an awareness raising activity, two activities for developing knowledge of how advice is given in English, and two production activities, along with a set of explicit tips on advice giving. These activities can be used in conjunction with a lesson on health, or they can be adapted to the current teaching situation.

Activity 2: Raising Students' Awareness

This activity is an inductive exercise designed to increase the students' awareness of English advice-giving strategies. In Worksheet 2 (see Appendix A), students identify the three different types of advice giving in familiar situations. When students have completed the worksheet, the teacher can discuss each level with them, explaining that when speaking English, advice should be given carefully. Indirect advice is usually given to superiors, and indirect or softened advice is used with peers. Direct advice is used sparingly. It may be necessary to explain that in Anglo-American culture, advice giving does not foster group cohesiveness and is generally not used for small talk.

Activity 3: Improving Students' Advice-Giving Skills

In Activity 3, students practice identifying examples of the three strategies that were previously discussed in Activity 2. Worksheet 3 (see Appendix A) focuses on individual sentences or utterances and requires students to determine which of three approximately identical statements is direct, which is softened, and which is indirect. As teachers check the students' responses, special attention should be given to the association of the following strategies and forms:

- Direct advice: *should, had better*
- Softened / Hedges (softeners): *we should, why not, you could, could you*
- Indirect: wait to be asked, then use *I would* or *I might*; or simply give a reason for an action or restraint from action
- Opting out: no advice or suggestion is given to the hearer

Note that direct advice with softeners such as *maybe*, *I think*, and *perhaps* sometimes functions as softened or hedged advice; however, these are often still perceived as rather direct.

Activity 4: Identifying Advice-Giving Strategies in Spoken Dialogues

In Activity 4, a time constraint is introduced. Students listen to prerecorded dialogues (see Appendix B for the transcript) in which advice is given. As they listen the first time, they identify the situation as represented in Worksheet 4 (see Appendix A); the second time, they focus on the level of directness of the advice. Here the students are required to recognize the strategies "on line" while also focusing on meaning.

Activity 5: Producing Appropriate Advice

In production activities, students respond to various scenarios, either orally or in writing. For the first production activity (see Worksheet 5 in Appendix A), students are asked to write their own responses to written scenarios. Students are expected to decide on one of the three strategies and produce a corresponding form. Students can then write their responses on the whiteboard and discuss their choices, drawing attention to the different levels of directness. When the teacher compares responses, students can see which responses were appropriate, depending on the situation.

Activity 6: Producing Appropriate Advice in a Role-Play

In Activity 6, students produce their own responses orally. They perform the open-ended role-plays described on Worksheets 6A and 6B (6A for Role A, 6B for Role B; see Appendix A), which involve opportunities for advice giving, applying their knowledge of the appropriate forms to online production. After observing several of the role-plays, the teacher and the class can discuss the students' choices.

Activity 7: Following Up

After students have completed the activities described in this chapter, their teacher can provide them with some general tips for advice giving in English. The following tips serve as simple reminders of what students have learned. However, they can also be used in a class that is focusing only on consciousness raising.

- **Think** before you give advice. Is the advice necessary?
- Use **indirect** advice with superiors.
- Use **indirect** advice or **softened** advice with friends.
- Avoid giving direct advice using *should* or *had better.*
- Don't give advice just to make small talk.

Finally, after presenting the activities designed to develop students' knowledge or production of a particular act, teachers may want to assess how effective the lesson has been. This can be accomplished using activities similar to the ones used at the practice stage.

REFLECTIONS 

Although a brief lesson, such as the one presented in this chapter, will obviously not result in students consistently producing sensitive acts that employ correct grammar and situationally appropriate forms, it can provide students with the awareness of the strategies and forms they need to successfully develop the knowledge and skills required to recognize and produce these acts. In Fujimori's case, after completing the advice-giving activities, students displayed an increased awareness of the constraints on advice giving in English and a better understanding of the implications of different forms. Although the ability to adapt strategies and forms to different situations will come only with experience, these students were able to produce forms that reflected a consciousness of the distinction and knowledge of the linguistic options available to convey the distinction.

Possible Modifications

Factors such as time, student level, and context can affect a teacher's approach to advice giving.

Depending on the amount of time available for supplementing course materials with advice-giving instruction, teachers may choose one or more of the exercises described in this chapter. For example, if time is limited, the most expedient choice would be to make students aware that giving advice may be considered rude or inappropriate, and that it is best to avoid it whenever possible. A second option is to develop students' ability to recognize some of the alternatives available for producing the act (i.e., direct, softened, and indirect strategies). The most ambitious choice is to guide students in producing advice appropriate to situations in which the opportunity to give advice may arise. In this case, the teacher needs to provide students with the opportunity to practice some of the forms and strategies in familiar situations.

Hinkel's (1994) three types of advice-giving strategies were considered appropriate for EFL high school students. If learners are more advanced, teachers may want to include more of the "conventionally indirect" strategies, such as the suggestory formula (e.g., "Why not"); hearer ability questions or statements with *could* or *can* (e.g., "You could take an alternate route"); and hearer want or need statements, especially with *might* (e.g., "You might want to call the office and explain").

To make the lesson relevant to different student audiences, teachers can make two basic types of adjustments. First, they can substitute situations that are meaningful to their students for those in the text. They can also use linguistic forms that are already familiar to the learners (e.g., use of *might* to replace *should*) or phrases that can be easily learned as chunks (e.g., "Why not").

Depending on the context, teachers may want to make learners aware of the constraints on advice giving in their own community. For instance, in adult education, students could be instructed not to give advice in the workplace and to offer English-speaking friends indirect advice. High school teachers might want to emphasize that advice to adults is frequently considered disrespectful. Students could be engaged in deciding what forms of advice giving to focus on by collecting data on advice giving from original English texts.

In addition, ESL learners should be informed that different regions and social groups often have different advice-giving norms. Thus, observation of advice giving by English speakers who are similar to them in situations similar to theirs is ideal. The results of their observations can be used as the basis for modification of the exercises. On the other hand, if students do not have access to native English speakers, the teacher might want to use DVDs of movies with characters with whom students can identify. If clips of films are used, EFL students should be encouraged to discuss the artistic uses of giving advice. A character in a film may use elaborate language in giving advice where most native speakers would use a simpler form. Also, a character might give direct advice because he or she is rude, not because it is appropriate to do so in real life.

ACKNOWLEDGMENTS 

We owe a significant debt of gratitude to Jana Moore and Chris Sullivan for recording the dialogues for the listening activity and heartfelt thanks to Megumi Horikoshi for providing the artwork for Worksheet 4.

Noël R. Houck is associate professor in the English and Foreign Languages Department at California State Polytechnic University Pomona in the United States. Her research centers on cross-cultural pragmatics and discourse analysis, with a focus on microanalysis of classroom discourse. She has taught and conducted research in Brazil, Mexico, and Japan.

John Fujimori teaches at Meiji Gakuin High School in Tokyo, Japan. His research interests include pragmatics, vocabulary acquisition, task-based language learning, and materials development. He is currently examining the content and format of government approved high school English textbooks and their effect on L2 learners.

APPENDIX A: WORKSHEETS AND ANSWER KEYS 

Worksheet 1: Advice Giving—Diagnostic

This worksheet presents three situations. Read each situation and think about what you would say to the other person. Write your answer.

Situation 1: It's not raining right now, but you know that a big storm is approaching. Your teacher is about to leave without his umbrella. You think he hasn't heard about the storm. What would you say?

You: ____

____

Situation 2: Tomorrow you and your friend have a very important test. You have studied hard, so you're confident you'll do well. Your friend hasn't studied at all and may fail the class. Tonight is the last chance to study. Your friend says:

Friend: Let's go sing some karaoke.

You: ____

____

Situation 3: You are walking down the street and meet Mr. Suzuki, your principal. You talk for a minute or two. He looks very sick. What would you say?

You: ____

____

Worksheet 1: Answer Key

What follows are suggested answers. Answers may vary.

1. I hear there's a storm approaching. I have an extra umbrella if you need one.
2. Aren't you going to study for the test tomorrow? If you want, I'll stay and help you.
3. (a) There's a pretty bad flu going around. I'm trying not to catch it. (b) Nothing.

Worksheet 2: Recognizing Directness Levels

Part I: Read the following three conversations. Is the advice *direct*, *softened*, or *indirect*?

Situation #1: You are at a DVD rental shop with a friend. Your friend decides to rent a movie. You've already seen it, and you think it's a boring movie. You say, "You should rent something more interesting."

Question: Was your statement direct, softened, or indirect?

Situation #2: Tomorrow is graduation day at your school. A new teacher will also be attending. This is a formal occasion. However, the teacher always dresses very casually. You suggest he should wear a suit.

Student: Will you be attending the graduation ceremony tomorrow?

Teacher: Yes, I'm looking forward to being there.

Student: So am I. It'll be exciting. Everyone will be dressed up, the students, parents, and teachers. And we'll be taking lots of pictures. See you tomorrow!

Question: Was your statement direct, softened, or indirect?

Situation #3: Every day you and your friend eat junk food after school. You now think it's unhealthy. You say, "I think we should go on a diet."

Question: Was your statement direct, softened, or indirect?

Part II: Now think about and answer the following questions:

1. What makes the advice **direct**? ______________________________
    a. Who is the addressee? ______________________________
2. What makes the advice **indirect**? ______________________________
    b. Who is the addressee? ______________________________
3. What makes the advice **softened**? ______________________________
    c. Who is the addressee? ______________________________

Worksheet 2: Answer Key

Part I

1. Direct
2. Indirect
3. Softened

Part II

1. It tells someone what he or she should do without any softening words.
    a. friend
2. The speaker doesn't directly give advice, but instead suggests behavior by describing an expectation.
    b. teacher
3. *I think*, collaborative implication of *we*
    c. friend

Worksheet 3: Identifying Appropriate Directness Levels for Advice Giving

Read the following sentences. Is the advice *direct (D)*, *softened (S)*, or *indirect (I)*? Which type would you use in the situation?

1. Suggest that your English teacher shouldn't wear such strong cologne.
   (a) You should not wear such strong cologne. ______
   (b) You might want to try a lighter cologne. ______
   (c) So many of my friends have allergies to cologne that I never wear it. ______

2. Advise a sick acquaintance to go see a doctor.
   (a) When I feel sick, I usually go to a doctor right away. ______
   (b) I think you'd feel better if you got some medicine from a doctor. ______
   (c) You look sick. You had better see a doctor. ______

3. Suggest that your friend shouldn't buy a bright shirt.
   (a) You know, plain shirts are really in fashion this season. ______
   (b) Perhaps we should look for another shirt.______
   (c) You shouldn't buy the striped shirt. It's ugly. ______

Worksheet 3: Answer Key

1. (a) direct
   (b) softened
   (c) indirect

   [Only (c) could be used. Students might want to refrain from making this comment at all.]

2. (a) indirect
   (b) softened
   (c) direct

   [Any one of these three could be OK, depending on the relationship with the friend.]

3. (a) indirect
   (b) softened
   (c) direct

   [(a) would be appropriate in most situations.]

Worksheet 4: Identifying the Directness Level of Advice

1. Listen to the five examples of advice giving (available at http://www.tesolmedia.com/books/pragmatics). Write the letter of the picture in the order that you hear it below. There are three extra pictures.
2. Listen again. Is the directness level of the advice given in each case: *direct*, *softened*, or *indirect*? Circle your answers.

a. b. 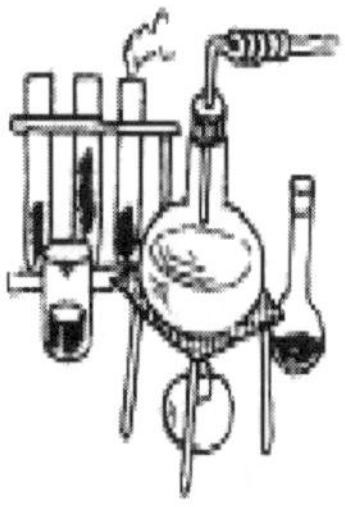 c.  d.

e.

f. 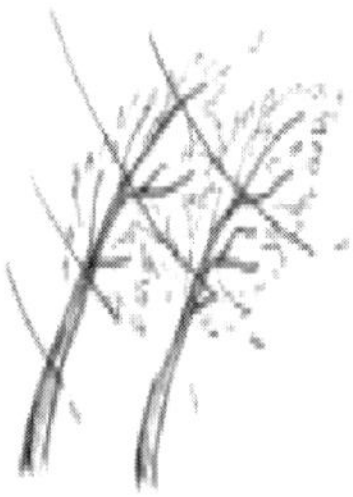 g.  h.

1. _______ direct, softened, indirect
2. _______ direct, softened, indirect
3. _______ direct, softened, indirect
4. _______ direct, softened, indirect
5. _______ direct, softened, indirect

Worksheet 4: Answer Key

1. (f); direct
2. (a); indirect
3. (g); softened
4. (c); indirect
5. (d); direct

Worksheet 5: Practice Giving Appropriate Advice

Write your own advice for each of the following situations.

1. A 5-day holiday is coming up. Your oral communication teacher, who recently moved to the area, is planning to drive to a vacation spot. You know the highways will be very crowded.

   ____

   ____

2. Your friend has an allergy. She's allergic to cedar pollen. Her eyes are puffy and she's constantly sneezing.

   ____

   ____

3. Your father's friend is visiting your home. He's in his 40s and is worried about losing his job. He has to learn how to use computers as soon as possible.

   ____

   ____

Worksheet 5: Answer Key

Suggested answers; answers will vary.

1. My family and I are taking a holiday, too. We're leaving really early to avoid the awful traffic.
2. You might want to talk to Dr. Grove. He treated my cousin's allergy, and she's doing really well.
3. I heard that the University has a really good basic computing course that's not awfully expensive.

Worksheet 6A: Practice Giving Advice—Role A

Instructions: Read your role-play card information. Think about what you would say. Then perform the role-play with your partner. Remember that opting out of giving advice is an option. If you opt out, say something other than giving advice.

1. You and a friend are going to eat in a restaurant. Tell your friend that you love to eat *tempura*, so you're going to order the "*tempura* special."
2. You are a teacher. You are taking some students to summer camp in your car. It's an old car, but you like it.
3. You are the principal. You're picking grapes from the vines behind the school. You're very tired from all the work.
4. Your homeroom teacher is going to get married. You know the man or woman your teacher is going to marry. You think your teacher should marry someone else. Give appropriate advice, or opt out.

Worksheet 6B: Practice Giving Advice—Role B

Instructions: Read your role-play card information. Think about what you would say. Then perform the role-play with your partner. Remember that opting out of giving advice is an option. If you opt out, say something other than giving advice.

1. You and a friend are going to eat at a restaurant. Your friend says he or she will order the "tempura special." You've eaten there before, and the tempura wasn't very good. Give your friend appropriate advice, or opt out.
2. You are going to summer camp with your teacher. He or she he is going to drive you. When you see his or her car you're surprised that it's very old. You think he or she should buy a new one. Give appropriate advice, or opt out.
3. The principal is picking grapes from the vines behind the school. You think the principal shouldn't do that kind of work. Give appropriate advice, or opt out.
4. You are a homeroom teacher. You are engaged and planning to get married in a few months.

APPENDIX B: TRANSCRIPT 

Activity 4: Identifying Advice-Giving Strategies in Spoken Dialogues

1. A: Where are you going?

   B: I'm going to the park to fly my kite.

   A: You *had better* go some other time. It's too windy today. [direct]

2. A: What happened to you? Are you OK?

   B: I hurt my back playing basketball.

   A: That's too bad. Did you see a doctor?

   B: No. I've been too busy.

   A: I hurt my back when I fell last summer. I saw the doctor right away and he gave me some medicine. I got better right away. [indirect]

3. A: You look worried.

   B: Yeah. I'm worried about our math test next week.

   A: I think I understand it. If you need help, *why not* study together? [softened]

4. A: How have you been?

   B: Great. I've been busy taking ballet lessons and the teacher is really popular.

   A: That sounds interesting.

   B: It is, but my class is too big. What do you think I should do?

   A: I *might* talk to my teacher about a smaller class. [indirect]

5. A: Yumiko, it's nice of you to take me to this restaurant. I don't have many chances to talk with my students.

   B: I often come here with my friends. The cakes and pies are really good.

   A: I'll have to try some. Do you mind if I smoke?

   B: You *shouldn't* smoke here. The sign says no smoking. [direct]

CHAPTER 8

Moving Beyond "In My Opinion": Teaching the Complexities of Expressing Opinion

Kristin Bouton, Katy Curry, and Lawrence Bouton

The ability to recognize and express opinions appropriately is an important skill in a second language. Textbooks generally present the most basic expressions such as *I think* or *maybe*. These expressions are acquired early (Salsbury & Bardovi-Harlig, 2000), and learners may latch onto them and overuse them (Netsu & LoCastro, 1997). However, native speakers rely on a variety of linguistic resources to let others know what they think about a topic. And norms for expressing opinions vary across cultures. Wierzbicka (1991) noted that native Polish speakers have a "tendency to express opinions in strong terms, and without any hedges whatsoever" (p. 43), whereas Japanese speakers may express an opinion so indirectly that the English-speaking hearer does not recognize it as an opinion (Beebe & Takahashi, 1989, p. 215).

Learners of English need to be exposed to a variety of forms used by many native English speakers to express opinions that are recognized as opinions, but that are also appropriately modified. Some of the more common forms used for opinions in English are linguistically complex and may, therefore, benefit from being explicitly taught. This chapter seeks to expand students' repertoire by introducing an additional linguistic resource for expressing opinions (i.e., negative questions), as well as forms for softening or strengthening opinions such as *a little* or *really*.

CONTEXT 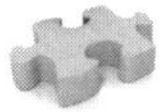

The activities presented in this chapter were first taught in the Intensive English Institute at the University of Illinois in the United States. This is a 20-hour-a-week program attended by students from all over the world, but primarily from

Asia. The students are usually at least 20 years old and are college educated. In particular, the materials were developed for and piloted on an upper intermediate, nonacademic listening–speaking class. Students reported finding the activities realistic and motivating. The use of audio clips[1] gives students a contextualized model that they find helpful as they try to put the new strategies into practice.

Opinions may be expressed on a variety of topics, ranging from personal preferences in music and clothing to choice of restaurant and political and religious beliefs. They can be unsolicited expressions, responses to another's opinion, or requests for an opinion. The activities in this chapter focus on two types of linguistic resources often used in the expression of opinions, but frequently ignored in discussions of opinion giving: (a) selected linguistic resources for softening and intensifying opinions and (b) negative questions as opinions.

Intensifiers and Softeners

In addition to adding to their repertoire of opinion-giving strategies, learners need to be able to modify opinions by softening or strengthening them. Softeners help speakers to mitigate or hedge strong opinions, whereas intensifiers strengthen the opinions they modify.

Although English has an extensive inventory of syntactic and lexical modifiers, this chapter focuses on a selection of common modifiers ranging from early acquired lexical items such as *very*, *so*, and *really* to later acquired forms such as *just* (Beebe & Waring, 2004). Before presenting these items, teachers need to be aware of their grammar, which can be much more challenging than is readily apparent to native speakers. Tables 1 and 2 provide a grammar overview of some softeners and intensifiers with examples. Teachers also need to note the different effect that the same form can have depending on the context and the item modified. Students may require extensive practice producing the items grammatically and appropriately before they are ready to use them productively.

Table 1. Softeners

Type of Softener	Examples
Modifiers of adjectives and adverbs: *a little, a little bit, kind of, sort of, not really, not so, not that*	*a little (bit)* tired, *kind of* unpleasant, *sort of* inspiring, *not really* interesting, *not that* crazy about it
Modifiers of verbs: *kind of, sort of* (occur before the verb)	I *kind of* like it, I *sort of* like it

[1]The audio files and transcripts for this chapter (including the transcripts for the videos mentioned in Handout 2) are available at http://www.tesolmedia.com/books/pragmatics. In addition, the transcripts for Activity 2 appear in Worksheet 3, and the video transcripts appear in Appendix C.

Table 2. Intensifiers

Type of Intensifier	Examples
Modifiers of verbs, adjectives, and adverbs: *really, really not*, so, too* (for a negative opinion)	*really* enjoy, *really* interesting; *really don't* appreciate; *so* quickly; *too* tired (note that *too* and *so* are not used to modify verbs)
Modifiers of nouns: *so much, such (a)*	*so much* fun, *such* pleasure, *such an* enjoyable experience
Modifiers of comparative adjectives: *so much*	*so much* better

*Note that *really not* often intensifies the negative, whereas *not really* usually serves as a softener.

General Modifier Just

Just can be used as a softener or an intensifier. Linguistic context, particularly the modified word or phrase, determines which way it is taken (see Table 3). As already mentioned, *just* is usually acquired late by learners of English.

The effect of softeners and intensifiers on a statement of opinion is identical regardless of whether the opinion is positive or negative: They soften or intensify the positive or negative force of whatever they modify (e.g., *not so* bad, *not so* good; *really* great, *really* awful).

Negative Questions

Besides modifiers, an additional resource for expressing an opinion is the negative question, which is rarely focused on in language classes. Although negative questions are a fairly common means to express an opinion in English, learners may find them difficult to process, much less produce correctly and appropriately. The difficulties associated with negative questions are related to several characteristics of negative questions, which are presented here:

- Negative questions may be acquired late in English (Pienemann & Johnston, 1987).
- English responses to negative questions behave differently from responses to negative questions in many other languages. In English, the response agrees with the polarity of the response, whereas in many other languages, the response agrees with the polarity of the question. This difference alone can result in serious miscommunication. For example: "Don't you like shrimp?"
  - — English response: Yes (I do like shrimp); No (I don't like shrimp).
  - — Japanese response: Yes (I don't like shrimp); No (I do like shrimp).

Table 3. General Modifier *Just*

Type of General Modifier	Examples
Softener: As a softener, *just* often conveys a minimizing meaning, such as *only* (modifies many types of phrases, e.g., adjective phrase, verb phrase, noun phrase, adverbial modifier).	*just* tired, *just* looking, *just* a student, *just* a little worried
Intensifier: As an intensifier, *just* can intensify the meaning of an adjective or adverb phrase, verb phrase, or noun phrase.*	*just* terrific, *just* awful, *just* too fast; *just* walking on air, *just* drowning in work; *just* a miracle, *just* an awful day
Just can also intensify a negation.	I'm *just* not interested.

*Note that both *just* and *such* precede the complete noun phrase they modify (e.g., *just* a simple man, *just* a boy, *such* a simple man, *such* a boy).

- Negative questions can be used to ask a real question or to express an opinion. Forms with more than one distinct meaning or function are often difficult for nonnative speakers to interpret (McCarthy, 1990). For example: "Wouldn't you like to have a convertible?"
  - — Real question: The speaker thinks that the hearer would not like to have a convertible and asks the hearer if that is true.
  - — Opinion question: The speaker thinks it would be great to own a convertible (and expects the hearer to agree).

  In addition, real negative questions can be used to express criticism. Thus, although "Can't you help me?" is a polite request in some cultures such as in Japan, it often has critical overtones in English.

- Negative opinion questions occur primarily in oral interaction or reports of interaction (e.g., "So he said, 'Wouldn't you like to have a convertible?'"). Thus, students have few opportunities to familiarize themselves with the characteristics and behavior of negative questions outside of dialogue-rich novels or observed interaction.

Even though negative questions are often difficult for learners to interpret or to use appropriately, their frequent appearance in conversation makes them an important form for learners to become familiar with.

CURRICULUM, TASKS, MATERIALS 

The activities in this section include a set of theme-based listening and speaking activities on softening and intensifying opinions, as well as activities on recognizing and producing negative questions that express an opinion. The theme for the softening and intensifying activities is music. Most people have an opinion on this topic, and students of all ages usually find it easy and fun.

The sequence of activities starts with a discussion activity designed to help students think about what they know about expressing an opinion. Students then listen to one or more audio clips with opinions expressed by different people in different contexts and discuss the specific strategies employed in these situations. Next, they practice using the strategies they have learned in a variety of activities. Finally, students complete a role-play or series of role-plays that demonstrate their ability to express opinions appropriately in a variety of contexts.

Activity 1: Raising Awareness of Opinion-Giving Strategies

Activities 1A and 1B represent two options for raising students' awareness of opinion-giving strategies. Activity 1A allows students more freedom of expression, whereas Activity 1B is more controlled.

Activity 1A

This activity (see Worksheet 1 in Appendix A) encourages students to think about how opinions are expressed both in their native language and in English. (Suggested answers for all worksheets are provided in Appendix A.)

Activity 1B

This activity offers teachers another version of the awareness-raising activity with a worksheet (see Worksheet 2 in Appendix A) that provides more focused questions to guide the students. The teacher can preface Activity 1B by explaining to students that the relationship between speakers will affect discussion of the same topic, so students need to consider each situation carefully and avoid generalizing about what is appropriate. For example, a student might feel very comfortable speaking to a particular teacher but use very formal language to another. Best friends might soften their language depending on personality or topic. Students can work through Worksheet 2 alone or in pairs.

For Activities 1A and 1B, students should be advised that that there is no polite or impolite way of answering. Each situation must be judged according to its context, and speakers from different cultures may assess situations differently. (See answer key, in Appendix A, for answers given by native English speakers.)

Activity 2: Recognizing Softeners and Intensifiers

In this activity, students listen to dialogues in which the characters express their opinions about music, as well as other topics. In these short conversations, students are exposed to some very direct and some softened opinions. After the sound clips have been played once or twice (depending on the students), students begin working on Worksheet 3 (see Appendix A), which includes the transcripts for the scenes they just heard. The strategies appear in italics on the transcripts so that they are easier to identify and analyze.

Students then answer the comprehension questions about the clip. Before focusing on the linguistic resources used to express the opinions, students need to have a good grasp of the content of the conversation.

After students have answered the comprehension questions, they listen to the dialogue again. Using the transcript, students identify and analyze how the softeners and intensifiers are used in the given context.

When students have completed Worksheet 3, the teacher can present some or all of the information in Handout 1 (see Appendix B) and discuss with students how individual softeners and intensifiers can be used, using examples from the dialogues as reinforcement, when possible. Teachers with lower level students may wish to present only a few softeners and intensifiers at this point.

Note that teachers can also use scenes from movies or television shows in which characters express opinions. Transcripts for additional movies and television shows can be found on the Internet (e.g., http://www.simplyscripts.com, http://www.imsdb.com, http://www.script-o-rama.com). It is important when choosing video sources for teachers to keep in mind that students need to see a variety of contexts to focus their attention on the factors that affect how opinions are expressed (i.e., mainly topic and speaker).

Another approach to familiarizing students with resources for softening or intensifying opinions is to have students watch and listen to a more lengthy model of native speakers discussing music, either alone (for lower level students) or in a conversation. This can be done in class or as homework. Two videotaped interviews (with Pam and Julian) with discussions of music preferences are available on the Internet. Handout 2 (see Appendix B) provides the specific websites and Appendix C provides the transcripts.

Activities 3–5 provide students with practice producing opinions in a variety of circumstances. Instructors may want to choose one, several, or all of the activities to help students gain more confidence and fluency in using the opinion-giving strategies.

Activity 3: Producing Softeners and Intensifiers

Activity 3 is a listening and speaking activity intended to elicit a variety of opinions from students in a fairly natural conversation. In the activity, students listen to two songs. They then discuss a series of questions designed to elicit descriptions of the songs and students' opinions.

To prepare for the activity, the teacher asks students to write down their three most and three least favorite songs and artists. From this list, the teacher chooses two songs that students will probably have differing opinions about. Before introducing Activity 3, the teacher needs to obtain a copy of the songs and their lyrics. These are usually easily downloadable from the Internet. (For lyrics, see http://www.azlyrics.com and http://www.metrolyrics.com. Song sites include http://www.music.com, http://new.music.yahoo.com, and http://music.aol.com.)

For this activity, students receive the lyrics to both songs and then listen to the songs as they are played in class. Students then brainstorm lists of vocabulary that can be used to describe music. The lower the students' level, the fewer the vocabulary items that will be introduced. Some possible vocabulary follows, although teachers should add vocabulary appropriate for describing their specific songs.

> **Adjectives:** soft, sweet, hard, fun to dance to, political, romantic, upbeat, depressing, uplifting, loud, noisy, slow, fast, emotional, beautiful, catchy, sentimental, dark, moody, poetic
>
> **Nouns:** lyrics, beat, melody, a hit, guitar solo, voice
>
> **Genres:** country, hip hop, bluegrass, rock, alternative, punk, funk, rhythm and blues, blues, pop, folk, jazz, reggae, heavy metal, world music, classical

Students then discuss the songs with a partner, explaining which song they liked best and why they liked it. For this discussion, students should have a copy of Handout 1 (see Appendix B) or a simplified version available. Before they begin the discussion, each student chooses a few of the intensifiers or softeners to incorporate into the conversation

Activity 4: Expressing Agreeing and Disagreeing Opinions

Activity 4 focuses on using softeners and intensifiers in agreeing and disagreeing opinions. Worksheet 4 (see Appendix A) offers students two different scenarios, one in which they agree with a friend's opinion about a popular singer, and the other, in which the student and his or her friend have different opinions. Students are given the opportunity to write and practice sentences expressing a softened or strengthened opinion, according to the scenario.

The final activity offers students opportunities to recognize and produce negative questions that function as opinions. Although recognizing negative questions that express opinions can be relatively straightforward once students have understood the concept, producing appropriate negative question opinions is tricky. Therefore, it is recommended for only very advanced students.

Activity 5: Recognizing Negative Questions Used to Express Opinions

The goal of Activity 5 is for students to understand the difference between a real question and a question as an opinion, a difference that can be difficult for learners to recognize. The teacher may want to review the explanation of negative questions used as opinions on Handout 3 (see Appendix B).

Then, if students need some practice in seeing the relationship between a particular negative question and the opinion it expresses, teachers can have students practice on the following sentences. Students hear or read the negative question and then rephrase it as a direct statement of the opinion, as in the following examples:

Isn't he a nice guy?	Students produce ⇨	*He's a nice guy.*
Wasn't that movie funny?	Students produce ⇨	*That movie was funny.*
Don't you love red cars?	Students produce ⇨	*I love red cars.*
Didn't he do a great job?	Students produce ⇨	*He did a great job.*
Hasn't it been an awful day?	Students produce ⇨	*It's been an awful day.*

Once students feel comfortable understanding negative questions to express opinions, they can work on Worksheet 5 (see Appendix A), which provides them with a dialogue between a husband and wife. Students must determine which questions could be an expression of an opinion rather than a real question.

REFLECTIONS 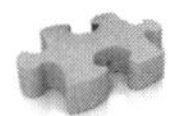

This chapter has introduced some aspects of opinion giving that are rarely taught as conversational tools. The dialogues presented in this chapter are especially appropriate for students at the intermediate to advanced levels. However, the activities can be used at a variety of levels from low intermediate to advanced. For lower level students the activities need to be simplified and fewer expressions presented, but the idea that context influences the way opinions are conveyed can be taught at any level.

It is also important to take into account the English-speaking culture to which students will be exposed. Johnson (2006) has pointed out that different English-speaking cultures may use opinion-giving strategies differently. She offers the example of British West Africans living in London, who tend to use fewer hedge expressions than British Whites. Thus, teachers should not assume that opinion-giving strategies are used in the same way in all English-speaking environments. The activities that teachers use may need to be adapted to the realities of the English environment that their students will encounter.

Ultimately, the goals of the activities in this chapter are not only to help students begin to express opinions appropriately, but also to raise students' awareness that opinions are expressed in a myriad of ways. With this new awareness, they can begin to take notice of these and other strategies on their own outside the English class.

Kristin Bouton has been with the Intensive English Institute at the University of Illinois, in the United States, since 1996 and is the coordinator for the upper level listening and speaking classes. She has a master's in English literature from the University of Illinois and has been an ESL and EFL teacher since 1984. She first began teaching English in Spain, where she lived for 12 years.

Katy Curry is currently teaching at KAUST schools in Saudi Arabia. She has had teaching positions from Grade 1 through university at various institutions in Germany, Japan, Saudi Arabia, and the United States.

Lawrence Bouton is a professor emeritus from the Division of English as an International Language at the University of Illinois–Urbana-Champaign, in the United States. His research interest focuses on pragmatics in language use, especially in cross-cultural communication, and the extent to which it can be taught in the ESL and EFL classroom.

APPENDIX A: WORKSHEETS AND ANSWER KEYS 

Worksheet 1: Expressing Opinions in English and Other Languages

Read and respond to these questions:

1. When you express an opinion, what might affect what you say and how you say it?
2. What are some strategies or expressions that you might use to express your opinion?
3. What are ways to make your opinions sound strong or weak? How do you soften a strong opinion?

Worksheet 1: Answer Key

1. Possible answers include:
    - The relationship you have with the person you are talking to (e.g., Am I close to this person or simply an acquaintance? Is he or she my superior?)
    - The sensitivity of the topic you are discussing (e.g., Do I think the hearer agrees with me? Is the topic sensitive, such as religion, or not, such as where to go to lunch?)

   (Answers will center on the student's relationship with the hearer—difference in power or status, difference in degree of intimacy, possibility that hearer may feel strongly about the topic, may disagree with you, etc.)
2. See Handout 1 "Expressing Your Opinion" in Appendix B for examples. (Depending on their level, students may offer different linguistic items: e.g., lower proficiency students are often aware of expressions such as "I think" and "In my opinion"; advanced students may offer more complex strategies such as "Don't you think . . . ?")
3. See Handout 1 "Expressing Your Opinion" in Appendix B for examples. (Lower level students may suggest linguistic forms such as *maybe* for weakening and *very* or *so* for strengthening. More advanced students may suggest modals or adverbial phrases such as "*not that* + positive or negative adjective" for weakening and "*just* + positive or negative adjective" for strengthening.)

Worksheet 2: The Influence of Context When Expressing an Opinion

When getting ready to express your opinion, you need to think about two things:

1. What is your relationship with the person you are talking to?

   Look at the three relationships that follow and discuss how direct or indirect these people might be when expressing an opinion about their favorite style of music. How might this change if they enjoyed the same kind of music or different kinds of music?

   - Best friends
   - Classmates in class together for the first time
   - Professor and student

2. How sensitive is the topic you are discussing?

   With a partner, imagine that two friends are talking about these topics. Rank them from 1 (*most sensitive*) to 4 (*least sensitive*) and discuss how they might express their opinions on this topic.

   - Your friend gave a terrible presentation.
   - You don't like your friend's boyfriend/girlfriend because he or she is not nice to you.
   - You need to decide where to eat today for lunch.
   - You need to choose a topic for your group presentation.

Worksheet 2: Answer Key

(a) Your friend gave a terrible presentation **(2)**

Possibly sensitive depending on how close the friendship (closer might mean more open and direct is possible) and how important the presentation was (more important might mean less candor and more supportive comments).

(b) You don't like your friend's boyfriend/girlfriend because he or she is not nice to you **(1)**

Very sensitive—might need to acknowledge that you know that they have strong feelings about the person but that your experiences have not been positive—or just avoid the topic completely.

(c) Where to eat today for lunch **(4)**

This is not very sensitive because every one should have some idea about what and where they might like to eat.

(d) What topic to choose for your group presentation **(3)**

This is a fairly neutral topic—no one should feel threatened by suggestions—as long as everyone's suggestions and opinions are accepted as possible and not ridiculed or dismissed without consideration.

Worksheet 2: Teacher's Note

Teachers need to stress that there is no polite and impolite way. Participants need to judge each situation by its context.

Worksheet 3: Identifying Softeners and Intensifiers

Part I: Read and listen to the following conversation (available at http://www.tesolmedia.com/books/pragmatics). Then answer the questions.

Dialogue 1

Boy: Have a seat while I put on some music.
Girl: Oh . . . I love this song!
Boy: Really?
Girl: Yes, Celine Dion!
Boy: Yeah, Celine's great isn't she?
Girl: You know, I went to her concert when she was in town and she was *just so* . . . moving!
Boy: I know. Her show was the best show I've ever seen. And she sounds *so much* better live than she does on the album doesn't she?
Girl: Yes, yes, you are **so** right, she sounds totally different.

Questions:

1. Listening for Content
   In this audio clip, the Boy has invited the Girl over for coffee. They have a conversation about music. Listen to the conversation, and discuss the following question: They both like Celine Dion. What are some of the things they like about her?

2. Listening for Intensifiers
   Pay attention to how the Boy and the Girl express their opinions about Celine Dion. Answer the following question: Which intensifiers do the Boy and the Girl use to express their opinions about Celine Dion?

Part II: Listen to or read the following dialogue (available at http://www.tesolmedia.com/books/pragmatics), then answer the questions below.

Dialogue 2

Bill: Hey Susan . . . Hey, hey, wow! What's that?
Susan: What's what?
Bill: What are you playing?
Susan: *Just* something I've been fooling around with.
Bill: You wrote it?
Susan: Yeah.
Bill: Well let's hear the whole thing.
Susan: Nah, it's *not that* good . . .
Bill: Come on, I want to hear it.
Susan: OK, but I'm *not really any* good . . .

Questions:

3. Listening for Content
   In this clip, Susan is playing the piano. Bill hears a short segment and asks her about what she is playing. Why doesn't Susan want to play her music?

4. Listening for Softeners
   Listen for Susan's opinion about her music, and answer the following question: What softeners does Susan use to express her opinion about herself?

Worksheet 3: Answer Key

1. Answer: a. The song that is playing in this scene
   b. She is so moving (expressive)
   c. She's better live (puts on a good performance)
2. Answers: *just, so*; (lines 6–7); *so much* (lines 8–9), *so* (line 10)
3. Answer: She doesn't think it's very good, doesn't think she's a good player
4. Answer: *just* (line 4), *not that* (line 8), *not really any* (line 10)

Worksheet 4: Expressing Agreeing and Disagreeing Opinions

Take one of the following sentences: "I like Britney Spears" or "I don't like Britney Spears." Read the following scenarios. Then, by yourself or with a partner follow the instructions.

1. <u>Scenario</u>: Imagine that you are talking with your friend and you both have the same opinion about Britney Spears.

   <u>Instructions:</u>
   a. Write a sentence that expresses this idea in a very strong way (using strong vocabulary and one other strategy that we've discussed).

   b. Practice saying the sentence out loud. Think about appropriate stress and intonation.

2. <u>Scenario</u>: Imagine that you are talking with your friend and you know that you have different opinions about Britney Spears.

   <u>Instructions</u>
   a. Write a sentence that expresses your opinion about her in a weak way (using weak vocabulary and one other strategy that we've discussed).

   b. Practice saying the sentence out loud. Think about appropriate stress and intonation.

Worksheet 4: Answer Key

1. Sample answer: Britney Spear's music is *so* fantastic (OR so awful).
2. Sample answer: Well . . . I'm *not that* crazy about Britney Spear's music. OR I don't know. I *kind of* liked her last song.

Worksheet 5: Recognizing Negative Questions to Express Opinions

Look at the italicized questions in this conversation and decide whether each question is a true question (asking for information or confirmation) or an opinion. (You may want to look at the response to the question to see how the respondent interpreted the question.)

Situation: A couple is shopping for a family car.

Tom: (1) *Don't you love this 2-door convertible?* It's so sporty and has a really powerful engine.

Sue: I don't know. (2) *Wouldn't it be impractical to have a convertible in Illinois?*

You'd only be able to drive it with the top down 3 months of the year.

(*Note:* Illinois has four seasons and is cold much of the year.)

Tom: (3) Yeah, but *wouldn't it be great during those 3 months?*

Sue: Come on, honey. I don't think there's enough space for the children.

Tom: There's plenty of room in the back! (4) *Don't you think they'd love driving around with the top down?*

Sue: (5) *Maybe, but what about the gas mileage?*

Tom: I'm sure it's fine. Let's ask the salesman. (to salesman) (6) *Excuse me, what kind of gas mileage does this car get?*

Salesman: 15 miles a gallon

Sue: Thank you. (to her husband) (7) *Don't you think we can do better than that?*

Tom: You're right, that is pretty low. OK, (8) *what kind of car were you thinking about?*

Sue: I was thinking about a sedan or a minivan, maybe even an SUV.

Tom: (9) *Don't SUVs get terrible mileage too?*

Sue: That's a good point. (10) *Then, do you think a minivan or a sedan would be better?*

Tom: I guess a minivan. I was hoping to avoid it, but it looks like that will be our best option.

Answer Sheet

Use the box below to record your answers. In the left-hand column, indicate whether the question is a true question or an opinion. If a question is an opinion, state the opinion in a plain sentence in the right-hand column. The first one is done for you.

Question	Is this a true question or an opinion? How do you know?	If it is an opinion, state it in a plain sentence.
1	Opinion. Negative question. (Tom supports the opinion immediately afterward)	I love this 2-door convertible.
2		
3		
4		
5		
6		
7		
8		
9		
10		

Worksheet 5: Answer Key

1	Opinion. Negative question. (He supports the opinion immediately afterward.)	I love this 2-door convertible.
2	Opinion: Negative question	It would be impractical in Illinois.
3	Opinion: Negative question	It would be great to have a convertible even for only 3 months.
4	Opinion Negative question	The kids would love driving with the top down.
5	True question	Asking for information
6	True question	Asking for information
7	Opinion	We can do better than that.
8	True question	Sue treats Tom's question as a real question, answering it with what she was thinking about.
9	Opinion	SUVs get terrible mileage too.
10	True question	Tom treats the question as a true question, answering it with his opinion.

APPENDIX B: HANDOUTS 

Handout 1: Expressing Your Opinion: Some Softeners and Intensifiers

When expressing an opinion, one of the most important things you need to consider is the **context**. Think about the following questions:

1. What is the relationship you have with the person you are discussing with?
2. How sensitive is the topic you are discussing?

Depending on the context, you will want to use other expressions to soften or emphasize your opinion:

1. **Softeners**—To soften an opinion, use softeners such as the following:

   For lower proficiency students:

   - *A little bit*, or *a little* (modifying an adjective)
     — Example: It might be *a little* distracting.
   - *Kind of*, *sort of* (modifying an adjective)
     — Example: The music is *sort of* loud.

   For more advanced students:

   - *Not really* (modifying adjectives, verbs)
     — Example: She's *not really* ready to play in the band.
     — Example: They *don't really* play the type of music we want.
   - *Not that* (modifying an adjective)
     — Example: It's *not that* good.
   - *Such, such (a)* (modifying a noun or noun phrase)
     — Example: That is *such* idiocy.
     — Example: Bob Dylan is *such a* great composer.
   - *Just*—meaning "only" (modifies many types of phrases, e.g., adjective phrase, verb phrase, noun phrase, adverbial modifier)
     — Example: *just* tired, *just* looking, *just* a student, *just* a little worried

2. **Intensifiers**—To strengthen an opinion, use intensifiers such as the following:

   For lower proficiency students:

   - *So* (with simple adjectives), *so much* (with comparative form of adjective)
     — Example: She was *so* . . . wild! She's *so much* better live . . .

- *Such (a)* (with nouns)
  - Example: She is *such a* nice person.
  - Example: That's *such* good cheese.
- *Really* (with adjectives, adverbs, verbs)
  - Example: It's *really* hot today.
  - Example: They go out for dinner *really* often.
  - Example: I *really* like that new movie.

For more advanced students:

- *Just* (with other intensifiers)
  - Example: She's *just* **so** wild
- *Just* (before negative expression)
  - Example: He *just* **doesn't** have the talent to be in the band.
- *Too* (for a negative opinion): *Too* implies an undesirable situation, even when paired with a positive adjective. Being "too beautiful" or "too happy" is a bad thing.
  - Example: She'll never go out with him. She's *too* good for him.

Handout 2: Videotaped Interviews With Pam and Julian

Note: The following two videos are in Flash format. For the transcripts, see Appendix C or visit http://www.tesolmedia.com/books/pragmatics.

Conversation with Pam:

http://flash.atlas.illinois.edu/video.html?src=/iei/iei-v-2010-1/Pam&player=SDNC

Conversation with Julian:

http://flash.atlas.illinois.edu/video.html?src=/iei/iei-v-2010-1/Julian&player=SDNC

Lyrics to the songs discussed by Pam and Julian and videos of performances are available at the following websites:

Pam's preferred music: "The Sound of Silence"

- Lyrics: http://www.lyricsfreak.com/s/simon+and+garfunkel/the+sound+of+silence_20124712.html
- Video: http://www.youtube.com/watch?v=eZGWQauQOAQ&feature=related

Julian's favorite music: "Where the Streets Have No Name"

- Lyrics: http://www.lyricsfreak.com/u/u2/where+the+streets+have+no+name_20141525.html
- Video: http://www.youtube.com/watch?v=QQxl9EI9YBg

Handout 3: Recognizing Negative Questions to Express an Opinion

Negative questions are very common in English. They often express an opinion and imply that you think the answer to the question is "yes" (meaning that you agree).

- Isn't he the best dad in the world? ⇨ He's the best dad in the world.
- Don't you think he's the best dad in the world? ⇨ He's the best dad in the world, (isn't he?)
- Hasn't he improved a lot this year? ⇨ He's improved a lot this year.
- Wouldn't it be (great/nice/fun/awful/boring, etc.) to (infinitive) etc.?
  Example: Wouldn't it be fun to see *School of Rock* in a live show?
  ⇨ It would be fun to see *School of Rock* in a live show.

Note that not all negative questions are used to express an opinion. For example, the following negative questions are real questions:

- Hasn't Greg finished the report yet?
- Isn't Jack a vegetarian?

The meaning of the real negative questions above can be paraphrased as follows:

Is it true that Greg has not finished the report yet? (I thought he had.)

Is it true that Jack isn't a vegetarian? (I thought he was.)

APPENDIX C: TRANSCRIPTS OF VIDEOS 

Handout 2: Videotaped Interviews With Pam and Julian

Conversation With Pam:

Kristin: Hello Pam.

Pam: Hi Kristin.

Kristin: Why don't you tell me about the music that you like.

Pam: OK, I think mostly what I listen to are old singers that I sort of grew up with but I buy their newer albums if they have it. And I listen to . . . soundtracks, show tunes, Broadway musicals, movie . . . movie themes and so forth. Who do I like? I like Paul Simon of Simon and

Garfunkel. And I think I have everything that he's ever composed and I don't think he's done anything recently. I liked him better when he was with Simon and Garfunkel because Garfunkel had a wonderful harmonizing voice and Paul Simon can't carry it by himself. Paul Simon is the writer and he writes music and he writes lyrics and I think Art Garfunkel doesn't, which is why he's disappeared. So I have some of the old Simon and Garfunkel, but I listen to Paul Simon a lot.

Kristin: Do you have a favorite song of Simon and Garfunkel?

Pam: Oh . . . of course, "Sound of Silence" absolutely one of my favorites. "Bridge Over Troubled Waters" . . . the . . . the . . . I'm trying to think . . . the *Graceland* album is good. The other thing, actually, I like about Paul Simon is that he takes a theme. For example, he did that whole theme with the South African singers in *Graceland* and so you have their harmonizing in the background which is really cool. He did . . . in *Rhythm of the Saints* he went . . . he has Brazilian . . . I think he went to Brazil in fact and recorded in Brazil. So he's got a lot of that . . . different kinds of Brazilian music which is really neat. So he changes. It's . . . It's . . . He continues to use . . . He's continually Paul Simon and he writes his songs . . . and another thing I like about it are his lyrics. He always tells . . . he usually tells a pretty good story in his songs, which is fun to listen to. And the fact that he changes a lot. Now I know he wrote the music to a Broadway play, a Broadway musical that flopped. I don't even think . . . I don't even think it stayed . . . I don't think it stayed more than a week or a month on Broadway. So I never heard that musical, although I've been sort of interested in finding out about it.

Kristin: OK.

Pam: OK?

Kristin: Alright, thank you!

Pam: You're welcome!

Conversation With Julian:

Kristin: Hi Julian.

Julian: Hi Kristin.

Kristin: Why don't you tell me about some of the music that you like.

Julian: OK. One group that I like is U2. I have some of their CDs here. U2 is a group from Ireland. Four . . . four guys who were childhood friends got together more than 20 years ago to form this group and they've been making what I think is good music ever since then, for almost 25 years. Their music is not all the same, you know, some of their songs are kind of slow and nice, and some of their songs are loud and fast. But I like pretty much all of their songs. I have almost all of their CDs. I've seen them in concert a couple of times. They've won a lot of Grammys; you know, they are pretty popular around the world.

Kristin: Uh-huh.

Julian: But another reason why I like them is because the lead singer of the group—this guy who calls himself Bono—is very politically active and he's involved in things like trying to get industrial nations like the US to give a lot of money to cure AIDS in Africa and trying to forgive third-world debt and things like that, so he travels around the world, and meets with President Bush and prime ministers of countries and, you know, he uses his celebrity status to try to do a lot of good for lots of different people.

Kristin: Do you have a favorite song of theirs?

Julian: Um, maybe one of their songs from one of the older CDs like this one—*the Joshua Tree*—which is from 1987. Maybe, maybe the first song on here—"Where The Streets Have No Name." It's a really nice song.

Kristin: What do you like about it?

Julian: I like the lyrics. They are kind of like poetry and the guitar sound. The guy who plays guitar in this group is really really talented.

Kristin: Cool.

Julian: Yeah.

Kristin: Thank you very much.

CHAPTER 9

Teaching Constructive Critical Feedback

Thi Thuy Minh Nguyen and Helen Basturkmen

This chapter introduces the notion of constructive critical feedback by peers, a type of activity which, when preceded by some initial training, has been found to be effective in improving production in first language (L1) academic classes, particularly composition courses. Although a great deal of research has been devoted to orienting students to the content of peer feedback and the structure of peer-feedback sessions (Liu & Hansen, 2002; Mendonca & Johnson, 1994; Rollinson, 2005), little attention has been focused on the language used to provide this feedback. This chapter addresses this lack by providing a set of activities designed to orient learners on how to offer appropriate constructive critical feedback in an English-speaking academic context.

Constructive criticism in general refers to a negative assessment of an individual's current work with the aim of improving current or future performance. It usually involves the identification of a problematic action, choice, or product, as well as advice on how to change or correct the problem. In institutional settings (e.g., classrooms) advice from a superior (e.g., a teacher) on how to improve one's work is expected. At the same time, advice giving by one peer to another is often tricky. In particular, advice on personal subjects is frequently unwelcome in most English-speaking cultures (see Houck & Fujimori, Chapter 7 of this volume, for more information on advice giving). Students who are asked to assess a peer's work are apt to be uncomfortable and may convey their message inappropriately. This is especially true for nonnative speakers. Research has shown that whereas students from some countries may find giving feedback that can improve a colleague's work a positive exercise, students from other cultures (particularly Asian cultures) are uncomfortable expressing criticism of another's output (Nelson & Carson, 1998; Soares, 1998).

Other studies have indicated that learners of English may give constructive criticism very differently from native speakers, softening criticism less frequently and aggravating criticism more often, as well as using intensifiers such as *too* and *very* and modal verbs such as *must, should,* and *have to* inappropriately (Nguyen, 2005). In addition, learners' compliments may be simplified to the point of appearing insincere and lukewarm by native speakers (Takahashi & Beebe, 1993).

To address some of the problems that second language (L2) learners may have with constructive critical feedback, this chapter introduces activities designed to increase learners' sensitivity to the cultural issues involved in offering critical feedback to peers in English and to help them identify language for expressing critical feedback in academic contexts that is both appropriate in the L2 context and comfortable to the learner.

CONTEXT

The activities described in this chapter were originally devised for and employed successfully with a group of 20 highly motivated young Vietnamese students, ages 17–20, who were learning Australian English as a foreign language (EFL) in an English for academic purposes program in Hanoi, Vietnam. The learners had been studying English between 4 and 10 years, but had received limited exposure to English outside the program and had never visited an English-speaking country. They had scored at an intermediate level of English on the International English Language Testing System with scores ranging from 5.0 to 5.5.

The 6-month program was designed to prepare the students for future university study in Australia. The curriculum included writing classes and classes that required oral presentations by students. In these classes, the students were often required to give feedback to their peers, for example by reading and commenting on the written draft of a fellow student.

One of the areas in which these students had problems was in giving critical feedback to their peers. Problems arose from learners' L1 influence, as well as from their lack of familiarity with the ways constructive criticism is performed in the target language. Constructive criticism in English is usually performed using strategies and softeners.

The activities in this chapter were thus designed to address problems that these students encountered when giving critical feedback. The critical feedback that the students gave to their peers in subsequent classes demonstrated that they improved considerably in their ability to provide appropriate constructive critical feedback to their peers.

Strategies

The two main strategies for constructive criticism are identification of the problem and advice on how to resolve it. Examples include the following:

Identification of problem:

- "I thought you had two conclusions."
- "I don't think the comma should've been here."

Advice:

- "Why don't you decide on just one conclusion."
- "You might want to delete the comma."

Mitigation

Among the means of mitigating a criticism are softeners, linguistic devices that limit potential offense. Softeners that may be used in identifying a problem include external modification such as compliments; softeners also include internal modification such as expressions of uncertainty (e.g., using phrases such as *I don't know*, certain modals such as *may, might*, and questions); problem minimization; and other linguistic devices such as use of past tense or conditional that can also serve to diminish the negative effect of the criticism. A complete description of mitigation devices can be found in Handout 1 (see Appendix A).

Teachers should be aware that *I think* is very easy for novice learners to add to a statement. However, as they become more proficient, students need to be encouraged to master a variety of softeners.

Whereas the use of mitigation alone does not guarantee that the feedback will be appropriate, criticism without mitigation is often too direct and blunt (although the degree of mitigation expected will vary even among native-English-speaking [NES] communities). The content of the feedback will also have an effect, as will the inclusion of intensifiers such as *too, very,* and *rather* (e.g., "You put it *too* strongly here").

CURRICULUM, TASKS, MATERIALS 

This section presents the sequenced set of activities for (a) getting students to start thinking about how they offer constructive criticism, (b) raising awareness of the strategies commonly used for peer criticism, (c) recognizing softeners, and (d) practicing softening critical feedback. The activities are based on authentic language samples (Nguyen, 2005).

Activity 1: Warming Up—Reflecting on Giving and Receiving Feedback

Activity 1 encourages learners to reflect on their own experiences with constructive critical feedback and on their knowledge of this speech act in their L1 and the L2. The teacher might start off by explaining the notion of constructive critical feedback, using the explanation and examples previously presented. Students are then ready to work in groups of 3–4 students on Worksheet 1 (see Appendix B).

After 10–15 minutes, the groups submit their answers to the teacher. Groups' ideas can be displayed on an overhead projector or read aloud. Teachers will want to refrain from making any comments on the groups' responses at this stage.

Activity 2: Raising Awareness of Strategies Employed in Giving Feedback

Activity 2 engages learners in analyzing authentic language samples and working out the rules for giving constructive critical feedback in a range of classroom situations. It aims to raise awareness of the resources for giving critical feedback in English and to teach the linguistic forms for realizing and softening critical feedback.

Students work on Worksheet 2 (see Appendix B) in small groups. The comments on Worksheet 2 are constructive criticisms made by one learner to another learner on the second learner's essay. The comments are taken from transcriptions of naturally occurring feedback by native English speakers in university settings (Nguyen, 2005).

After students have read the instructions, and gone over the first excerpt with the instructor, the groups will need about 15–20 minutes to reach an answer to the four questions on each of the remaining turns. When each group has finished, the members can present their responses. As students present, the teacher can elicit comments from the rest of the class, give feedback, summarize the points raised, and list these points using the terms for strategies and softeners mentioned in the previous section (and elaborated on in Handouts 1 and 2; see Appendix A). The teacher may wish to distribute this information to students before they complete the exercise so that students can use it in recognizing strategies and softeners. Information on strategies is included as Handout 2. Information on selected softeners is covered in Handout 1 in the Context section.

As teachers review the information on the handouts with learners, they may want to discuss to what extent students want to adopt NES ways of giving critical feedback and how their choices might affect their communication with native English speakers. In some cases, divergence from the NES norm may cause communication breakdown. Thus, although it is totally acceptable for learners to express their systems of values and beliefs, they might also want to be sensitive to the L2 rules of speaking and adjust their behavior where necessary.

Activity 3: Recognizing Softener and Directness Levels

Activity 3 aims to provide learners with practice in identifying relative degrees of softening. Using Worksheet 3 (see Appendix B), the teacher can guide the whole class through the analysis of the first situation, reviewing the softeners on Handout 1 (see Appendix A). Students can then analyze the remaining situations individually and compare their responses in pairs before going over the activity with the whole class. Finally, the teacher can lead the class discussion of how they feel about each of the responses (A–C) to the four situations and whether they would feel comfortable giving those responses. The teacher should emphasize that this is a personal decision and there is no right answer.

Activity 4: Practicing Softening Criticism

This activity provides intensive practice in using softeners in critical feedback. On Worksheet 4 (see Appendix B), learners are asked to suggest appropriate softener markers for each turn. Learners may complete Worksheet 4 individually first and then compare and discuss their answers in pairs before the teacher checks the answers with the whole class. Note that for lower level learners, the teacher might want to focus only on a few forms, such as compliments and perhaps modals that soften versus those that strengthen or the verb *seem*.

REFLECTIONS 

The activities in this chapter were developed in an EFL context in classes in which the teacher was familiar with learners' L1 language and culture. However, they can easily be used in mixed-L1 classes such as those in many English as a second language (ESL) contexts. At the same time, teachers should be aware that research suggests that students in an EFL setting may respond differently to assignments requiring peer critical feedback from students in a university ESL class that includes students from other cultures (Levine, Oded, Connor, & Asons, 2002). Thus, it can be helpful if the learners themselves find and present samples of critical feedback in their L1 to compare with the L2.

For nonacademic contexts or younger groups of learners (e.g., middle school students), the activities can be adapted to include giving feedback on other types of peer performances such as dramas and role-plays. For students who live in an environment in which English is spoken, the teacher can encourage learners to collect more samples of feedback as used by native English speakers that they hear in real life, note down the contexts of use, and bring the samples to share with the class.

Providing constructive critical feedback to a peer or colleague can be a daunting experience for L2 learners. Awareness of some of the strategies and linguistic forms commonly used in many English-speaking cultures can give learners some much-needed confidence and offer the possibility that they may profit from both offering and receiving such feedback.

Thi Thuy Minh Nguyen is an assistant professor in the English Language and Literature Academic Group at the National Institute of Education, Nanyang Technological University in Singapore. She is currently researching the learning of pragmatics in Singapore's English-medium classrooms. She has taught in Vietnam and Singapore.

Helen Basturkmen is a senior lecturer in the Department of Applied Language Studies and Linguistics at the University of Auckland, New Zealand. Currently, she is involved in a funded research project to investigate teachers' use of authentic spoken texts in pragmatics-focused instruction. She has taught in Turkey and Kuwait.

APPENDIX A: HANDOUTS 

Handout 1: Constructive Criticism—Mitigation Devices

Mitigation devices are linguistic devices that can reduce the potential offence of a speech act. They include external mitigating devices such as additional comments; and internal linguistic softening devices such as uncertainty markers, shifts in tense or condition, and softening lexical items or phrases.

1. **External modification:** additional comments, separate from the problem identification and advice giving

   <u>*Compliment*</u>: Say something good about the thing you are going to criticize. Avoid bluntness or frankness.

   Ex: It's an interesting paper.
   Ex: That was a great presentation.

2. **Internal modification:** linguistic softeners

   a. <u>*Uncertainty markers*</u>: Show hesitation or uncertainty about the criticism.

   i) Use explicit statements of uncertainty.

   Ex: *I'm not sure* about that; *maybe* it needs a transition word.
   Ex: *I don't know* that I agree with the third point you made.

   ii) Use modal verbs, adverbs, and phrases that indicate uncertainty: *might, could, may, possibly, probably.*

   Avoid modal verbs and phrases such as *must, should,* and *have to* when you are trying to soften problem identification and advice; these modals are usually associated with directness.

   Ex: This section *could* be clearer. (Problem) You *might* add a transition word here. (Advice)
   Ex: Your presentation *may* be too long. (Problem) *I'm not sure* but *maybe* you *could* cut out the second section. (Advice)

   iii. Use questions, rather than bald statements or imperatives, to identify a problem or propose a potential solution.

   Ex: *Did you summarize the main ideas?*
   Ex: *Could* this work?

   b. <u>*Past tense, conditional*</u>: Create a sense of distance between the speaker and the comment.

   Ex: Past tense: I *thought* it *would* make more sense that way.
   Ex: Conditional: *If you added a few more examples, your presentation would be stronger.*

<u>*Other linguistic softeners*</u>:

i. Use modifying words and phrases such as *kind of, a little, sort of.*
    Ex: This sentence is *sort of* confusing. It's *kind of* unclear.
    Ex: Your second point is *a little* too direct.

ii. Use the verb *seem.*
    Ex: Your introduction *seems* too long.

iii. Use parenthetical phrases such as *I think, I'm afraid.*
    Ex: *I think* you need more examples.

    (Note: *I think* is a very weak softener, and may have little or no effect.)

Handout 2: Strategies for Offering Constructive Criticism

The two main strategies for offering constructive criticism are (1) identifying the problem and (2) giving advice for correcting the problem.

1. **Identifying the problem**

   State the problems or errors found with the hearer's choice, work, or products. Be as specific as possible. Avoid using negative words such as "wrong," "weak," and so on.

   The following examples illustrate acceptable problem identification statements.
      Ex: I thought you had two conclusions.
      Ex: I didn't see your introduction.

2. **Giving advice: One "do" and some "don'ts"**

   Explain how the problem can be repaired.

Problem	**Advice**
Ex: You wrote "their"	but I think "t-h-e-r-e."

Peer feedback can be tricky, especially between speakers of equal status. To avoid sounding imposing, native English speakers often choose to avoid the following:

- Don't use the modals/phrasal modals *should, must, have to, ought to.*
  — Too strong: You should elaborate more on this.
- Do use the modals *could, may, might.*
  — Softened: You might want to give more examples.
- Don't use imperatives.
  — Too strong: Give more examples.

APPENDIX B: WORKSHEETS AND ANSWER KEYS 

Worksheet 1: Warming Up

Work with your group to answer the questions below.

Group A: Discuss your experience in giving constructive critical feedback to peers in English learning contexts, for instance, when you are asked to comment on your peer's work or performance. If you have never experienced this in an English context, use your experience in your L1, or try to imagine what would happen. Specifically, explain:

a. What difficulties have you had giving constructive critical feedback?

b. What are some typical ways in which you have delivered critical feedback?

Write your answers on a piece of paper to turn in.

Group B: Discuss your experience in receiving constructive critical feedback from peers. Recall a time when you received constructive critical feedback and explain:

a. How did you feel about the feedback?

b. What type of feedback have you felt is effective?

c. What kind of feedback is not helpful? Why not?

d. What are your expectations of "good" critical feedback?

Write your answers on a piece of paper to turn in.

Group A and Group B: How are your native language and culture and the English language and culture similar in regard to giving critical feedback? How are they different? Write any differences you can think of on a sheet of paper to turn in.

Worksheet 1: Answer Key

Some suggested responses:

Group A: Giving critical feedback
- Difficulties might involve the decision about how direct and specific the criticism should be. A direct criticism might cause offence to the hearer but an indirect one might not be effective because the hearer might not recognize the speaker's intention.
- Some typical ways to deliver critical feedback that could be mentioned: stating the problems, expressing disagreements, giving advice or suggestions for change, hinting about the problems, etc.

Group B: Receiving critical feedback
- Effective criticisms are often well-grounded with specifics and softened. They also suggest how to make changes possible.
- Ineffective criticisms are either too harsh, thus putting off the hearer or too indirect for the hearer to recognize them.
- Learners may expect that feedback will be comprehensible and helpful.

Groups A and B: Cross-cultural differences
Some cultures prefer a direct approach while others prefer an indirect one. But they might all appreciate criticisms that are delivered in a tactful manner that do not hurt the hearer's feelings. Note that what constitutes "tactful" may vary from culture to culture.

Worksheet 2: Identifying Constructive Criticism

Read the constructive criticism from one native speaker to another native speaker and, for each comment, determine the following:

(a) What aspects of the essay did the speaker give feedback on (i.e., what problem does the speaker identify)?

(b) What advice did the speaker use in giving feedback (i.e., what advice did she give on how to correct or improve the problem)?

(c) How did the speaker soften her critical comments?

Here's an example of how you might do it:

1. Anne: OK, well, I think it's a pretty good paper, pretty good argument, so most of the problems I have are probably with the organizational structure and a couple of grammatical things. Um to start, I think it seems like both of these introductory paragraphs may be put together as just one paragraph. It would be easier because they're both good paragraphs. They're both introductory ones so I think if they were together they would make more sense (laugh).

Sample answer:

(a) Identify problem(s): "Organizational structure and a couple of grammatical errors"

(b) Identify advice: "Combine both of the introductory paragraphs together into just one paragraph."

(c) Identify Softeners:
- Compliment ("pretty good paper," "pretty good arguments," "they're both good paragraphs")
- *I think, probably, seems, may, would*
- Conditional ("If they were together, they would make more sense.")

2. Anne: And I thought you had sort of two conclusions as well. But they're both good so I thought maybe if that one came after that one, because that was more of a conclusion than that one, perhaps that would be better.

3. Anne: Then just a couple of the other problems were grammatical, like I think *is* is better than *are* there because *traffic* is single. I think I'm not sure about that (laugh). It's just what I think. You might want to check that.

4. Anne: And yeah this phrase here, I wasn't sure that was the best phrase you could've used. So you could think of one.

5. Anne: And ah you put "their" but I think "t-h-e-r-e." Yeah that's just a grammatical thing.

6. Anne: Um and down here I don't think the comma should've been there. It could've been better without the comma so ah . . . (laugh).

Worksheet 2: Answer Key

2 (a) Two conclusions
 (b) Put one conclusion after the other
 (c) Past tense: *thought . . . had, sort of;* Compliment: *they're both good*; others: *maybe, perhaps, would*

3 (a) A couple of grammatical problems
 (b) use *is* after *traffic*, not *are*
 (c) *just, I think*, I'm not sure, *it's just what I think*, *might*

4 (a) "this phrase here"
 (b) Move or delete the phrase
 (c) *I wasn't sure, could've, could*

5 (a) You put "their"
 (b) instead of "t-h-e-r-e"
 (c) *I think*

6 (a) "I don't think the comma should've been there"
 (b) It could've been better without the comma. (Rather indirect way of saying "delete the comma.")
 (c) *I (don't) think, should've, could've*

Worksheet 3: Recognizing Softeners and Directness Levels

Each situation below is followed by three possible constructive critical comments (a–c). For each situation,

1. Identify all the softeners in the responses to each situation.
2. Calculate a relative directness level between 1 (*most direct*) and 5 (*most softened*). Note that perceptions of the directness level may vary.

direct				softened
1	*2*	*3*	*4*	*5*

Example Situation
In a writing session, Student A had to give critical feedback to Student B's English essay. Student A thought that Student B's essay presented only one-sided arguments, which could make it hard for her to convince her readers. In her feedback, she said:

(a) *I think* everything *must* be seen from two sides but in this essay you presented only one-sided arguments. So you *have to* address the opposing points of view as well.

Answer:

1. Softeners: *I think*
2. Level of relative directness: Level 1 (due to use of strong modals *must, have to* in direct statements). Note that simply using *I think* does not soften this response.

(b) Your arguments are not well-balanced so they can't convince the readers. Can you address the fact that there is a very strong voice against your opinions?

Answer:

1. Softeners: Use of question to offer advice. (Use of question softened what would otherwise have been very direct constructive criticism.)
2. Level of relative directness: Level 2–3

(c) *You wrote very to the point* but *I think* you didn't *sort of* address the fact that there was another point of view, you know. So you *might* not convince someone who doesn't agree with you.

Answer:

1. Softeners: Compliment: "You wrote very to the point"; *I think, sort of, might*
2. Level of relative directness: Level 5

Situation 1
After a classmate's presentation you were asked to give her some feedback. You thought that the presentation was not very well organized and sometimes she wandered off the topic. You said:

(a) I think what you said was really interesting but sometimes your points seemed to stray from the topic. So it'd probably be easier to follow it if you limited your arguments to just a few strong points.

Answer:

1. Softeners: ______________________________
2. Level of relative directness: Level __________

(b) To tell the truth, your talk lacked a focus and sometimes you went a bit too far from the topic.

Answer:

1. Softeners: ______________________________
2. Level of relative directness: Level __________

(c) I think some of your points are not related to the topic, so you should organize your talk more carefully and try to stick to the topic.

Answer:

1. Softeners: ______________________________
2. Level of relative directness: Level __________

Situation 2
The teacher asked you to help a weaker peer to edit his essay. You found the concluding paragraph not very well written because it did not summarize the main points and restate the thesis. You two were not very close although you got on quite well. You said:

(a) Generally, I think you wrote a very good essay but I found your conclusion pretty weak. A good conclusion must summarize your main ideas and restate your thesis.

Answer:

1. Softeners: ______________________________
2. Level of relative directness: Level __________

(b) I think it may be useful to summarize your main ideas and restate your opinions in the conclusion. I think that'd be a very nice way to wrap up things. But generally, I found the essay very interesting to read. It was very well thought out.

Answer:

1. Softeners: ______________________________
2. Level of relative directness: Level __________

(c) I found this concluding paragraph a bit confusing. Did you summarize the main ideas? I wasn't sure if there was a restatement of the thesis.

Answer:

1. Softeners: ______________________________

2. Level of relative directness: Level __________

Situation 3

When helping a friend to edit her essay, you found that the essay contained many grammatical errors. This was a very close friend of yours. You said:

(a) If I could be blunt, this essay contained quite a few grammatical errors. I think you should probably spend time proofreading your essays more carefully if you don't want to be marked down.

Answer:

1. Softeners: ______________________________

2. Level of relative directness: Level __________

(b) Did you check your grammar carefully? I'm afraid I got a bit lost with your meaning here and there. For example, what were you trying to say in this sentence?

Answer:

1. Softeners: ______________________________

2. Level of relative directness: Level __________

(c) I thought your essay was pretty good, especially taking into consideration that we had pretty limited time writing it. You had a few grammatical mistakes here and there—but I think that's because you were writing pretty fast. So if you could've spent a few minutes in the end checking what you'd written, I'm sure you'd be able to correct them all.

Answer:

1. Softeners: ______________________________

2. Level of relative directness: Level __________

Situation 4

You were working on a team project. Each member of the team completed a part of the work and then brought it together. You thought one of the parts would need some revision because the arguments were not developed very well. You and the friend who wrote that part were quite close. You said:

(a) I thought the arguments were pretty logical but they seemed to be kind of repeated. So I think if you go and do it again, you're going to figure it all out and put it straight. It's nothing too major.

Answer:

1. Softeners: ______________________________

2. Level of relative directness: Level __________

(b) Here you presented very interesting arguments but I guess you didn't have time to develop them more. How about giving a few examples to support them and finding a way to link them together?

Answer:

1. Softeners: ______________________________

2. Level of relative directness: Level ________

(c) Frankly speaking, I don't think these arguments were developed well enough. You talked about a bit of the problem in the first paragraph and then you talked about it again in the next paragraph. Why don't you find a way to connect your arguments? Also, try to explain them more.

Answer:

1. Softeners: ______________________________

2. Level of relative directness: Level ________

Worksheet 3: Answer Key

Situation 1

(a) Compliment: *sometimes, seemed to, probably;* conditional (Note: *just* doesn't seem to be used as a softener here.)
Suggested Level 5 (Note: Perceived levels may vary among speakers.)

(b) *a bit*
Suggested Level 2

(c) *I think*
Suggested Level 1–2, especially with the strong modal *should*

Situation 2

(a) Compliment: "you wrote . . . essay"; *pretty*
Suggested Level 2 (Note use of strong modal *must.*)

(b) *I think, may, would;* compliment: "I found . . . out."
Suggested Level 5

(c) *a bit*; question for advice: "Did you summarize . . . ?"; uncertainty: *I wasn't sure*; directness forms: none
Suggested Level 5

Situation 3

(a) *I think, probably*
Suggested Level 1; bluntness, intensifier *quite a few*, use of *you should*

(b) Advice stated as question; *I'm afraid, a bit*
Suggested Level 3

(c) Weak compliment: *pretty good*; *a few*, *I think* + excuse; advice in conditional *if*-clause
Suggested Level 2

Situation 4

(a) Compliment: "I thought . . . logical"; *seemed, I think*
Suggested Level 4–5

(b) Compliment: "Here . . . arguments"; *I guess;* advice: *how about* question
Suggested Level 5

(c) *I don't think;* advice: *why don't* question
Suggested Level 2 (Note effect of strengthening imperative "try to explain them more.")

Worksheet 4: Practicing Softening Criticism

How might you modify the following ways of giving critical feedback to include softeners? Look at the underlined forms and write them in a more softened form (some already incorporate some softeners). Two possible sample answers are provided to the first feedback example.

1. You know, in this paragraph you changed from passive to active voice and then back to passive, so it was inconsistent. I think you should keep one or the other.

   Sample answer: Below are two possible answers. The first is less softened; the second is more so. Both are appropriate.

   (a) You know in this paragraph you changed from passive to active voice and then back to passive, so it was *sort of* inconsistent. You *might just* keep one or the other.

   (b) You know in this paragraph you changed from passive to active voice and then back to passive, so it *may seem sort of* inconsistent. *Do you think it would be a good idea* to *just* keep one or the other?

2. It wasn't clear what you think about the topic. I can see how you've given two sides of the arguments but you can stress one side more.
3. There are quite relevant arguments that you presented but you didn't back them up. They are personal opinions but you stated them as if they were facts.
4. Look at this sentence here. I think it's wrong. Can you improve it?
5. This example was very vague. Can you explain it?
6. I didn't think your paragraphs were sequenced logically enough. They can be sequenced much better. For example, if this one comes before this one, they will flow more naturally.
7. In the introduction you didn't put what you thought about the issue. You left it until the very end. So yours was not a clear introduction
8. That point doesn't strengthen your arguments. Why don't you leave it out?

Worksheet 4: Answer Key

Answers will vary. Below are some possible responses.

2. (a) It wasn't clear what you think about the topic. I can see how you've given two sides of the arguments, but *maybe* you *could* stress one side more.

   (b) It wasn't clear what you think about the topic. I can see how you've given two sides of the arguments, but *maybe* you *could perhaps just* stress one side more.

3. (a) There are quite relevant arguments that you presented, *but I thought you could've backed them up better. . . .*

   (b) There are quite relevant arguments that you presented, but *I am not sure that you backed them up enough. . . .*

4. (a) Look at this sentence here. I think it *could be* wrong. *You might want to check that.*

   (b) Look at this sentence here. *I'm not sure it's quite right. You might want to check that.*

5. (a) This example was *pretty* vague. *Could* you explain it?

   (b) *I wasn't sure about the example. You might want to explain it.*

6. (a) I didn't think your paragraphs were sequenced *quite* logically enough. They can be sequenced much better. For example, if this one comes before this one, they *may* flow more naturally.

   (b) I think the paragraphs were *perhaps* not sequenced *quite logically*. They can be sequenced much better. For example, if this one comes before this one, they *may* flow more naturally.

7. (a) In the introduction you didn't put what you thought about the issue. You *sort of* left it to the very end. So yours was not a clear introduction.

   (b) In the introduction you didn't put what you thought about the issue. *I thought* you *sort of* left it *a bit late*. So yours was not a clear introduction.

8. (a) That point doesn't *do much* to strengthen your arguments. Why don't you leave it out?

   (b) *I'm not sure* that point *does much* to strengthen your arguments. Why don't you leave it out?

CHAPTER 10

Indirect Complaints as a Conversational Strategy

Dana Saito-Stehberger

This chapter provides resources[1] for introducing learners to a common activity among many North American social groups: indirect complaining. Coined by D'Amico-Reisner (1984, as cited in Boxer, 1993a), *indirect complaining* refers to a type of complaint that focuses on situations or problems for which the hearer is not responsible (e.g., "I just hate this weather"; "I can't believe my manager asked me to work this weekend"). This activity is sometimes referred to as "grousing" (DuFon, 1995) to differentiate it from *complaining* to the person responsible, an act that can be realized indirectly (e.g., "I wish you'd consulted me before canceling my reservation"). However, the term *indirect complaint* has been widely adopted and will be used in this chapter. The pervasiveness of this activity was noted by Hatch (1992), who found that 87% of all verbal communication on a university pool deck one afternoon was either a complaint or a response to a complaint, both of which Hatch refers to as an "indirect complaint speech event" (p. 143).

Although indirect complaints have received considerable attention from speech act researchers (see particularly Boxer, 1993a, 1993b), they are rarely mentioned explicitly in language textbooks. Boxer and Pickering (1995) surveyed seven textbooks that were organized on a function-based syllabus and found that the few complaints addressed in the textbooks tended to be direct complaints, rather than indirect. Even if indirect complaints constitute a markedly smaller proportion of everyday informal conversation than was found in Hatch's (1992) data, they compose a significant part of conversation and as such are worth addressing in English language classrooms not only because of their frequency, but because responses to indirect complaints may vary across cultures in ways that may affect conversationalists' mutual perceptions of each other (Boxer, 1993b). This chapter

[1] The audio file and transcripts for this chapter are available at http://www.tesolmedia.com/books/pragmatics. The transcripts also appear in Appendix B.

addresses the lack of material on indirect complaints by explaining the act and its functions in North American contexts and by providing students with opportunities to recognize not only the act itself but, more importantly, to select the type of response that is most supportive (and most frequent) in North American interactions.

CONTEXT

The activities in this chapter on indirect complaints and their responses were created for a conversational English course; however, they are applicable in many different settings. The activities have been used in a higher level speaking–listening course and a public speaking course. Indirect complaining and responses to indirect complaining were taught to improve students' comfort with making small talk as well as to introduce them to this aspect of North American culture. An interesting response to this curriculum was that many of the students did not feel comfortable complaining. Complaining is frowned upon in many of their cultures and is even seen as a sign of weakness, as it is also sometimes perceived here in the United States. The class discussed how indirect complaints could reflect positively on the speaker. One student suggested that indirect complaints could draw attention to things that needed to be changed, such as in the following example: "I can't believe that so many people in our office throw away a brand new paper cup every time they get a drink of water. Why can't they just bring a glass and wash it every evening?" Such a complaint demonstrates the speaker's awareness of the environment and his or her concern for being economical. At the end of the unit, students mentioned that practicing indirect complaints was very helpful for them because, even though they choose not to make negative comments themselves, all of them had experienced someone directing an indirect complaint toward them. This unit informed them of various ways they could respond to such complaints. One student commented: "It was helpful to learn how to respond to indirect complaints. Before I learned, I couldn't respond by using contradiction and humor. It allowed me to communicate flexibly and to escape unwanted arguments."

Indirect Complaints

Complaining is usually defined as an expression of dissatisfaction or disapproval toward some situation for which the speaker considers the addressee responsible (Trosborg, 1995) and for which the speaker may expect some type of solution or redress. Indirect complaining, on the other hand, is an expression of dissatisfaction with someone, including oneself, or a situation in which the addressee is not considered responsible, often times with the result of building solidarity between the speaker and the addressee. If the speaker and the addressee have an intimate relationship, they may share indirect complaints about personal situations, such as frustrations in personal relationships, a serious illness, perceived unfairness, perceived intrusiveness, a cancellation of an important event, or job pressure; if the speaker and the addressee do not have an established relationship, more impersonal topics of indirect complaints include: bad weather, poor drivers, being made to wait, or political opinions (Boxer, 1993a).

Imagine the following example of an indirect complaint between teachers who already have an established relationship. They are complaining about a job situation. A teacher may complain to fellow teachers about the lack of authentic language in textbooks. In doing so, he or she does not expect to change the content in textbooks; rather, an expression of dissatisfaction is being communicated to colleagues who have similar objectives, who face similar challenges, and who can relate to his or her frustration.

Thus, although complaining is generally viewed as negative and tiresome, this sort of complaining to someone who is not the target of the complaint and who may be expected to be sympathetic is part of the fabric of interaction in many speech communities. Language learners who become familiar with the characteristics of indirect complaints and their responses can enhance their ability to get to know others in their second language (L2) environment and decrease their sense of alienation in the foreign culture.

Responses to Indirect Complaints

Responding appropriately to indirect complaints can be complicated. Boxer (1993a) collected responses to indirect complaints by native English speakers, categorized them into six categories (see Table 1), and described the general social circumstances in which the responses took place. She found that the social distance between the speaker and the addressee, their social status, and the gender of the speakers strongly affected the type of response that was given. Although responses 1–5 in Table 1 are used in intimate and informal conversation, at times these responses can come across as being rude and insensitive. Language learners need to be reminded that the sensitivity varies among individuals.

See Handout 1 in Appendix A for examples of these six categories of responses to indirect complaints and typical expressions. Note that most of the example indirect complaints in Handout 1 begin with a formulaic expression; however, approximately 80% of indirect complaint responses do not begin with a set formulaic or slang expression, according to Boxer (1993a).

Given the circumstantial complexity and the infrequencies of most of the categories of responses, teaching nonnative English speakers to produce all six types of responses does not seem like responsible use of valuable class time. However, with 44% of all the responses falling into the *commiseration* category, it does make sense to spend time teaching students to respond to indirect complaints in ways that will communicate agreement and reassurance of the speaker. In addition, it has been found that, although commiseration is by far the most frequent response of native English speakers to indirect complaints, Japanese speakers' most common response was to ignore the complaint by changing the subject or not to

Table 1. Responses to Indirect Complaints by Native English Speakers

Response Type	% Observed	Function	Relationship
Null response or topic switch response	10%	— May indicate boredom	Sometimes between — Intimates — People separated by large social distance
Challenge or question	12%	— Challenges complainer — Requests elaboration	— By higher status speaker — By interested listener
Contradiction	15%	— Challenges complainer	— Between intimates — Speakers of unequal status/ high degree of social distance
Joking or teasing	6%	— Creates a relaxed atmosphere	— People who are familiar with one another — Between strangers in service situations
Advice or lecture	14%	(Not really advisable)	— Manner of delivery depends strongly on relative social status/ social distance between speaker and addressee
Commiseration	44%	— Agrees, assures, or seeks to make the speaker feel better	— Most common between equals and with subordinates, but be careful with superiors

Note: Adapted with permission from Boxer (1993a, p. 102).

acknowledge it (Boxer, 1993b). The disparity between the way native English speakers and Japanese speakers responded to indirect complaints indicates that the direct instruction of commiseration responses to indirect complaints may be a worthwhile topic to teach to all English as a second language (ESL) and English as a foreign language (EFL) students as they seek to fit into a peer group using American English.

CURRICULUM, TASKS, MATERIALS 

The learning activities presented in this chapter are designed to meet the following goals: (a) to introduce the concept of indirect complaints and to help students recognize them in authentic situations, (b) to familiarize students with the six categories of responses to indirect complaints, and (c) to encourage students to initiate indirect complaints in a positive way and to give commiserating responses.

The activities described in the following sections include: (a) an awareness raising activity, (b) an activity to familiarize students with indirect complaint forms and response types, and (c) guided and independent practice where students actually use the indirect complaint forms and responses.

Activity 1: Raising Awareness

To introduce the concept of the indirect complaint, the teacher can write the word *complain* on the board and ask students what it means, when people do it, and what they have complained about or heard others complain about recently. After students have discussed complaints for 5–10 minutes, they can be asked why people complain. One reason that should be mentioned is that people complain to share their frustrations with others to build community with them.

Students then listen to a compilation of true complaints sung by the "As It Happens Complaints Choir" in class or at home, as long as there is access to the Internet (see Appendix B for song lyrics). A performance of the song, which is the eighth choir listed, can be viewed at the following websites:

- http://www.youtube.com/watch?v=yChwJyOL9vc
- http://www.complaintschoir.org/choirs.html

Instructions on how to save the video to a hard drive are available at the author's website (Saito-Stehberger, 2010). To practice their listening skills, students write down all the complaints that they hear in the Complaints Choir's song; for example: "slow passport applications," "can't open childproof bottles," "hidden cell phone fees," and "advertising that fills up the singer's e-mail box." See the lyrics in Appendix B for more instances. Disseminate lyrics to students and listen again.

At this point the class can discuss why this choir has put so much effort into communicating these complaints. Some possible responses are: realizing that other people have similar frustrations creates a sense of inclusion or it is relieving to talk about issues that are bothering us. This creates an opportunity to teach the following idioms: "we're in the same boat," "to get something off one's chest," and "to blow off steam."

The goals for the unit on indirect complaining should then be discussed: students will understand what indirect complaints are, what they look like structurally, and which situations they are used in (considering setting, context, and interlocutor). Depending on the students' needs, objectives may include the following: (a) Students will identify indirect complaints in English and become aware of common responses, (b) Students will respond to indirect complaints with a commiserating response in written and verbal form, or (c) Students will produce appropriate indirect complaints in English in written and verbal form.

Activity 2: Recognizing and Responding to Indirect Complaints

At this point students should understand the concept of indirect complaining and the purpose it serves, but they have not yet seen how it is used in actual conversation.

Activity 2 begins with students receiving Handout 1 (see Appendix A) and then Worksheet 1 (see Appendix C). The class reads through the 11 example expressions on Worksheet 1 that can introduce indirect complaints, noting that some are only used in informal contexts, whereas others are neutral. Because there is a risk of being socially inappropriate when using indirect complaints in a formal situation, students should not be encouraged to do so.

The teacher then reads or plays a list of previously recorded statements,[2] and students put a check on Worksheet 1 (see Appendix C) next to the expressions they hear. This recording (see Appendix B for transcript) exposes students to a variety of native English speakers and provides a consistent sample to analyze for intonation, speed of delivery, and clarity.

At this point, the students are ready for Worksheet 2 (see Appendix C). You can play the audio file just mentioned as students read through the indirect complaints. Students should understand what the speakers are complaining about. (See the answer key in Appendix C for sample answers.)

If time permits, the complaints can be replayed in order for students to pay particular attention to intonation, speed of delivery, and clarity. Just knowing a vocabulary item is not enough to communicate effectively in English. Students need to be reminded that their use of intonation communicates their involvement (or lack of) in a conversation, that speaking too slowly or too fast may discourage listeners, and that if they do not enunciate and speak clearly, their listeners will need to strain to understand them.

Once the indirect complaints have been practiced, the class then discusses the circumstances in which these statements would be acceptable. Students consider the place, the speakers, and the situation. For example, one appropriate context of the first indirect complaint on Worksheet 2, "It's not fair that he didn't get the promotion. He works harder than anyone," is at home between a husband and a wife as they discuss what happened during the day. It would be inappropriate for this comment to be made in the work environment, between two gossiping colleagues or directly to the boss who gave the promotion. Discussing the contexts in which indirect complaints are appropriate often leads to an interesting discussion comparing how indirect complaints are viewed and handled in the students' own cultures.

For the next part of Activity 2, the teacher leads a discussion in which students are asked if they have ever heard complaints similar to the first four complaints on Worksheet 2 in their native language. If so, students are asked about common

[2] The audio file for Activity 2 is also available at the author's website (Saito-Stehberger, 2010). The link is labeled "Indirect Complaint Examples."

responses to these complaints. Next, students are asked to imagine how they would respond to the first four complaints on Worksheet 2 in an English-speaking setting. It may motivate students to know that different cultures tend to respond to indirect complaints differently. Boxer (1993a) found that native English speakers tend to use the commiseration strategy, whereas Japanese speakers tend to ignore the complaint and change the subject. Students then work in pairs to come up with responses to the remaining four indirect complaints.

Now students receive Handout 2 (see Appendix A) and discuss it as a class. Students then read the example dialogues in pairs, practicing intonation, speed of delivery, and clarity.

For homework, students can review the different kinds of responses and then come up with at least two additional responses that they could imagine themselves actually saying. In formulating their answers, they should refer to Handout 1 (see Appendix A). They should be encouraged to use commiseration responses. Lecture or advice is included on the handout for completeness and comprehension purposes. Students should be discouraged from responding with advice, as it may be resented.

During the next class period, the teacher can review the concept of the indirect complaint by having students think about situations they encounter throughout the day. Students then make a list of the situations including the people involved and an indirect complaint they can imagine themselves actually making. The teacher can collect the students' papers in order to give individual feedback on the grammatical correctness and on the appropriateness of the complaint.

Activity 3: Matching Indirect Complaints and Responses

The goals of the next activity are to provide more examples of indirect complaints and to offer students an opportunity to recognize and identify the six types of responses.

The activity begins with students receiving Worksheet 3 (see Appendix C). In Part I, the students match each indirect complaint with the most likely response. This is not a difficult task because the context for each statement is fairly distinct. The benefit is that students need to read and reread these complaints and responses in order to complete the worksheet, thus receiving multiple opportunities to acquire the forms.

In Part II, the students label each of the responses in Part I as a commiseration, question, advice or lecture, contradiction, humor, or no response. They may want to consult the examples on the worksheet. (See the answer key in Appendix C for the correct responses.)

Activity 4: Practicing Indirect Complaints and Responses—Guided Practice

This activity provides an opportunity for students to work together to produce indirect complaints and responses. Students need to be particularly careful to keep their indirect complaints short; otherwise, they may be accused of whining or ranting. They should also be warned to carefully choose topics and listeners so that there is no possibility that their indirect complaint will be perceived as a direct complaint.

Students receive Worksheet 4 (see Appendix C) and work in pairs to write an indirect complaint and dialogue for three of the five situations provided. Students should be encouraged to commiserate with the speaker. Sample answers are provided in the answer key (see Appendix C).

Students then perform their dialogues in front of the class. Teachers may want to remind them to pay particular attention to their body language, eye contact, and intonation.

Activity 5: Creating Indirect Complaints—Independent Practice

In Activity 5, students demonstrate their ability to create indirect complaints that are relevant in their lives and to give appropriate responses in English. Students receive Worksheet 5 (see Appendix C). Using the worksheet as a guide, students brainstorm in pairs a problematic situation which they are likely to encounter. Some example situations of dissatisfaction may include: the difficulty of their homework, lack of time, a relationship with siblings or parents, or financial frustrations. This is a good time to discuss taboo topics that may be inappropriate as an indirect complaint; for example, complaining about specific political groups, religions, or ethnicities or giving details of a personal illness. The teacher can either create an example dialogue working together with the class, or use the dialogue in Handout 2 (see Appendix A).

Students will develop a dialogue in pairs. Each dialogue needs to have at least one indirect complaint. Each person needs to have at least three turns, as was modeled in the example. When the dialogue is complete, students should record it (if possible). If a computer lab is available, they can record their performance using Audacity software (2006).

The teacher then instructs students to assess their own performance using the Self-Assessment Chart in Worksheet 5 (see Appendix C). The self-assessment and the audio recording should be submitted to the teacher, who can listen to the recording and provide his or her opinions of the students' assessments.

REFLECTIONS 

This lesson systematically introduces the concept of indirect complaints and gives students opportunities to apply these types of complaints in their own individual contexts. As previously mentioned, indirect complaints are a part of the North American culture and are used by everyone, including businessmen, middle-school children, homemakers, and travelers alike. The set of activities is appropriate for various audiences and can be adapted to different learning environments, as the parts of the lesson can be taught in longer or shorter periods of time.

During the development and the teaching of this curriculum, some issues surfaced, leading to insights that may be of value to readers. One important discovery was that, as discussed in the Context section, the teacher needs to emphasize the positive aspects of learning about indirect complaints. Students living in an English-speaking environment will frequently be confronted by indirect complaints. As teachers provide students with response choices, they can help students deflect negativity and encourage solidarity.

Teachers should also emphasize the fact that topics that are acceptable in some social situations may not be acceptable in others, as was discussed in Activity 2. Students need to consider the place, the situation, and the addressee when deciding if a particular indirect complaint is appropriate or not. For example, an indirect complaint by a teaching assistant about the shockingly low ability of some students may be appropriate in talking with a professor or other teaching assistant, but would be inappropriate to discuss with other students.

The activities in this chapter focus primarily on the production of the commiseration response because it is the most common response, as well as the one that is most likely to build community among the participants. However, more advanced students can be challenged to brainstorm indirect complaints that they have heard recently, and then to create responses that are humorous or that contradict the complaint.

Dana Saito-Stehberger is an ESL instructor and teacher trainer at the University of California Irvine Extension in the United States. She received a doctorate of education in TESOL at Alliant International University in San Diego, California. Her research interests include the instruction of pragmatic competence, online instruction, and ESOL in faith-based communities.

APPENDIX A: HANDOUTS 

Handout 1: Types of Responses to Indirect Complaints With Examples

Type of Response	Example Responses	Some Typical Responding Expressions (Degree of Formality)
No response or change of topic	IC*: A: One thing that drives me crazy is getting phone calls from telemarketers* at home. R*: B: What's keeping you busy at home? A: I'm renovating* our kitchen. It should be finished in a couple weeks.	
Question Clarification or elaboration requests, or questions expressing doubts about the validity of the complaints (often don't require response)	IC: A: Unfortunately, it's impossible to do anything here without a car. R: B: Oh, really? My bike and the bus system work fine for me.	• Really? • You think? • Don't you think that . . . ? • What about . . . ?
Contradiction Disagreeing with the complaint or defending the object being complained about	IC: A: I am sick and tired of her backing out* of the plans we have made. This is the third time in the last 2 weeks. R: B: Don't be so hard on her.* You know that she's going through a really difficult time at home.	
Using humor, joking, or teasing	IC: A: Oh, my gosh! That movie was so boring that you couldn't pay me to sit through it again. R: B: Look on the bright side.* If anyone ever asks you the worst movie you ever saw, you'll have an answer!	• Look on the bright side . . . (neutral) • At least . . .
Advice or lecture	IC: A: I can't believe my computer froze again last night and I lost my entire assignment. R: B: Have you tried programming your computer to save your work every 10 minutes or so?	• You might try . . . • You probably need to . . . (formal) • Why don't you . . . ? • Did you ever consider . . . ?
Commiseration Agreeing with or reassuring the speaker	IC: A: I have no idea how these crazy drivers managed to get a driver's license. That guy just cut me off*! R: B: I know what you mean. The other day I was almost hit by someone who was talking on his cell phone.	• I know what you mean. • You can say that again. • I hear you. • That's true./That's for sure. • I'm with you on that one.

**IC* = indirect complaint
R = response
telemarketers = people who sell things or advertise by calling people on the phone
renovating = to make something like new
to back out = to refuse to do something that was agreed to earlier
to be hard on someone = to be unforgiving
look on the bright side = be positive
to cut someone off = to suddenly drive in front of another car; it is a rude and dangerous action

Handout 2: Example Indirect Complaint Sequence

Situation: dissatisfaction with an early 8:00 a.m. class

Place: in the cafeteria

Speaker and addressee: two students (A and B)

A: Hey, Jamie, is this seat taken?

B: No. Go ahead and sit down. Have you picked up your new schedule yet?

A: Oh, my gosh. It's not fair. My English class starts at 8:00 in the morning. That's what time I usually wake up in the morning!

B: Oh, no. Did you request a later class?

A: Of course I did. I've already tried to change classes, but all three other sections are completely full.

B: Actually, I'm taking the same course at 3:00 in the afternoon. I'd love to be finished with my classes earlier. Maybe we can ask the registrar if we can change classes.

A: Really? That would be terrific!

B: I think so too!

APPENDIX B: TRANSCRIPTS 

Activity 1: Raising Awareness

The Complaints Choir concept began with two Finnish artists who were working in Birmingham, England. They pulled together the first ever Complaints Choir. Then Helsinki and Hamburg started one. Hosts of the radio program *As It Happens,* Carol Off and Barbara Budd, who introduced the choir on the air, gathered close to 80 singers in the Glen Gould theater in Toronto on February 21, 2007, to sing the song that was written from the hundreds of complaints sent in to the Canadian Broadcasting Corporation (CBC) listeners. The composer and lyricist is Eric Robertson, who accompanies on the piano. The choir's conductor is Kelly Galbraith.

As It Happens
Canadian Complaints Choir

VERSE 1

I just think that you ought to know,
Canada leaves me feeling low;
Winter slush;
People who don't flush;
Passport applications that are slow.

Chorus
Why are my feet so cold—tell me why do . . .
My hands feel so numb?
I hate plastic bags;
I hate the word called Referendum;
Hidden cell phone fees;
Expensive cars that have no signal lights;
Why can't things just be right?

SHOUT OUTS 1
I can't open childproof bottles!
Whatever happened to being polite?
Why can't people use apostrophes properly?
Air Canada sucks.

VERSE 2
I hate car alarms that will not quit;
Stephen Harper's clothes that just don't fit;
Static on my cat;
Vomit on the mat;
The single men who can't commit.

Chorus
Why are my feet so cold—tell me why do . . .
My hands feel so numb?
I hate plastic bags;
I hate the word called Referendum;
Hidden cell phone fees;
Expensive cars that have no signal lights;
Why can't things just be right?

SHOUT OUTS 2
The other line moves faster!
Everything's so hard. Can't something be easy?
My boss is pathetically pedantic.
Why don't people have proper escalator etiquette?

VERSE 3
Fierce dogs used as weapons of attack; why
Can't I be as rich as Conrad Black?
Spam spam, spam, I'm fed up

I am; won't someone
Please, oh please, give me my office back?

Chorus
Why are my feet so cold—tell me why do . . .
My hands feel so numb?
I hate plastic bags;
I hate the word called Referendum;
Hidden cell phone fees;
Expensive cars that have no signal lights;
Why can't things just be right?

Chorus reprise
Why are my feet so cold—tell me why do . . .
My hands feel so numb?
I hate plastic bags;
I hate the word called Referendum;
Hidden cell phone fees;
Expensive cars that have no signal lights;
Why can't things just be right?
Why can't things just be right?

Vocabulary

Feeling low is an idiom that means "feeling mildly depressed."

Slush is partly melted snow, often mixed with dirt.

Pedantic means "overly concerned with small details."

A *referendum* is a political term that asks the people to vote directly for or against a proposal. Because this word is capitalized, it is likely that this term refers to the 1995 Quebec Referendum that asks voters to decide if Quebec should secede from Canada and become an independent state.

Stephen Harper is the twenty-second Prime Minister of Canada.

Conrad Black is a controversial figure in Canada who acquired great wealth in the newspaper industry.

Spam is the commercial advertising that is sent as e-mail.

Activity 2: Recognizing and Responding to Indirect Complaints

1. It's not fair that he didn't get the promotion. He works harder than anyone.
2. You know what? I left my lunch at home again! I think I am losing my mind.*

* "losing my mind" = I'm going crazy

3. Don't you hate it when the weather is beautiful all week, then Saturday rolls around and it's grey and cold outside?
4. Why is it that every time I get into a line at the store, the other lines move twice as fast?
5. I can't stand how noisy it is in here. I can barely hear myself think.
6. This is not my day. The one day I didn't make it to class, the teacher gave a 100-point quiz.
7. I can't believe how much airfare costs these days.
8. I am sick and tired of sitting at home every day.

APPENDIX C: WORKSHEETS AND ANSWER KEYS 

Worksheet 1: Introducing Indirect Complaints

Note that the following expressions are formulaic. They will familiarize you with some of the ways that indirect complaints can be introduced. However, the majority of indirect complaints are not introduced by an easily recognizable formula.

Check the box if you hear the expression as your teacher reads or plays a recording of some sample indirect complaints (available at http://www.tesolmedia.com/books/pragmatics).

(a) I'm sick and tired . . .	(informal)	☐
(b) It's not fair . . .	(informal)	☐
(c) One thing . . .	(neutral)	☐
(d) Unfortunately . . .	(neutral)	☐
(e) You know what?	(informal)	☐
(f) I can't believe . . .	(informal)	☐
(g) Oh, my God/gosh . . .	(informal)	☐
(h) I can't stand . . .	(informal)	☐
(i) This is not my day!	(informal)	☐
(j) Why is it that . . .	(neutral)	☐
(k) Don't you hate it when . . . ?	(informal)	☐

Worksheet 2: Identifying the Complaint

Part I: Play the audio file (available at http://www.tesolmedia.com/books/pragmatics) and listen for the indirect complaints in context. What is the person complaining about?

1. It's not fair that he didn't get the promotion. He works harder than anyone.
2. You know what? I left my lunch at home again! I think I am losing my mind.*
3. Don't you hate it when the weather is beautiful all week, then Saturday rolls around and it's grey and cold outside?
4. Why is it that every time I get into a line at the store, the other lines move twice as fast?
5. I can't stand how noisy it is in here. I can barely hear myself think.
6. This is not my day. The one day I didn't make it to class, the teacher gave a 100-point quiz.
7. I can't believe how much airfare costs these days.
8. I am sick and tired of sitting at home every day.

Part II: Consider each of the indirect complaints above. In what situations do you think the indirect complaint would be socially acceptable? In what situations do you think it would be unacceptable?

Worksheet 2: Answer Key

Part I: The speaker is complaining . . .

1. that someone did not get a promotion that he deserved.
2. about being very forgetful lately.
3. that good weather comes when it cannot be enjoyed during the week and bad weather tends to come on the weekend when there is more free time.
4. that he or she always gets into the slowest lines at the grocery store.
5. that it is too noisy.
6. about a bad day he or she is having.
7. about how expensive airfare is these days.
8. that he or she doesn't like staying at home every day.

* "losing my mind" = I'm going crazy

Worksheet 3: Matching Indirect Complaints and Responses and Identifying Complaint Responses

Part I: Match each complaint with the most likely response.

Complaints

1. _____ "It's crazy how much homework we are expected to do in just one week."
2. _____ "Why can't people simply put their paper in the recycle bin instead of the trash can?"
3. _____ "I can't believe I locked my keys in my car again!"
4. _____ "If gas prices keep going up, I'm going to have to find a second job!"
5. _____ "How on earth did he become a teacher's assistant? I could barely understand a word he said."
6. _____ "Even though there are 200 television channels, there is hardly ever anything worth watching."
7. _____ "We spend more time at the airport in this line for the security check than we do actually flying in the plane."

Responses

(a) "Do *you* always put your paper into the recycle bin?"

(b) "What kind of job do you think would be most interesting as a second job?"

(c) "It's a good thing you have AAA to unlock your car for you. They must know your name by now!"

(d) "This is nothing compared to the last school I was at."

(e) "You mean he was speaking English?!"

(f) "I know what you mean. I flipped through all 200 channels last night for an hour and ended up turning the TV off and actually reading a book for entertainment."

(g) "Ya think? This line is actually moving faster than I had expected."

Part II: Label the responses in Part I as commiseration (COM), question (Q), contradiction (CONT), advice or lecture (A/L), humor (H), or no response or change of topic (N).

(a) _____ (b) _____ (c) _____ (d) _____ (e) _____ (f) _____ (g) _____

Worksheet 3: Answer Key

Part I: 1. (d); 2. (a); 3. (c); 4. (b); 5. (e); 6. (f); 7. (g)

Part II: (a) question, (b) no response, (c) humor, (d) contradiction, (e) humor, (f) commiseration, (g) question

Worksheet 4: Writing a Dialogue in Pairs

Imagine yourself in the following situations. Write an indirect complaint for three of the following five situations. Then refer to Handout 1 to come up with an appropriate response. If time permits, continue the dialogue for two or three turns.

1. You are talking to your good friend on the phone and telling him or her about the new city that you just moved to. It isn't very exciting. There isn't much to do on the weekends there.

2. You are at a restaurant with two classmates and the service is extremely slow. You have been waiting for a waiter or waitress to come to your table for 15 minutes.

3. You are at a bus station waiting for the bus to school. There are two other people your age waiting with you. The weather is uncomfortably warm and humid.

4. You are at the supermarket with a friend. Another customer is blocking your path with his cart and he doesn't realize it because he is on his cell phone. You don't like that people are always on their cell phones and don't notice the people and things in front of them.

5. You just got out of class and you are eating lunch with two classmates. You are annoyed that the teacher assigned a whole essay to be written over the weekend.

Worksheet 4: Answer Key

Sample responses

Situation 1

A: The city is a comfortable place to live. The people are nice and the weather is warm. The problem is that there is absolutely nothing to do on the weekends. It's so boring here!

B: There isn't much happening here either. There aren't even any good movies playing right now. Hey, do you have Internet access yet? There are a few new computer games we can play together online.

A: Actually, yes! It was installed yesterday. Let's meet online so we can decide which game we want to play.

B: OK, see you online in a minute!

Situation 2

A: How long've we been waiting for someone to come and take our order? (with a frustrated intonation)

B: About 15 or 20 minutes.

A: This is ridiculous. We'll never get back in time.

B: I just caught the waiter's eye. He's coming right now.
("To catch someone's eye" = to make eye contact with someone)

Situation 3

A: Man, it is pretty hot today.

B: It's humid too.

C: At least it's not as hot as it was last week!

A: That's true. Here comes the bus now.

Situation 4

A: Geez, there should be a law against talking on cell phones in public places.

B: I know what you mean. I can't tell you how many close calls I've seen when people were driving and talking on their cells phones.

A: (to the woman in the supermarket) Excuse me, ma'am. Do you mind if we move your cart so we can get by? Thank you!
("Close call" = an accident that almost happened, but didn't)

Situation 5

A: Can you believe that he expects us to write the whole essay over the weekend?

B: I was surprised when he said that it was due on Monday morning. We usually have time to write our essays in class.

A: That's right. I've already made plans to help a friend move during the day on Saturday and to celebrate another friend's birthday on Saturday night.

B: I know what you'll be doing all day on Sunday!

Worksheet 5: Creating Original Indirect Complaints and Responses

Part I: Self-Assessment

Up to now, you have been given examples of indirect complaints, responses, common expressions, and possible situations they are used in. Now you and a partner think of your own indirect complaints that you can imagine saying to someone. You and your partner will:

1. Think about something or someone that you are dissatisfied with.
   - (a) What are you dissatisfied with in your life?
   - (b) Where would you be likely to make an indirect complaint about this situation?
   - (c) Who would you be talking to about it?
2. Create a dialogue about one of the situations you have discussed. Each speaker must have at least three turns. At least one indirect complaint must be used in the dialogue.
3. Record your dialogue.
4. Self-assess your performance by answering the questions on the Self-Assessment Chart.
5. Hand in your self-assessment and e-mail the audio file to your teacher.

Self-Assessment for ______________________________

Part II: Self-Assessment Chart

Read the following statements. Put an "X" on the line to communicate how much you agree or disagree with the statement.

(a) We chose an indirect complaint that we would really use in our lives.

Agree ____ Disagree

(b) We made a believable response to the complaint.

Agree ____ Disagree

(c) I spoke clearly and I am easy to understand.

Agree ____ Disagree

(d) I used intonation to express my emotion.

Agree ____ Disagree

(e) I had at least three turns.

Agree ____ Disagree

(f) It is easy to think of indirect complaints to use in my life outside of the classroom.

Agree ____ Disagree

The next time you make an indirect complaint, in what ways would you like to improve?

Responding Acts

CHAPTER 11

I'm Sorry—Can I Think About It? The Negotiation of Refusals in Academic and Nonacademic Contexts

J. César Félix-Brasdefer and Kathleen Bardovi-Harlig

The objective of the activities introduced in this chapter is to develop learners' pragmatic ability by raising their awareness of the structure of refusals and their use in specific situations. Because refusals are usually negotiated, this chapter promotes the learning of refusals at the discourse level by looking at how strategies are used to express pragmatic intent across turns. We explore two main contexts: refusing offers from advisors in an academic context and refusing invitations from friends in a social context.

Refusals differ from many of the acts discussed in previous chapters in that they are responding acts—acts uttered in response to initiating acts such as invitations, suggestions, requests, and offers. This has consequences that are particularly challenging for learners. Because practically any reply is interpreted in terms of the act preceding it, it is often difficult to opt out of a refusal. In addition, refusals are often negotiated across many turns in a conversation, and they may require "face-saving maneuvers to accommodate the noncompliant nature of the act" (Gass & Houck, 1999, p. 2). Moreover, what is considered appropriate refusal behavior may vary across cultures.

CONTEXT 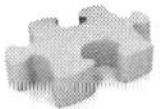

The refusal data that informed the pedagogical activities included here were gathered in academic and nonacademic settings at Indiana University (Bardovi-Harlig & Hartford, 1993) and the University of Minnesota (Félix-Brasdefer, 2004, 2008). The participants in these studies were English as a second language (ESL) and English as a foreign language (EFL) learners at intermediate and advanced proficiency levels, and none had received instruction in refusals. In addition, production data from native English speakers were collected to establish norms for refusal behavior in English in the same contexts. These data were supplemented by retrospective verbal reports that reflect the sociocultural values of the U.S. culture with respect to how native English speakers perceive refusals in formal and informal situations.

Using the production and reflection data of native English speakers as a source of pragmatic input, we developed pedagogical activities to raise learners' awareness of appropriate ways to refuse in advising sessions and informal invitations. In line with Rose's (1994) pragmatic consciousness raising approach, these activities help "sensitize learners to context-based variation in language use and the variables that help determine that variation" (p. 57). The activities presented here for ESL and EFL students were first developed for teaching refusals to learners of Spanish and were successfully tested with 4th-semester Spanish classes in a university foreign language context (Félix-Brasdefer, 2006). The examples that focus on refusing academic advice are geared toward university-bound ESL and EFL students; the invitation examples may be used with all intermediate or advanced students.

Refusals are a speech act by which a speaker fails "to engage in an action proposed by the interlocutor" (Chen, Ye, & Zhang, 1995, p. 121). In this chapter the term *refusal* includes both general refusals, such as refusing to do something, and refusals for which there are special verbs in English, such as *declining* an invitation and *rejecting* advice. The linguistic resources used may vary according to the situation (e.g., refusing a professor's advice or a friend's invitation), topic of conversation, participants' gender, setting (e.g., a university vs. a grocery store), and relationship between the participants.

Refusals may be direct or indirect. Direct refusals are often short and clear (e.g., "No, I can't," "I can't," "No") and are frequently softened or mitigated (e.g., "*Unfortunately, I don't think* I'll be able to come"). Because any response that indicates nonacceptance or noncompliance will be interpreted as an attempt to refuse, refusals are often indirect, with no expression of negative willingness or ability. Thus, they require interpretation by the listener. Indirect refusals include the following strategies:

1. Reason or explanation ("But—the problem is that summer classes meet daily.")
2. Alternatives ("Well, I'd kind of thought of taking another class." "Why don't we go out for dinner next week?")
3. Expression of regret or apology ("I'm really sorry." "I apologize.")

4. Avoidance—There are a variety of avoidance strategies such as the following:
   (a) Postponement ("Can I think about it?")
   (b) Hedging ("I don't know.")
   (c) Request for clarification ("Did you say Saturday?")
   (d) Request for additional information ("Can you tell me more about the class?")
   (e) Partial repeats of previous utterance (A: "I'm having a party on Monday and I would love it if you could come." B: "*Monday*?" [partial repeat in italics])
5. Indefinite response ("Maybe." "That's a possibility.")

If these strategies occur with a direct refusal such as "no" or "I can't," they function as external modifications of the direct act. Refusals can be preceded or followed by expressions of gratitude (e.g., "Thanks for the invitation, but . . ."), positive remarks (e.g., "That's a good idea, but . . ."), expressions of willingness (e.g., "I'd love to, but . . ."), partial agreements ("Yes, I agree, but . . ."), or minimal vocalizations or discourse markers and expressions ("*Oh, darn it*, tomorrow I can't"). The preference for strategy use and the degree of internal modification also vary according to the situation and the relationship between the participants.

Refusals in Advising Sessions

The two most dominant refusal strategies used by native speakers to reject the advice of their advisors during academic advising sessions are (a) reasons or explanations and (b) alternatives (Bardovi-Harlig & Hartford, 1991). Native-speaker rejections in advising sessions are frequently mitigated by *downgraders* such as mental state predicates (e.g., *I think*) and modal adverbs (e.g., *probably*; Bardovi-Harlig & Hartford, 1991, 1993; Félix-Brasdefer, 2008). Postponement, characterized by a request to delay a response, is typically used in the advising context by nonnative speakers but is also used by native speakers in other settings. Examples 1–4 provide example refusals (softeners are in italics):

(Ex. 1) Reason or explanation

"Shoot! That's the one that conflicts with what I have to take."

(Ex. 2) Alternatives

"Well, I *kind of* thought of taking phonetics."

(Ex. 3) Mitigated direct rejection

"OK, well, I, I, I'm actually looking at doing some grad school, in—the literature field, um, so: *I think probably* I'm not gonna take the class."

(Ex. 4) Avoidance: Postponement

"Can I think about it?" "Can I decide next week?"

Native speakers of American English tend to avoid refusals in advising sessions, but when they occur, they are short and typically unambiguous as in Example 5, in which a native speaker rejects the advisor's suggestion to take a class (Bardovi-Harlig & Hartford, 1993; the refusal is included in the box).

(Ex. 5) Advisor accepts rejection (native speaker to native speaker interaction)

A: Advisor; S: Student. (A suggests that S take Mary Smith's class.)

Advice 1 A: Um . . . what you might want to do is
2 S: yeah
3 A: is go over and talk to them, um, . . . I could call Mary
4 and ask, that's Smith, and ask her. But . . . let me see if
5 S: um-hm
6 A: she's in

Reason 7 → S: Except that that's a clash, 10:20 to . . . yeah

8 A: Oh it is? Oh, okay, so

In this example, the successful native-speaker rejection is accomplished through an explicit and appropriate explanation that effectively rejects the professor's advice and that is also delayed across the interaction. There are pauses by the advisor in lines 3 and 4 where the student could have made a contribution, but did not. This rejection is accepted by the professor (line 8). Example 5 shows that when native English speakers reject a professor's advice, their refusals are mitigated but firm and provide legitimate reasons or explanations for the rejection. In contrast, when rejecting advice in advising sessions, nonnative English speakers show a preference for avoidance strategies such as requesting repetition of information or postponement of a response, as in "I'm sorry. Can I think about it?"

Refusing an Invitation

Similar to rejecting a professor's advice, declining invitations in English generally entails the interaction of direct and indirect strategies, as well as expressions that preface or follow the refusal. Strategies include (a) direct refusals that are often mitigated or softened (e.g., "*Unfortunately*, I can't make it to the party"); (b) indirect refusals including reasons or explanations, suggestions or alternatives, expressions of apology or regret, and postponements or avoidance; and (c) expressions that preface or follow a direct or indirect strategy such as partial agreements, expressions of gratitude, positive remarks, indications of willingness, and demonstrations of empathy (Beebe, Takahashi, & Uliss-Weltz, 1990; Félix-Brasdefer, 2008). In the e-mail in Example 6, Anne declines Emily's invitation (lines 1–9) for their families to go to the park. Notice that Anne does not refuse directly. (The refusal is included in the box [lines 14–20].)

(Ex. 6) Invitation refusal by e-mail

Emily's invitation:

	1 Hi Anne! How are you guys? Hope you're doing well.
	2 It was great to see you at the Trike-A-Thon the other day.
	3 I just realized that with no class on Monday, we would be free
	4 for a play date if you guys are going to be in town.
	5 Mark would love to have Alex over (or we could meet at a park
	6 or something) if you guys are going to be in town.
Invitation →	7 Would you like to get together on Monday afternoon?
	8 Let me know if you guys want to get together and then
	9 we can make plans. Have a great day!—Emily

Anne's refusal:

Opening →	10 Hi Emily!
	11 Hope you're having a great weekend with this beautiful weather.
	12 Sorry it has taken me so long to get back to you,
	13 we've had a busy few days again.

Gratitude →	14 Thanks for the invitation for tomorrow afternoon,
Reason →	15 but we already have plans for the day since Stephen rarely gets time off.
Suggestion →	16 I know you must be really busy with your classes and all,
	17 so I hope that we will have a chance to get together soon.
	18 What does next weekend Saturday/Sunday look like for you?
	19 Of course, we'll have to play it by ear with the weather and all,
	20 but as far as I know we don't have any plans for then.

Closing → 21 Let me know what works for you and we can plan from there.
22 Enjoy the rest of the weekend, Anne.

The e-mail response consists of three moves (lines 10–22): a greeting and message initiator (lines 10–13), a refusal to the invitation (lines 14–20), and a closing move (lines 21–22). The actual refusal to the invitation is presented later in Anne's turn (lines 14–20). It is prefaced by an expression of gratitude followed by the reason or explanation (lines 14–15), concluding with an initiated suggestion to make plans that leaves the interaction open for further negotiation (lines 16–20). The refusal structure in Example 6 (Gratitude + Reason + Initiated Suggestion) is common among North Americans in refusals to invitations (Félix-Brasdefer, 2008).

Without instruction, the refusals produced by learners of English and other languages show frequent unmitigated direct forms, avoidance strategies that yield nonnative-like refusals, and a lack of alternatives. Learners generally use a small set of expressions to downgrade refusals, and they use them less frequently than native speakers (Bardovi-Harlig & Hartford, 1993; Félix-Brasdefer, 2004). Moreover, nonnative speakers often end refusal sequences abruptly, which can hinder the negotiation of the refusal (Bardovi-Harlig & Hartford, 1991; Félix-Brasdefer, 2004; Gass & Houck, 1999).

CURRICULUM, TASKS, MATERIALS 

This section presents a four-step lesson[1] (Activities 1–4) to raise learners' pragmatic awareness of refusals, using academic advising sessions as the context. A follow-up activity expands the context to refusing a friend's invitation. This lesson was designed for intermediate learners who are learning English in both ESL and EFL classrooms. The lesson can be completed in two to three 50-minute class sessions: 1–2 class sessions devoted to teaching rejections in advising sessions, with a follow-up class to teach refusals to an invitation. For the following activities, teachers and students listen to role-play interactions and follow along in written transcriptions. These and other activities can also be accessed directly from the Indiana University website (see Félix-Brasdefer, 2010a, 2010b).[2]

To begin, the teacher explains that in conversation we use language to request something, apologize for something, or refuse something, and the way we do this may vary across cultures. The expressions used to carry out these actions vary according to the situation and the relationship between the interlocutors. The teacher explains that the focus of the class for that day will be on learning about English refusals in a college or university environment between students and professors. For example, refusing a professor's advice to take a class or revising a final paper.

[1] The audio files and transcripts for this chapter are available at http://www.tesolmedia.com/books/pragmatics. The transcripts also appear in Appendix B.
[2] The online materials and exercises for this chapter were created by the first author.

The activities included here are divided into four phases: raising awareness, recognizing refusal strategies, identifying softeners, and producing refusals.

Activity 1A: Raising Awareness

In the first part of Activity 1, the teacher builds on the introduction to speech acts by explaining that there are various ways of saying "no" in response to requests, suggestions, or invitations. (See the list of strategies in the Context section.) The teacher uses a warm-up activity in which the class brainstorms on various ways to say "no." At the end of the warm-up, the teacher introduces the key concepts: Refusals can be expressed directly or indirectly and can convey different degrees of politeness.

Activity 1B: Perceptions of Refusals

During the second part of Activity 1, students listen to refusals by North American university students in two role-plays[3] (see Appendix B for transcripts) and then read comments by the same speakers on their refusal strategies. In this way, students are exposed to the structure of refusals and the reasons speakers used them. Worksheet 1 (see Appendix A) includes introspections by some of the speakers in the role-play refusals. Students read the comments and identify the expressions that North American students used, the degree of politeness students tried to convey, and the directness level students aimed for. After 5–10 minutes of discussion among the students, the teacher asks the class to comment briefly on the questions as a group. (See Appendix A for answer keys.)

Activity 2: Recognizing Refusal Strategies

In the recognition phase, students analyze rejection sequences in advising interactions with a North American professor. Activity 2 exposes students to relevant pragmatic input to raise their awareness of the pragmalinguistic resources commonly used in rejections of advice. Pragmatic input is presented in two parts: analysis of written input (e.g., analyzing refusals) and listening comprehension (e.g., analyzing *mitigators* and refusal strategies at the discourse level; the examples of rejection sequences are taken from data collected by Bardovi-Harlig & Hartford, 1991, and by Félix-Brasdefer, 2008).

In Worksheet 2 (see Appendix A), students read the examples of rejections to advice (Part I, 1–8), and then work together in pairs to complete a matching activity (Part II). Once students have completed Part II, the teacher reviews the answers with the class.

[3]To access the audio files and transcripts from Félix-Brasdefer (2010a), go to "Listen to Refusals" and scroll down the drop-down menu to "A Professor's Advice 1 and 2." Then click on the audio icon above the text to hear the interactions.

Activity 3: Identifying Softeners

Activity 3 raises awareness of certain expressions utilized in refusals to soften the rejection of a professor's advice.

In preparing learners to listen to native-English-speaking (NES) students' refusals, the teacher points out that when refusing a professor's advice to take an extra class, North Americans soften the negative effects of a direct refusal and present the refusal more tentatively by using expressions called *mitigators* or *downgraders*. These expressions may occur in reasons or explanations, alternatives or suggestions, and indefinite replies or acceptances that function as refusals, as well as in mitigating direct refusals.

The activity begins with an awareness-raising task (see Worksheet 3 in Appendix A) in which students identify softening expressions before they listen to a role-play.[4] The teacher can distribute the transcript (see Appendix B) as a handout for students working on Part III of Worksheet 3 or have students find it online.

Activity 4: Producing Refusals

During Activity 4, students can practice up to five role-plays using the practice activities.[5] Three of these activities involve refusing a professor's advice, and two involve refusing a friend's invitation. The main part of the activity, which is discussed here, focuses on the three situations that involve refusing a professor's advice.

1. Selecting a linguistics class: Students hear a professor suggest that a graduate student take a linguistics class. (See Worksheet 4 in Appendix A.)
2. Selecting an English class: Students hear a professor recommend a writing and composition class to an English major.
3. Final-paper review: Students hear a professor offer advice to a student on revisions of a final paper.

Each situation has an audio component in which the professor speaks, followed by silence during which the student responds, followed by a second turn for both professor and student. The teacher plays the audio file and asks a volunteer to respond to the simulated role-play. The different situations elicit various types of rejection responses.

After the three role-plays are completed, the class comments on the effec-

---

[4] To access the audio file and transcript from Félix-Brasdefer (2010a), go to "Listen to Refusals" and scroll down the drop-down menu to "A Professor's Advice 1." Then click on the audio icon above the text to hear the interaction.

[5] These five audio files and transcripts are available from Félix-Brasdefer (2010b). See "Refusing a Professor's Advice" and "Refusing a Friend's Invitation." The audio files and transcripts for the three situations discussed in the chapter are also available at http://www.tesolmedia.com/books/pragmatics. In addition, a transcript of Situation 1 appears in Worksheet 4.

tiveness of the students' responses in light of the information discussed in the previous activities: (a) selection of linguistic resources to perform the refusal and (b) appropriateness of the response and content of strategies used. The teacher encourages students to practice these activities outside of class.

Follow-Up Activity: Refusing Invitations

The activities presented in this chapter can be extended to other contexts, such as refusing a friend's invitation. In the follow up session, the teacher shows that the strategies that were identified for refusing advice from a professor can also be used when refusing an invitation from a friend, but with different distribution. The most frequent strategies for refusing a friend's invitation to a birthday party (and other contexts) include (a) reasons or explanations, (b) direct refusals, (c) postponements and (d) alternatives, along with expressions that preface the refusal, such as (e) partial agreements, (f) expressions of gratitude, or (g) statements of empathy. The teacher can adapt the discussion questions for the advising session presented earlier to declining invitations. (For a general classification of strategies commonly used in refusal responses and examples of these strategies, see Félix-Brasdefer, 2010a). The teacher should again convey that an invitation–refusal sequence is complex and has a structure similar to that of advising sessions. The teacher presents the following five sequenced parts for refusing an invitation in English:

1. Opening
2. Invitation–refusal sequence
3. Insistence–response (optional)
4. Suggestion to make plans–response
5. Closing

Three refusals to invitations according to the participants' gender (male–male, female–male, female–female), can be found online (see Félix-Brasdefer, 2010a).[6] A sample transcript of an invitation–refusal interaction, featuring the five sequences just described, is included in Appendix B.

Finally, the website (Félix-Brasdefer, 2010b)[7] offers two role-plays similar to the one described in Worksheet 4, in which students can practice

[6] These three audio files and transcripts are available from Félix-Brasdefer (2010a). Go to "Listen to Refusals" and scroll down the drop-down menu to "Refusing in English." See "A Friend's Birthday Invitation." The female–male interaction and transcript are also available at http://www.tesolmedia.com/books/pragmatics.

[7] Scroll down the page. See "Refusing a Friend's Invitation." These files are not available on the book's website.

invitation–refusal sequences. Students select activities according to their gender (male–male or female–female):

1. Refusing a male friend's invitation to a birthday party (male–male)
2. Refusing a female friend's invitation to her graduation party (female–female)

REFLECTIONS 

This chapter presents activities that attempt to raise learners' pragmatic awareness of linguistic resources that are used to make refusals in accordance with the sociocultural expectations and norms of interaction in a specific academic or social context. Such activities can serve as supplements to academic and other curricular content.

The activities described here can be used in ESL and EFL contexts. We recommend that in an EFL context the teacher expose learners to various forms of pragmatic input including e-mail refusals (see Example 6 in the Context section), films, YouTube, and online radio discussions where other types of disagreements occur. In addition, students should be encouraged to listen to and practice interactions in a variety of refusal situations.

César Félix-Brasdefer is associate professor in the Department of Spanish and Portuguese and adjunct associate professor in the Department of Second Language Studies at Indiana University, Bloomington, in the United States. His current research projects include the assessment and teaching of second language pragmatics, interlanguage request modification, the pragmatics-prosody interface, and the pragmatics of service encounters.

Kathleen Bardovi-Harlig is professor of second language studies at Indiana University, in the United States, where she teaches and conducts research on second language pragmatics. Her work on the teaching and learning of pragmatics has appeared in TESOL Quarterly, ELT Journal, Pragmatics and Language Learning, *and* Language Learning.

APPENDIX A: WORKSHEETS AND ANSWER KEYS 

Worksheet 1: Analyzing Native English Speakers' Reflections After Refusing a Professor's Advice

These are comments from the students in the dialogues you just heard: "A Professor's Advice 1 and 2" (available at http://www.tesolmedia.com/books/pragmatics). In them, they explain what strategies they used to refuse to take an extra class as recommended by their professor. Read them and do the following.

1. Identify some expressions that students use in their rejection of a professor's advice.
2. Comment on the degree of politeness and respect that native English speakers try to convey when rejecting advice from a professor.
3. Comment on the native English speakers' degree of directness or indirectness when rejecting advice from a professor. Should a student be direct or vague when conveying the final rejection?

Comments

(a) "I was trying to politely let him know that I couldn't [take the course] this semester, that it wasn't working out and it seemed to me that he thought it'd be a good idea, rather than I needed to take it, so I thought that I was trying to be very polite and trying not to offend him, but at the same time letting him know that I can't do it."

(b) "Thinking that I put a lot of time into organizing my schedule and he had a suggestion, I asked him if it was going to affect graduation; I appreciated his input and I wanted to make that known, but at the same time I wasn't willing to change."

(c) "I wanted to convey a certain amount of respect and appreciation to the professor for making a recommendation to me, but at the same time I knew I didn't want to take the class and I wanted to make that clear."

(d) "[In my rejection I was] indirect at the beginning—[you] cannot be direct right away (. . .) [I tried] to be polite by asking questions, asking for explanations, (. . .) [you] need to be sincere with a professor, but not give a 'no' bluntly."

Worksheet 1: Answer Key

1. Reason or explanation, suggestion, *I don't know, could, probably, possibly, I think, maybe*
2. Native English speakers try to be polite, state appreciation, and convey respect.
3. Try to be indirect first. Then be clear.

Worksheet 2: Recognizing Refusal Strategies in Advising Sessions

The examples in Part I (1–8) include refusals used by students during advising sessions. The arrow (→) indicates the student's refusal response. Read the refusals listed in Part I (1–8) and match them with the refusal strategies in Part II (1–8). Select the strategy that best describes each refusal and complete the blanks.

Part I: Student Refusals

(1) Advisor: So, I'd like you most up-to-date in the area that you will be pursuing um

→ Student: Definitely. So, I have to decide which area I want to pursue and, uh, I'm still thinking a little about that.

(2) Advisor: Here, Educational Psychology, P501, page 49.

→ Student: I've taken that.

(3) Student: That might be a solution.

(4) Student: I should try to work something out for the summer which is where I will need your advice if I want to do these three.

(5) Student: That's the one that conflicts with what I have to take.

(6) Student: By the way, I *could* look into the *possibility* of having that requirement waived . . .

(7) Student: OK, well, I, I, I'm actually looking at doing some grad school, in—the literature field, um,

→ so: *I think probably* I'm not gonna take the class.

(8) Student: OK, *could* you—just tell me *a little bit* about it?

Part II: Refusal Strategies

For each example number on the left, fill in the blank the with appropriate strategy letter from the right-hand column.

Example #	**Strategy**
1. _______	(a) asking for explicit advice
2. _______	(b) direct short rejection
3. _______	(c) postponing the rejection
4. _______	(d) offering an alternative
5. _______	(e) requesting additional information
6. _______	(f) offering an indefinite reply
7. _______	(g) making a mitigated refusal
8. _______	(h) offering a reason or an explanation

Worksheet 2: Answer Key

Part II: Refusal Strategies

1. (c); 2. (b); 3. (f); 4. (a); 5. (h); 6. (d); 7. (g); 8. (e)

Worksheet 3: Identifying Expressions, Softeners, and Strategies

Part I: Focusing on Softeners

With a classmate, discuss the function of the expressions in italics in the following examples. What do these expressions do? How does the speaker use them?

Student: By the way, I *could* look into the *possibility* of having that requirement waived . . .

Student: OK, well, I, I, I'm actually looking at doing some grad school,
in—the literature field, um,
→ so: *I think probably* I'm not gonna take the class.

Student: OK, *could* you—just tell me *a little bit* about it?

Part II: Listening

Listen to the audio file "A Professor's Advice 1" (available at http://www.tesolmedia.com/books/pragmatics). In this role-play interaction, a North American student refuses his professor's advice. Read along on the transcript (also available online). You will hear the interactions twice. Complete the following activities as you listen to the conversations.

1. Write down the various expressions that the student used to soften his refusal.
2. Compare your list of expressions with a classmate's and decide what strategies were used in those expressions (e.g., reasons or explanations, mitigated refusals, postponements, expressions of uncertainty, or others).

Part III: Postlistening

This activity consists of four sections:

1. Listen to the role-play interaction again. This time, follow along on the role-play transcription (available at http://www.tesolmedia.com/books/pragmatics). While you listen, underline or write down all the forms used by the student to soften a refusal response or to present the refusal more tentatively.
2. Compare your responses with a classmate. Make sure to include those expressions that are used at the beginning of each of the native-English-speaking (NES) student's turns.
3. Class discussion. Discuss all the mitigators identified in the role-play. Your teacher will write these expressions on the board.
4. Finally, with a classmate compare the three refusals by the NES student (see lines 5–7, 11–15, and 17 on the transcript). How is each of these responses different? What strategy does the student use to make his last refusal?

Worksheet 3: Answer Key

Part II: Listening

1. *Could, possibility, I think, probably, a little bit*
2. Some strategies include: soften, sound less certain, start a negotiation.

Part III: Postlistening

1. *I don't know, kind of, I guess, well*
2. Compare answers with partner
3. Compare answers with class
4. Lines 5–7, explanation and alternative; lines 11–15, explanation; line 17, postponement

Worksheet 4: Refusing a Professor's Advice—Situation 1

For the following situation imagine yourself at your advisor's office. Read the situation carefully. Take a minute to look over the conversation. You will have 15 seconds to respond. Press [start] on the audio when you are ready to begin the advising session (available at http://www.tesolmedia.com/books/pragmatics).

Situation 1: Selecting a linguistics class for next year

> **Advisor–Student:** It is class registration time and you go to your advisor's office to finalize your schedule for next year. After exchanging greetings, your professor begins the advising session.

(Student hits Play button to begin the advising session.)

ADVISOR: [Professor begins advising session]

[Tone]

YOU: Respond: Briefly agree with your professor's suggestion and provide a reason for not taking the class.

[Tone]

ADVISOR: [Professor responds]

[Tone]

YOU: Respond. Provide a partial agreement response, then an alternative or a suggestion.

[Tone]

ADVISOR: [Professor ends advising session].

Worksheet 4: Answer Key

Sample responses provided by a North American female graduate student. An audio file is also available at http://www.tesolmedia.com/books/pragmatics.

ADVISOR: [Professor begins advising session.]

YOU: Respond: Briefly agree with your professor's suggestion and provide a reason for not taking the class.

Student's response:

Oh—yeah, I think I think it would be helpful—um—however it's at the same time as um this brilliant important seminar that I'm—that I'm taking in theoretical linguistics—um—

so I think I'd probably better take that one.

ADVISOR: [Professor responds.]

YOU: Respond. Provide a partial agreement response, then an alternative or a suggestion.

Student's response:
OK, maybe I can—um—talk to the—theoretical linguistics professor to see if he is going to offer another s—um—section of the class—is there another time that the second language class would be offered?

ADVISOR: [Professor ends advising session.]

APPENDIX B: TRANSCRIPTS 

Note: Activity 1B: Perceptions of Refusals uses "A Professor's Advice 1 and 2." Activity 3: Identifying Softeners also uses "A Professor's Advice 1."

A Professor's Advice 1

Advisor: Taylor, I've looked over your—transcript and I've noticed
that you've taken a lot of—literature classes but you haven't
taken any linguistics classes, and there's a Spanish linguistics class
that I think it would be really beneficial for you to take this semester↓
→ Student: Yeah, I don't know—I thought about that, but I really—I really felt
that I've, I've learned enough—linguistics before in my other classes
so::—I—I kind of felt like I wanted to take a literature class.
Advisor: Yeah, well this focuses not just on the linguistics that you've learned
but it applies to Hispanic Linguistics—so I think it would be
really beneficial if you had some other linguistics background.
→ Student: M-kay—well—I don't know—I'm really—I'm really not—
I don't feel completely ah—like I need—ah—I guess I feel
like I can—get enough out of the books that I've read and—
just from previous classes
so:: I'm st—I'm still kind of unsure about it ((laughs))—uh
Advisor: OK, well I just think that it would—it would be very beneficial.
→ Student: OK, well, I'll—I'll look into it—I'll think about it some more.
Advisor: OK.

A Professor's Advice 2

Advisor: Well—I've been reviewing your transcript and uh while you've taken a lot
of Spanish classes, a lot of literature classes for your Spanish major, you
you haven't taken any linguistics classes yet—and uh—I think it'd be a real
good idea for you to take this linguistics class that's being offered,
it's a really good class.
Student: OK, when does that meet?
Advisor: Um, it meets um Tuesdays, Thursdays in the afternoon.
Student: OK um, my Tuesdays and Thursdays are really wrapped up right now,
um I'm not gonna be able to do that this semester, um, hopefully
I can get around to it next semester—if that's a necessity for . . .
Advisor: Well it's not a requirement, but it's a really good class and it's it's
something that I REALLY think you should take.
Student: OK, do you think that it would be helpful in me doing better
in these classes?
Advisor: It's gonna help you understand the Spanish language better, yeah.
Student: OK, um, well like I said—maybe next semester, I can't do it now,
uh per se
Advisor: Um—I I think it'd be very beneficial for you to take it uh—
uh as soon as you can.
Student: OK, um, do you think I should try to rearrange my schedule . . .
or should—is it something [that I could put off?
Advisor: [Well, well, I think so,
I think you should take it uh—
you know—I think it would really be helpful for you
Student: OK, um . . .

Follow-Up Activity: Refusing Invitations

Erin (female) and Paul (male) are two college students at an American University in the southern United States. Erin invites Paul to her birthday party and Paul declines.

Erin:	Hey Paul—how's it going?		Opening
Paul:	hey, Erin how are you?		
Erin:	I'm fanta::stic		
Paul:	I haven't seen you in a long time—	[where you been?	
Erin:		[I—	
	I've just been working—going to class		
Paul:	[oh good—good		
Erin:	[the usual—		
	I'm so glad that I saw you—I've been trying to figure out how to get in touch with you cuz—um—I just turned 21—yesterday—and I'm gonna have a party this Friday night and I'm just trying to get in touch with everybody—um—from last semester—that we were all in class together and everything and I really wanted you to come—it's gonna be at eight o'clock at my house		Invitation–refusal
Paul:	ooh—this Friday?		
Erin:	yeah		
Paul:	ohh my goodness—it's my grandmother's birthday this weekend		
Erin:	you're kidding		
Paul:	and my grandmother lives out of town – too		
Erin:	oh— [no:::		
Paul:	[and—normally—you know—my parents go of course—you know		
Erin:	umhm		
Paul:	so—when we go, we spend the weekend with 'em		
Erin:	yeah		
Paul:	because I live so far away—		
	we just can't come back and forth on	[a day	
Erin:		[yeah	
	when are you leaving?		

Paul:	Thursday night	
Erin:	oh man::—	
Paul:	and we're gonna get there Friday morning and stay until Sunday	
Erin:	and—there's no way you can—like =	Insistence–response
Paul:	—oh, I wish I could—I—I wish I could make it because, you know—I haven't seen you for such a [long time	
Erin:	[yeah	
Paul:	and I'd like to get—you know—I'd like to get back with you but—um—maybe next—are you busy next week? I mean—I'll take you out for dinner or =	Suggestion–response
Erin:	—ohh ((laughs)) that's nice of you—um yeah we can just— we can get together—that's cool	
Paul:	would that work?	
Erin:	yeah	
Paul:	ok	
Erin:	well, I'm sorry you can't come, but have a good time with your grandmother	Closing
Paul:	alright—I'm sorry too—	
Erin:	alright	
Paul:	happy birthday	
Erin:	thank you.	

CHAPTER 12

They Made Me an Invitation I Couldn't Refuse: Teaching Refusal Strategies for Invitations

Emma Archer

Refusals to invitations can be highly face-threatening acts. Even native speakers may find refusing invitations a tricky task. However, language learners, particularly those in an English as a second language (ESL) context, may often find themselves in situations where they need or want to refuse an invitation. For English as a foreign language (EFL) learners, the task is further complicated due to the great deal of variation in how refusals are constructed and understood in different cultures. Furthermore, because refusals often occur between only two speakers, language learners may not be in a position to observe exchanges without participating directly—a factor that Bardovi-Harlig and Mahan-Taylor (2003) argued may hinder second language (L2) pragmatic development. As mentioned in previous chapters, pragmatic instruction can be useful for helping students learn appropriate pragmatic strategies.

This chapter uses videotaped activities to demonstrate how verbal strategies for refusals and their complementary adjuncts (e.g., statements that accompany refusals) can be strung together to soften the refusal of an invitation. For that, it employs a visual metaphor, which compares the "breaking" of a conversation with the breaking of an object.

CONTEXT

This lesson was used with ESL students who had advanced linguistic competence but low pragmatic ability. The students had spent several weeks in the United States participating in a summer intensive language program at a university. The program combined classroom instruction, cultural excursions, and informal conversation groups with U.S. students. Students interacted with North Americans in conversation groups, excursions, and dorms. In their everyday interactions with U.S. students, social situations arose in which they needed to refuse invitations without offending their hosts.

The activities included in this lesson helped to heighten students' awareness of a wider variety of refusal strategies and the reasons for using them. Also, students' overall awareness of the value and benefits of recognizing target language pragmatic norms increased. In a class discussion, one of the students commented on her new awareness that English speakers are not always as direct as she had previously learned, but rather that it is "necessary to take care in English" and choose appropriate language for different situations—strong support for teaching and studying pragmatics.

The materials for this lesson are grounded in the findings of Gass and Houck (1999); Beebe, Takahashi, and Uliss-Weltz (1990); and the writer's own data collected using native-English-speaking (NES) simulations of invitation and refusal scenarios, as well as the University of Minnesota Center for Advanced Research on Language Acquisition (CARLA, n.d.), which presents an analysis of refusal speech acts and metapragmatic strategies as observed in authentic language samples.

A person who does not accept an invitation needs to rely on culturally specific pragmatic strategies to avoid offending the person who offered the invitation. As native speakers may often be unaware of how these strategies are deployed, extensive research has documented how refusals are conducted in American English. It provides an empirical foundation for the development of pedagogical activities (Kasper & Rose, 2002). The four refusal strategies that occur frequently in both first language (L1) and L2 refusals are as follows:

1. Direct refusals ("no," "I won't be able to"; often softened)
2. Reasons or explanations ("I have to work," "I'm not feeling well")
3. Alternatives ("maybe next week")
4. Expressions of apology or regret ("I'm sorry")

(Beebe, Takahashi, & Uliss-Weltz, 1990; Gass & Houck, 1999)

In addition to these nonacceptance strategies, speakers often use *adjuncts* to soften the nonacceptance. These include the following, which are often prefaced with pause fillers such as *ummm, well,* and *you know*:

- Positive statements ("that would be great")
- Expressions of gratitude ("thanks," "I appreciate the invitation")
- Statements of empathy ("I know you've been planning this for a while")

Although refusals of invitations vary depending on the context of the conversation, a common formula for nonacceptance in American English is as follows:

1. Signal: Begin with an adjunct, such as *Well, Thank you, I'd love to.*
2. Refusal: Offer an apology or expression of regret (one of these by itself can function as a refusal), or a direct refusal can be given.
3. Follow-up: Provide an excuse.

In American English, giving at least a basic explanation ("I have plans," "I'll be out of town") for not accepting an invitation is especially important because it demonstrates that your refusal of the invitation is not a rejection of the inviter (CARLA, n.d.).

In addition to the verbal strategies previously discussed, Gass and Houck (1999) cautioned that the complex nature of nonacceptance speech acts makes them particularly dynamic and that nonverbal components such as facial expressions and intonation can play key roles in successfully maintaining face (i.e., attempting to avoid the embarrassment of either interlocutor). Therefore, in addition to studying the language of refusals, it is also important for the instructor to present appropriate models in which students can observe nonverbal features of the speech act, such as the speaker's tone of voice (e.g., questioning or hesitant), gestures (e.g., a shrug, nod, or head tilt), and facial expressions (e.g., a slight frown or scrunched eyebrows). This observation should be followed by a discussion of how these nonverbal cues make students feel, which can elucidate cultural differences students should be aware of concerning nonverbal components of refusals.

CURRICULUM, TASKS, MATERIALS 

Prior to the lesson, students should write a journal entry about refusals. This will activate students' background knowledge, provide opportunity for considering cultural differences, and reveal gaps in the students' knowledge. A sample prompt might ask students to describe what they would say to a friend if they could not attend the friend's birthday party, to reflect on how comfortable they feel about their ability to decline an invitation in English, and to think about a situation where a refusal did not go as well as they would have liked.

Activity 1: Eliciting Refusals

The lesson begins by eliciting student-generated speech samples. The teacher issues a personal invitation to each student to come to a special class very early on Saturday morning. (If students accept the invitation, the teacher should explain that attendance at the special class is entirely voluntary and that they are allowed and indeed encouraged to refuse.) Students reply orally and then record their refusals on the board. For example,

> Teacher: Yoojin, would you be able to come to school this Saturday morning at 5:00 for a review session?
>
> Yoojin: I'm sorry. I have to work late on Friday, so I won't be able to come.

Activity 2: Introducing Refusal Strategies

Once all of the students have responded, the teacher demonstrates the idea of refusal strategies in a visual-kinesthetic manner. A video recording of this demonstration is available on the Internet (Archer, 2009b). Given the large size of videos, we recommend that the teacher download them rather than using the website's viewer. This will minimize hesitation in the video due to buffering.

The video available at this site demonstrates visually the concept of *face* through using an object that breaks and can be put back together (e.g., Magnetix linking magnets). The teacher explains that because the inviter expects the conversation partner to accept the invitation, a refusal could result in embarrassment, hurt feelings, or a breakdown of the conversation and loss of face (here demonstrated with the breaking of the object). At this point, the object is dropped and breaks on a paper sheet labeled "Direct Refusal." Then the class considers refusal situations with different contexts that represent varying levels of power, distance, and imposition (e.g., refusing your employer's invitation to attend an important conference, refusing your brother's invitation to go to a movie). Students judge whether a situation is high or low stakes (i.e., very likely to cause loss of face or unlikely to cause loss of face), and the teacher represents this concept visually by moving the object higher or lower above the paper labeled "Direct Refusal."

The teacher then asks students what they might say to soften the blow of the refusal. The teacher matches student responses to categories of strategies (i.e., positive statement, offering an alternative, thanking, apology, direct refusal, and giving a reason), which are written on pieces of colored felt (see Figure 1). These pieces of felt are stacked on top of the paper labeled "Direct Refusal" to create a cushion (i.e., "refusal softeners"). When all the strategies are identified, the teacher drops the breakable object (i.e., "the conversation") onto this cushion, and it remains intact.

After this demonstration, students are given Handout 1 (see Appendix A) with the strategies listed in the same colors as the felt used in the demonstration. Students discuss the categories and compile additional phrases. Students then use colored chalk to underline examples of corresponding strategies used in the student-generated speech samples on the board. For instance, if a student had written "I'm sorry, I already have other plans" then *I'm sorry* would be underlined in red (apology) and *I already have other plans* would be underlined in green (giving a reason).

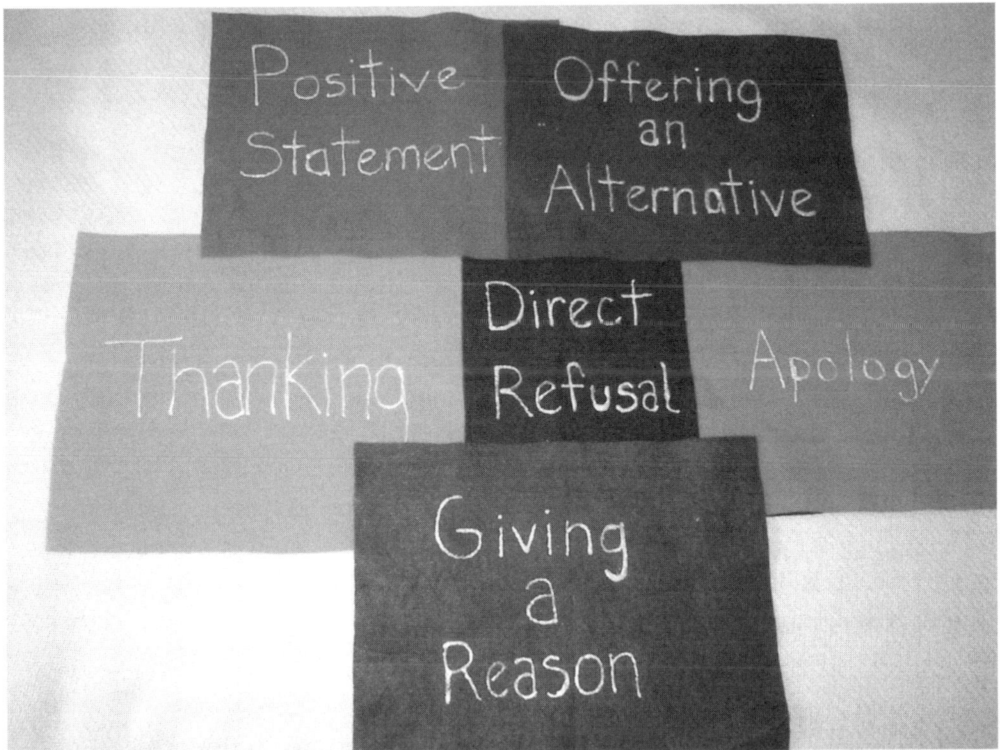

Color Key: positive statement = purple; offering an alternative = blue; thanking = orange; direct refusal = black; apology = red; giving a reason = green

Note: A color version of Figure 1 is available at http://www.tesolmedia.com/books/pragmatics.

Figure 1. Refusal Strategies

Activity 3: Sequencing Components of a Refusal

Next, students are asked to work in groups to compose a conversation out of phrases written on strips of paper that can be cut out and scrambled (see Worksheet 1 in Appendix B). Each phrase is also labeled with the type of strategy it represents. As students compare answers, some of the students can write their answers on the board. Note that variability in answers should be expected and should encourage a discussion of the degree of acceptability of the language used. Certain forms may be preferred, but there is not a single correct answer.

Activity 4: Practicing a Common Refusal Sequence

In the next activity, students practice a common refusal sequence in English (see Handout 2 in Appendix A and Worksheet 2 in Appendix B) whose structure is based on common NES practice.

Handout 2 (see Appendix A) should be accompanied by a discussion of the purpose of different strategies and sequences used in refusals. For example, the conjunction *but* after a positive opinion prepares the inviter for the coming refusal. On the other hand, an expression of appreciation in the signaling position may lead the inviter to expect acceptance.

Activity 5: Receptive Practice

If access to the Internet is available, then teachers and students can access refusal videos from the Internet (Archer, 2009a). These videos are simulations of refusals enacted by highly proficient speakers of English. Students can watch the videos more than once as they complete the chart (see Worksheet 3 in Appendix B), which requires them to draw on their new pragmatic knowledge. Transcripts of the conversations are available in Appendix C and at http://www.tesolmedia.com/books/pragmatics.

Though answers may differ somewhat from the examples given in the answer key (see Appendix B), they should demonstrate the students' awareness of various pragmatic features. Given that nonverbal elements often play a crucial role in interactions, this discussion can serve as a reminder to students of the importance of nonverbal communication and the necessity to observe and study nonverbal as well as verbal factors.

Activity 6: Productive Practice

Finally, students are given multiturn *discourse completion tasks* for refusals (see Worksheet 4 in Appendix B). For this activity, students will be given one speaker's part of a conversation and asked to complete the other speaker's part. This allows students to practice the strategies they have studied in a nonthreatening format, and offers the teacher an opportunity to assess students' understanding.

After finishing the discourse completion tasks, students could complete self-assessment sheets that incorporate the learners' intent (e.g., how the student wants the language to be perceived) to allow learners to express their individuality in pragmatic choice and to inform teachers as to whether the students' language serves the function that they intend (see Ishihara, Chapter 14 of this volume). The teacher could also offer feedback on the appropriateness of the refusal and recommend language and strategy use that would create a better match between the learners' intent and probable perception in the target language and culture.

REFLECTIONS 

This lesson provides an opportunity for university ESL students with little previous experience in a predominantly English language environment to learn appropriate strategies for refusing an invitation. However, the visual illustrations of its key concept make it suitable for adaptation for beginning to intermediate level students, provided that the instructor supplies the necessary scaffolding for vocabulary and grammar. The lesson may also be used in an EFL context because it includes video clips, audio recordings, and written dialogues that can provide students with opportunities to notice differences between their own pragmatic production and the target language use. For EFL contexts, it will also be necessary for the teacher to clearly demonstrate to students how knowledge of English pragmatics will prove useful to them, the specifics of which will vary depending on the students' context and language needs.

With my own students, I found pragmatic violations that were not directly addressed in the lesson. For instance, several of my students produced reasons that might be considered too vague for the context, such as "I can't go," in response to an instructor's request for a meeting. This is similar to the findings of Beebe, Takahashi, and Uliss-Weltz (1990). Other students were too direct in offering an alternative (i.e., "You will invite me next time"). However, such violations are useful in providing guidance for future pragmatics instruction that encourages students to build on what they have learned. To individualize instruction, the instructor could point out pragmatic violations and encourage students to conduct their own research on how people conduct specific speech acts.

Emma Archer is a Peace Corps volunteer in Mongolia serving as a teacher trainer at the Erdmiin Dalai Complex School. Her professional interests include teacher mentoring and critical reflective practice. She has taught in the United States and Mongolia.

APPENDIX A: HANDOUTS

Handout 1: Example Strategies and Adjuncts for Refusing Invitations

Positive statement (purple) That sounds wonderful, but . . . I'd like/love to, but . . . I wish I could, but . . .	**Offering an alternative (blue)** Maybe some other time. Would you want to _______ instead?
Thanking (orange) Thank you for the invitation . . . but Thanks, but . . .	**Apology (red)** I'm sorry, but . . . Sorry
Direct refusal (black) I can't go. I can't make it.	**Giving a reason (green)** I already have other plans. I have to . . .

Note: This handout was adapted from Beebe, Takahashi, and Uliss-Weltz (1990).

Handout 2: Invitation Refusal Sequences

To refuse an invitation politely, please follow this refusal sequence and the refusal strategies listed in it. Please note that it can change depending on the context.

1) **Signaling the refusal:** Prepare interlocutor for the refusal. Begin with a positive statement, words of thanks, followed by the word *but*.

   Example: "Oh, I'd love to go to your picnic, *but* . . ."

   Example: "Thank you for thinking of me, *but* . . ."

2) **Refusal:** Offer a direct refusal or an apology used instead of a direct refusal.

   Example: "I won't be able to make it."

   Example: "I'm sorry but I have another appointment at that time."

3) **Follow-up:** These statements tend to explain, justify, soften, or reinforce the refusal. An alternative may be proposed at the end.

   Example: "I already have plans with my family. My son is playing in his championship baseball game. Thanks for inviting me though! Maybe we can meet up for lunch some other time."

A Model Refusal

In refusing an invitation, North Americans often begin with a delay (e.g., words or vocalizations such as *oh, well, umm, uh*), an expression of thanks, and/or a positive statement. Then, they generally offer an apology followed by a reason for the refusal. Note that a direct refusal is sometimes not expressed.

This model can change depending on the conversation, but it is a very common form. In English, giving a reason for the refusal can be especially important. The person you are talking with will normally feel better about your refusal if they understand *why* you cannot accept.

> Example: "Oh, that sounds like a lot of fun, but I'm afraid I have to work tomorrow night. Maybe we can do something this weekend. I already have plans with my family. My son is playing in his championship baseball game. Thanks for inviting me though! Maybe we can meet up for lunch some other time."

APPENDIX B: WORKSHEETS AND ANSWER KEYS 

Worksheet 1: Responding to Invitations

An old friend who you have not seen in a while is in town and has asked you to go to lunch next week, but you have to work. How would you respond to the invitation? Work with your group to order the sentence strips. You do not have to use all of the strips.

Examples: "That sounds great, but I have to work. Thanks for asking me."
"That sounds great and maybe some other time, but I have to work."

Positive statement **that sounds great**	Thanking **thanks for asking me**
Apology **I'm sorry**	Alternative **maybe some other time**
Direct refusal **I can't go**	Reason **I have to work**
but	**and**
but	**and**

Worksheet 2: Invitation Refusal Sequences

Choose one of the refusals that your classmates wrote on the board. Does it have a clear signal, refusal, and follow-up? What types of strategies are used? Write the components of your classmate's refusal below:

Signal the refusal is coming: ______________________________

Refusal: ______________________________

Follow-up: ______________________________

Note: This worksheet was adapted from CARLA (n.d.).

Worksheet 3: Refusal Strategies and Nonverbal Behaviors

View the video (Archer, 2009a) available at http://www.youtube.com/watch?v=6yJGVjlj27g and complete the following tasks:

1. Fill in Columns 1 and 2 of the chart below. Focus on the speakers' verbal communication. What is the context and what refusal strategies do the speakers use?
2. View the video again. Fill in Column 3 of the chart below. Focus on the speakers' nonverbal communication.
3. Discuss what you observed with your classmates. Use your notes from the tables below. How did you feel about what you saw? How would people from other countries and cultures behave in this situation?

(1) Situation and Context Who are the speakers? What is their relationship? How did the speaker seem to perceive the refusal?	**(2) Strategies Used**	**(3) Nonverbal** What did you notice about the speakers' body language, facial expressions, or tone of voice?
(a)		
(b)		
(c)		

Worksheet 3: Answer Key

Answers will vary.

Column 1	Column 2	Column 3
(a) Professor Brady and Kelly Professor and student He didn't seem upset. He agreed to help find an alternative.	Giving a reason, positive statement, offering an alternative	Questioning tone, hesitation, leaning back, nodding
(b) Han Suk and Kate Good friends He quickly agreed and said that it didn't matter.	*Umm*, direct refusal, giving a reason	Hesitation, looking at the window for evidence of the reason, looking down, shrugging, slight frown
(c) Heather and Chrissy Acquaintances Heather seemed to understand and agreed to do something else with Chrissy.	*Well*, giving a reason, offering an alternative, apology	Audible drawing in of breath, shrug, tilting head and touching chest, gesturing to emphasize alternatives, looking away quickly

Worksheet 4: Discourse Completion Task

Complete the following dialogues using appropriate refusal strategies.

1. A close friend has asked you to come to her house to watch a movie, but you don't really want to go, because you've already seen the movie and don't like it.

   A: Do you have plans Friday?

   B:

   A: I was going to have some people over to watch a movie.

   B:

   A: I think Julie's going to bring *Silence of the Lambs.*

   B:

   A: It'll be fun. There'll be a bunch of people there and we're going to order pizza.

   B:

   How would the friend feel about this refusal? Why?

   Teacher feedback:

2. Your friend asks you to come to his graduation, but you have to work.

   A: So, do you think you're going to be able to make it to my graduation?

   B:

   A: It's on May 13th at noon. That's a Sunday.

   B:

   A: Yeah, next Sunday at noon. Think you can come?

   B:

   How would your friend feel about this refusal? Why?

   Teacher feedback:

3. Your neighbor invites you to a surprise birthday party that he's having for his wife, but you already have plans to go to New York with your friends.

   A: Don't tell my wife, but I'm having a surprise birthday party for her next Saturday afternoon.

   B:

   A: If you're free, you should come. I know she would love to see you there.

   B:

   A: Oh, OK. Well, if your plans change for any reason, feel free to stop by.

   B:

   A: Thanks. Have a nice trip.

   How would the neighbor feel about the refusal? Why?

   Teacher feedback:

Worksheet 4: Answer Key

Sample answers in italics. Answers will vary.

Dialogue 1:

A: Do you have plans Friday?
B: *I don't think so. Why?*
A: I was going to have some people over to watch a movie.
B: *Oh yeah? What are you watching?*
A: I think Julie's going to bring *Silence of the Lambs.*
B: *Uhh, I might have to pass. I don't really like scary movies.*
A: It'll be fun. There'll be a bunch of people there and we're going to order pizza.
B: *Sorry. Maybe some other time.*

How would the friend feel about this refusal? Why?
I think she would understand.

Teacher feedback:
This is an appropriate refusal. It's good that you explain why you don't want to watch the movie and suggest that you watch a movie another time.

Dialogue 2:

A: So, do you think you're going to be able to make it to my graduation?
B: *I'll definitely try. When is it?*
A: It's on May 13th at noon. That's a Sunday.
B: *Next Sunday?*
A: Yeah, next Sunday at noon. Think you can come?
B: *Sorry, I can't come.*

How would your friend feel about this refusal? Why?
I said I'm sorry, so he'll understand.

Teacher feedback:
Because this is an important event for your friend, he may be disappointed by your refusal. You would probably want to give a reason for why you can't go to the graduation and maybe offer an alternative way that you could celebrate.

Dialogue 3:

A: Don't tell my wife, but I'm having a surprise birthday party for her next Saturday afternoon.
B: *That's great. I'm sure she'll be thrilled.*
A: If you're free, you should come. I know she would love to see you there.
B: *Oh, I'd love to, but I'm going to be out of town.*
A: Oh, OK. Well, if your plans change for any reason, feel free to stop by.
B: *Thanks. Have fun at the party.*
A: Thanks. Have a nice trip.

How would the neighbor feel about the refusal? Why?
I think he would think I am busy but polite.

Teacher feedback:
This is an appropriate refusal. You give a good reason why you can't go to the party and express your positive opinion about how much fun it will be.

APPENDIX C: TRANSCRIPTS 

Activity 5: Receptive Practice

1) *Professor and Student: Professor Brady asks Kelly if she can attend a training.*

Prof: Um any other questions on the assignment?

K: Nope, I think that's pretty clear.

Prof: OK, well I'm sure you'll be fine. Oh (snap) before I forget, there's a workshop this Friday on Dreamweaver, and I really would like you to attend because umm I, I think they've got some new stuff that'll be very useful. Umm it's, it's at uhh 2:30 in the afternoon.

K: 2:30?

Prof: Yeah.

K: I think I have a doctor's appointment then. I think it'd, it'd be useful, but I can't miss Friday. Do you know of any other days that they're doin' it?

Prof: Umm no, not right off the top of my head, but let me check because, you know, they're pretty good about doin' these kinds of things again.

K: All right.

Prof: OK.

2) *Good friends: Han Suk asks Kate if she wants to go out for ice cream.*

HS: Hey.

K: Hey, how's it goin'?

HS: Very well. What's up?

K: Not too much.

HS: OK. Hey, would you go out for ice cream?

K: Ummm. I don't think so. It looks like it's gonna rain. [So . . .]

HS: [Oh, really?] Oh. I didn't know that.

K: Yeah.

HS: OK, never mind.

3) *Acquaintances: Heather asks Chrissy if she wants to go to a movie.*

H: Hey, Chrissy?

C: Yeah, Heather.

H: Umm, I was wondering. They're showing the *Devil Wears Prada* in Bethesda next week. Would you be interested in going to that movie with me?

C: Well, I don't know. It's August. It's kind of hot. I've already seen it. Is there anything else, maybe inside? Or uh a different, something else we can do? Maybe you wanna go shopping? Or, it's just.

H: We can [go shopping.]

C: [I don't know.] It's just, it's just, it's kind of hot for me.

H: Oh, I understand. That's OK. [We'll try something else.]

C: [I'm sorry.] OK.

CHAPTER 13

Online Collaboration for Pragmatic Development—Talkpoint Project

Emi Yamanaka and Kenneth Fordyce

This chapter introduces a series of collaborative activities to be used in conjunction with a freely available and customizable web-based tool, Talkpoint (http://www.talkpoint.org).[1] This tool has been developed for the purpose of teaching pragmatic aspects of a second language (L2; e.g., how to request, invite, apologize, refuse, or complain) through collaborative learning. It enables learners in different locations in the world to compare the pragmatic characteristics of their first language (L1) with those of the L2 they are learning, and to reflect on those differences and similarities through online discussions. So far, Talkpoint has been utilized for the study of speech acts by English-speaking learners of Japanese as a foreign language (JFL learners) and English as a foreign language (EFL) learners in Japan. However, the model of this website can easily be used by teachers of any language throughout the world.

Talkpoint was created in response to a growing body of research (Kasper & Rose, 2002), that shows that it is crucial for learners to be exposed to ample authentic examples of the L2 and then become aware of and notice (Schmidt, 1993) the differences and similarities between their L1 and L2 in order to acquire pragmatic competence. This includes, for example, comparing ways in which speech acts are expressed, meaning is negotiated, and viewpoints are expressed.

Thus, learners need to have access to appropriate authentic language examples. However, it is not always easy for teachers to collect naturally occurring data for the pragmatic feature they intend to focus on in class (Yamanaka, 2003). Furthermore, many textbook materials tend to follow cultural stereotypes (Matsumoto, Shimizu, Okano, & Kubo, 2004) and often lack authenticity. The Talkpoint

[1] This project was funded by the National Institute for Japanese Language e-Japan project fund from the Japanese government in 2004–2006.

website (see Figure 1 for an illustration of the system) provides an environment in which authentic language can be generated by learners. This language can then become the object of reflection, analysis, and discussion via direct communication with target language speakers in a partner class.

On the website, learners input how they would respond in a particular situation (e.g., requesting a schedule rearrangement, refusing an offer of help, or apologizing for dropping an item) in their L1. Then they compare their responses with the responses of other students (i.e., target language speakers), reflecting and commenting on the differences and similarities through online discussion.

Posted solutions can be sorted and downloaded anonymously with information about age range (if disclosed), gender, and native country for teaching material development or research purposes. A teacher support network has been set up for teachers to find possible partner teachers and classrooms through the website. The network is located at the bottom of the teacher's home page.

CONTEXT

The materials and curriculum described in this chapter are based on a project conducted with an EFL class in Japan and a JFL class in the United States for advanced learners at the college level. The EFL class had 30 students and the JFL class had 16. After both the EFL and JFL teachers created their teacher accounts and agreed on situations to use for the class, their students were directed to

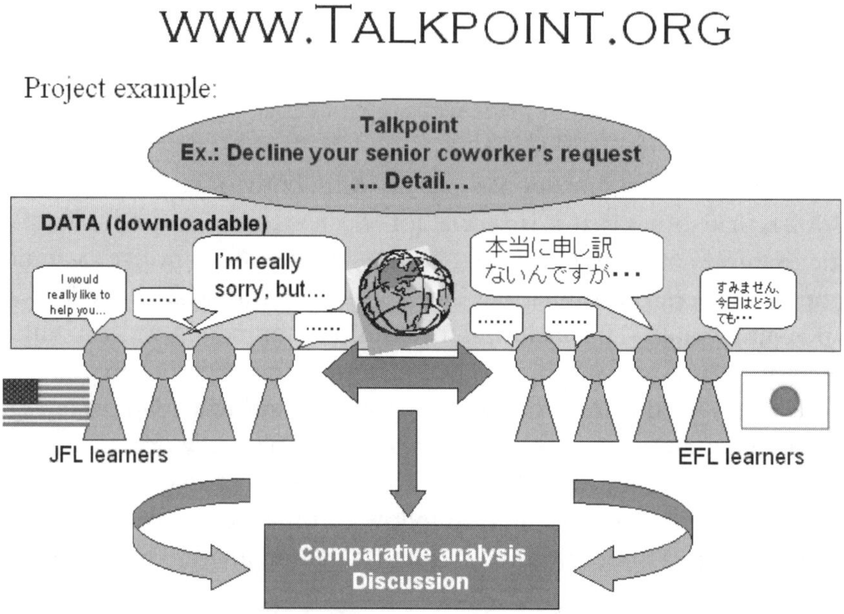

Figure 1. How the Talkpoint System Works

the same virtual classroom via randomly generated invitation codes. When the students created their accounts, they were asked to input a username, age range (optional), gender, and native country or region. The project was a small part of the curriculum of both courses. It took about 2 hours of class time in total over 4 weeks, including pre- and post-discussion activities.

Through the situation responses and discussion, students noticed points that they had not previously been aware of. Many who had hesitated to speak up in class were able to articulate their opinions more easily online.

CURRICULUM, TASKS, MATERIALS 

English teachers who are interested in developing a Talkpoint relationship with a class in another country should begin by taking the Flash website tutorial on the Talkpoint home page (http://www.talkpoint.org). After creating a teacher account, teachers need to find a partner teacher and set up a time frame for the project. Following the directions on the Talkpoint tutorial, teachers will do the following:

1. Create a class on the website. At this point, the teacher will obtain a Student Invitation Code.
2. Set up Talkpoint(s) by taking the following steps:
    a. Click on "Create Talkpoint" and choose situation(s), or Talkpoint(s).
    b. Give the Teacher Invitation Code(s) to the partner teacher(s). Note that each Talkpoint has its own, which is different from the Student Invitation Code.
    c. The partner teacher creates an account, clicks on "Join Talkpoint," and inputs the Teacher Invitation Code(s). Now the two teachers can share a virtual classroom.

The teachers choose a situation (i.e., the Talkpoint) to which their students will respond. In this example, one pair of teachers created a set of situations involving making a refusal to someone senior or superior whom the learner knows well. The learners were provided with the following two situations, which varied by the level of difficulty of refusing (i.e., Situation 1—lower level; Situation 2—higher level):[2]

> **Situation 1**
> You are a college student. You are going hiking with your seminar members. In the bus on the way to the hiking site the professor of the seminar,

[2] There are five categories in the situations (Talkpoints): invitation, apology, complaint, refusal, and request. Each category has multiple situations that are varied based on power, distance, and ranking of imposition factors (Brown & Levinson, 1987).

who is sitting next to you, puts sunscreen on himself or herself and asks you if you need to use it too. You have your own sunscreen, so you do not need to borrow it (adapted from Yamashita, 1996).

Situation 2
You are a new worker in a company. You have finished the day's work and you have an important appointment with your friend from abroad. You made this appointment a long time ago and your friend is relying on you. When you are about to leave, a senior worker asks you to stay for a couple of hours to help him or her. However, you really need to leave now.

The Japanese EFL students saw these descriptions in Japanese and typed what they would say in the situation in Japanese. The JFL students in the United States did likewise in English.

Activity 1: Pre-Talkpoint Warm-Ups

Classroom activities designed to increase students' awareness of the pragmatic aspects of language, as well as those designed to have students get to know the partner class students beforehand, are helpful in preparing students to participate in the virtual classroom. Worksheet 1 (see Appendix) offers a set of activities that focuses students on potential problems in producing particular speech acts and leads them to consult students in the partner class for their opinions. Note that for the Group Activity (see Activity 4 on Worksheet 1), the teacher provides students with some examples from the Talkpoint website database, which can be obtained by clicking on "View All Posts" on the index page.

Activity 2: Participating on Talkpoint

To orient students to the Talkpoint website, the teacher may wish to distribute Worksheet 2 (see Appendix) to students or go through the steps in a lab together. The instructions are also available online (see http://www.talkpoint.org/HowToTalkpoint.pdf [Yamanaka, 2004]). Depending on the students' needs, the teacher could determine the language to be used in the discussion. Postings could be submitted during class or according to a schedule. For example, one pair of teachers set up the following schedule:

Week 1: Introduction to Talkpoint; Pre-activities; Posting of responses for Situation 1

Week 2: Analysis of postings (L1 and L2); Online discussion 1 (in Japanese)

Week 3: Posting of responses for Situation 2

Week 4: Analysis of postings (L1 and L2); Online discussion 2 (in English); Post-activities

Sample Postings for Situation 1: Sunscreen

In English:

- No thank you, I have already brought some. (Male, USA, 20s)
- Oh, no thanks, I put some on before I left. Thanks though! (Female, USA, 20s)

In Japanese:

- *Go-shinsetsu ni arigatoogozaimasu. Keredo watashi mo hiyakedome o mottekimashita node kekkou desu.* (Thank you for your kindness, but I brought my own sunscreen, so it is OK; Female, Japan, 20s.)
- *A, arigatoogozaimasu. Demo boku wa jibun no hiyakedome ga aru node daijoobu desu.* (Oh, thank you. But I have my own sunscreen, so I am OK; Male, Japan, 20s.)

Sample Postings for Situation 2: Working Late

In English:

- Oh, I'm so sorry! I just can't stay late tonight—I've promised to pick up a friend from the airport, so I really have to leave on time. I apologize for walking out like this. Is there any way I can help with the work tomorrow, if I come in early? (Female, USA, 10s)
- I'm so sorry—I've really got to make this appointment right now, but I'd be happy to help out later tonight or first thing tomorrow morning. Here's my cell phone number and e-mail address; let's talk things over tonight. (Male, USA, 20s)

In Japanese:

- *Senpai, hontooni mooshiwakenai ndesu ga, kyou wa kyanseru dekinai yooji ga arimashite . . . Konkai wa kanben shite-kudasai! Ashita senpai no shigoto mo tetsudaimasu kara! Shitsureishimasu!* (I am so sorry *senpai* [one's senior], but I have an engagement that I just cannot cancel today . . . Just this time, please! I'll do your portion of work tomorrow. I'm sorry to leave!; Male, Japan, 20s.)
- *Hontoo ni moushiwakenai no desu ga, kyou wa hontoo ni chotto muri nandesu. Jitsu wa Narita ni Koronbia kara kuru chijin o mukaeni ikanakerebanaranai ndesu. Sumimasen ga, watashi igui ni kanojo wa tayoreru hito ga inai node . . . Hontoo ni sumimasen. Kono umeawase wa mata kanarazu sasete-itadakimasu node!* (I am really sorry, but it's really not possible today. Actually, I have to pick up my acquaintance coming from Columbia at Narita.

I'm sorry, but she has no one but me to rely on, so . . . I'm really sorry. I will definitely make up for this!; Female, Japan, 20s.)

After students post their answers, they can analyze the data from the postings from each language (as in Weeks 2 and 4 in the schedule), look for patterns of similarities and differences, and discuss any differences from what they expected to find. For example, discussion of Situation 1, which had seemed to be a fairly simple situation, led to various interesting analyses on stereotypes, gender, jokes, and use of specific expressions, such as the following:

- Stereotypes: The idea that "Americans decline more directly" was not actually true.
- Gender: Female speakers decline more politely in both Japanese and English (longer responses, more polite expressions); whereas Japanese responses contain words making the gender of the speaker explicit, this is not the case for English.
- Jokes: More English responses than Japanese responses included expressions to make light of the situation.
- Specific expressions: (a) Many English responses began with "no," whereas Japanese responses often started with reasons and then used *daijoobu* (OK); some of the Japanese students said they would not use "no" even with friends; (b) Japanese responses often included the conjunction *node* (because), making the response appear more polite to some students; (c) the use of *thanks* rather than *thank you* to a professor surprised some of the Japanese students; JFL students in the United States responded that they used it as the situation was casual, but in a classroom situation they would be more likely to use *thank you.*

A discussion of the refusals in Situation 2, carried out in English, focused on the frequency of apologetic words, reasons, working style, similarities, and so on.

- The JFL students in the United States were surprised by the recurrence of apology statements in the Japanese responses (there were at least two apology phrases in most Japanese postings). They claimed that in English it would sound insincere if they apologized too often, whereas the Japanese EFL students claimed that they tried to express their sincere feelings by repeating their apology.
- Specific reasons for having to refuse were given in many Japanese responses and in most English responses by females. Possible reasons for this were discussed.
- Working styles and situations in Japan and the United States were discussed.

- Many of the responses in both languages included mentioning an alternative plan to help the senior worker. Some Japanese speakers explained that although they said they would help later, actually, they did not intend to do so. On the other hand, the English speakers claimed to intend to do what they said.
- Stereotypes were reexamined.
- Students found many similarities in the construction of refusals for this situation as compared to the first situation; it was suggested that this was due to this situation being more formal.

It is not necessary for teachers to be involved during the discussion stage. However, if it is considered appropriate in a certain situation, a teacher can play a more directive role in a discussion.

Teachers will log into the teacher account and monitor the discussion closely for student involvement (i.e., to see if all students are participating), problematic comments, and aspects of the postings that students have not noticed. Teachers can facilitate the discussion if necessary and remove problematic postings by logging into their own account.

Activity 3: Following Up the Talkpoint Discussion

After each situation, the teacher can follow up the discussion with post-discussion activities in class, drawing students' attention to interesting cultural or linguistic features of the discussion. As shown in examples that follow, teachers can use pragmatic elements in comments in discussions and postings to further increase students' awareness of the pragmatic aspects of the L2 in a variety of types of post-discussion activities. Teachers can direct students toward more effective use of the language input they were exposed to during the project for their future L2 use, as well as point out factors that they noticed but their students did not. For instance, teachers can select some phrases or vocabulary and analyze their connotations (e.g., are these words or phrases formal/informal, masculine/feminine, positive/negative, strong/weak?) with an eye toward raising students' awareness of the importance of pragmatic aspects of the L2. Other suggestions for follow-up activities include examples provided by some of the participant teachers.

One teacher focused on participants' use of expressions for refusing politely. She brought up the comment from the discussion that female speakers tended to use more polite forms. Students were asked to find expressions that they could use when they want to decline politely. They listed these expressions on Worksheet 3 (see Appendix), which was designed for JSL students, and then practiced polite refusals.

Another teacher chose some formal phrases from the postings. EFL students in Japan were asked to consider alternative phrases that they would have used if the interlocutors were their friends (see Worksheet 4 in the Appendix). Students then practiced refusals in more casual situations.

Another teacher designed practice activities with expressions for giving opinions and making comparisons. In the context of the discussion forum, students used various expressions to express the (un)certainty of their viewpoint: *it might be, it seems, I feel, probably, perhaps,* etc. Students were asked to find such expressions in the discussion. They then practiced using them to express their opinions in other contexts.

These are only a few of the possibilities for follow-up activities. Various other linguistic and cultural aspects of speech acts could be focused on.

REFLECTIONS 

This online collaboration project gave learners an opportunity to be exposed to input directly from target language speakers of their age and exchange their thoughts with them. In the discussion, students could reconsider their own stereotypes and notice various pragmatic aspects of both their L1 and the L2. Furthermore, working with their own L2 data and comparing those to authentic language from native speakers of this language proved highly motivating to students.

By utilizing the Talkpoint website in collaboration with other classes, teachers can provide their students with ample examples of authentic language use and avoid stereotyping. Moreover, as students can post messages outside the classroom, the actual class time needed for a project can be short enough to warrant its inclusion even within a crowded curriculum.

The Talkpoint tool and its collaborative learning method are extremely adaptable to various groups of learners and learning contexts. The project discussed here was designed for advanced-level students. Less proficient or younger learners could also use this tool in simpler situations (e.g., ordering water at a restaurant or asking to borrow a pen) that require familiar language forms. If students have limited L2 vocabulary, they can express their opinions in their L1, making a more in-depth discussion possible. If time difference is not an issue, instead of using the website's forum, learners can use video conferencing, text messages, or voice chats as well. More than two classes can also collaborate. For example, EFL classes in Japan and JFL classes in the United States and the United Kingdom could work together. It can be beneficial for students to be exposed to various types of English from around the world. If the class size is too large for the purposes of discussion, teachers can divide their classes into smaller groups and create multiple Talkpoint classes for a project. The project time frame and number of situations can also be easily modified. If students' Internet connection is limited, teachers can download English examples from the website and utilize them in class.

The primary focus of this project is to increase learners' pragmatic awareness. Teachers need to guide learners not to overgeneralize from a limited number of postings and to focus not only on differences but also on similarities between the two languages. Teachers' own awareness of pragmatic features, their intervention in the discussion if needed, and the classroom pre- and post-discussion activities they design have an important role to play in making a Talkpoint project successful.

Emi Yamanaka has been teaching Japanese at Harvard University in the United States since 2000. Her research interests include pragmatics, second language acquisition, and language pedagogy. She is the creator of Talkpoint, a web-based language learning tool.

Kenneth Fordyce is an associate professor at the Institute for Foreign Language Research and Education at Hiroshima University in Japan. He has taught in the United Kingdom, Austria, and Japan. He is currently completing a doctorate on interlanguage pragmatic development and plans to research the application of task-based language teaching to pragmatics.

APPENDIX: WORKSHEETS 

Worksheet 1: Pre-Talkpoint Warm-Ups

1. Pair Activity: Fill out the following table individually and then share your information with a partner to see if he or she has had any difficult experiences when he or she had to request, refuse, complain, apologize, etc. in the second language.

Difficult Situation	Where, When, Who?	What was said? What happened?
Refusing		
Complaining		
Requesting		
Apologizing		
(other situations?)		

2. Class Activity: Choose one situation to focus on as a class and compile a collection of situation descriptions that were discussed in Activity 1.

3. Online Pair Activity: Go to the course website's discussion forum and write to a student from the Talkpoint partner class. Ask what he or she would say in one of the situations discussed in Activities 1 and 2.

4. Group Activity: What do you think about the examples from the Talkpoint website database? Discuss your opinions with your group.

Worksheet 2: Signing In on the Talkpoint Website

To participate on the Talkpoint website with students from another country who are learning your language, you will need to go to the Talkpoint website at http://www.talkpoint.org and do the following:

1. Create a Student Account

2. Enter the Student Invitation Code

   Each class has a unique Student Invitation Code. Your teacher will give you your class's Student Invitation Code. Once you have entered your code, you will be directed to your class's Talkpoint webpage.

3. Post Answers

   Your class's webpage will have a place where you can post your answer to the situation(s) on your class's Talkpoint. You will not be able to see other students' postings until you post your own answer.

4. Discuss Responses

   After posting your answer(s), you will see the "View Other Answers/Discuss" link(s). Click on the link to read and analyze other students' answers. You can select from the "View" pull-down bar to see postings from your class, your partner's class, or both.

   Click on the "Discussion" link on the upper right corner to go to the Discussion forum, which opens in a different window, and submit your analyses and exchange your thoughts with other students.

Worksheet 3: Declining Politely in Japanese

From the postings you read, find various phrases you can use to decline politely. Below are listed some possible examples in Japanese to get you started.

Go-shinsetsu ni arigatoogozaimasu.
(Thank you very much for your kindness.)

O-kizukai itadaki, arigatoogozaimasu.
(Thank you very much for your thoughtfulness.)

1. ______________________________
2. ______________________________
3. ______________________________
4. ______________________________

(*Note:* The actual worksheet was written entirely in Japanese.)

Worksheet 4: Using Formal and Informal Phrases in English

Look at the following phrases from the postings. All of the phrases included below are relatively formal. How could you say the same thing less formally?

More Formal	Less Formal (with friends)
I am really sorry for this unexpected conflict.	
I have a very important engagement that I am unable to break.	
However, I am willing to help tomorrow if possible.	

Assessment

CHAPTER 14

Assessing Learners' Pragmatic Ability in the Classroom

Noriko Ishihara

Classroom-based assessment of learners' pragmatic competence is an indispensable component of instruction, but it is no simple task. First, pragmatic norms of the target language that we might intend to use are dynamic and vary across individuals, so the range of acceptable behavior is not always clear-cut or accurately identifiable, threatening the reliability in the assessment. Second, in assessing learners' pragmatics, teachers need to be aware that pragmatic choice is intertwined with subjectivity (e.g., identity, values, beliefs, morals, and personal principles). Second language speakers are found to sometimes intentionally diverge from native-like pragmatic language use for assertion of their identity and maintenance of an optimal distance from the target community (Ishihara, 2009; LoCastro, 1998; Siegal, 1996). In addition, second language speakers' pragmatic behavior is sometimes assessed and interpreted differently from that of native speakers (Iino, 1996; McNamara & Roever, 2006). Thus, classroom assessment of learners' pragmatic ability warrants cultural sensitivity. A further validity issue that arises is how authentically language teachers could or should assess learners' socially and interactionally constructed language use in the classroom, with imagined, often unfamiliar situations and assigned roles. How authentic is a learner's imagined conversation with a spouse if he or she has never experienced marriage, for instance?

This chapter presents a set of classroom-based assessment strategies designed not only to assess learners' pragmatic language use and awareness, but also to provide constructive feedback to learners, leading them to self-reflection and language development. Some of the tasks capture learner language in action, directly evaluating it while learners perform the tasks. Other assessment examples are built on teacher–learner collaboration, taking learners' intent into consideration and using it as a basis of evaluation.

Because teacher feedback can focus on what learners are able to do, rather than what they are not yet able to, classroom-based assessment can be especially helpful in supporting learners' development of pragmatic competence over time. And because assessment can be diagnostic in nature, it can be useful to teachers in determining their next instructional move.

CONTEXT

The assessment tools in this chapter were originally constructed for intermediate to advanced English as a second language (ESL) learners with varying levels of exposure to different languages and cultures. The target audience is preacademic adult university ESL or English as a foreign language (EFL) learners with high literary and general language awareness. These instruments have been designed as part of everyday instruction and not as a one-shot test; so it is important that learners become familiar with their principles and instructions and are accustomed to the format prior to assessment. The assessment instruments were pilot-tested with a small number of ESL and EFL learners in a classroom or tutorial setting. Feedback from language teachers who participated in a summer institute on teaching pragmatics in 2006–2008 at the University of Minnesota in the United States was also incorporated into the assessment tools.

What to Assess

The following are possible pragmatics-related areas for which classroom assessment may be necessary. This list includes some of the evaluative foci associated with speech acts that classroom teachers might select to align with their instructional goals. Each area can be utilized singly or in combination with others depending on the learners' needs and capacities, instructional time, and other factors. (Ideally, the list will eventually be expanded beyond speech acts to include areas such as implicature, epistemic stance markers, and conversational management.)

- The extent to which the speaker's intentions (i.e., how they want to present themselves) match the hearer's most probable interpretation
- The extent to which the speaker's language use is likely to achieve his or her goal (e.g., what they want to achieve through the language use)
- Organization and discourse structure (e.g., introduction, body, closing)
- Directness, politeness, and formality
- Grammar structures (e.g., language form of requests)
- Semantic moves (e.g., a series of acts to realize a request such as *apologizing, requesting, thanking, leave-taking*)

- Word choice (e.g., request softeners such as *just a second, a bit*, discourse markers such as *by the way, speaking of*)
- Tone (e.g., level of sincerity through verbal and nonverbal cues)
- Sociocultural norms in the target culture
- Cultural reasoning behind pragmatic norms

How to Assess

Different areas for pragmatic-focused assessment may be assessed in a variety of ways in the classroom setting. This chapter will focus on the following types of assessment:

- Holistic assessment: Noting the general impression of the learners' pragmatic language use or awareness (encompassing all or most of the areas of pragmatics-focused assessment)
- Analytic assessment: Showing overall assessment with a breakdown of learners' performance in each dimension
- Focused assessment: Targeting one particular area (e.g., primary-trait rubric) or a narrow range of areas (e.g., multitrait rubric; O'Malley & Valdez-Pierce, 1996; Tedick, 2002)
- Peer- and self-assessment: As a means of enhancing learners' pragmatic awareness, metapragmatic analysis, and reflective critical thinking (applicable to holistic, analytic, and focused assessments)

CURRICULUM, TASKS, MATERIALS 

This section provides examples of classroom-based assessment using holistic, analytic, primary-trait, or multitrait rubrics, as well as some ideas for peer- and self-evaluation. Each example is structured as a response to a scenario to which students have been instructed to respond or which students have been told to evaluate. Many of the examples utilize teacher–student collaboration in the process of assessment. Samples in this section illustrate how the rubrics can be applied to performance-based and reflective tasks, such as role-plays, skits, writing samples, reflective journals, and teacher observations of authentic learner interactions.

Holistic Assessment

Holistic assessment captures the general impression of the learners' pragmatic language use or awareness as a whole through the use of a single score or a set of descriptions. The following sample set provides a scenario with a quantitative and descriptive rubric.

Quantitative and Descriptive Holistic Assessment

The scenario and the instructions in Worksheet 1 (see Appendix A) prompt learners to imagine a typical (and pragmatically competent) speaker or writer in the target-language community and to demonstrate the language that this character would be expected to use. This way, learners can avoid the issue of how native-like (or nonnative-like) they want to be in their target language use (e.g., whether they want to complain to the professor and if so, how), while teachers evaluate learners' pragmatic awareness and language-focused productive skills.

The teacher can assess the appropriateness of the student's e-mail in Worksheet 1 using a quantitative and descriptive holistic assessment based on a range of target community norms. Rubric 1 (see Appendix B) is an example of such an assessment, which can be shared with learners ahead of time. This rubric may be best suited for intermediate- to advanced-level learners.

Narrative Holistic Assessment

Although teachers are often required to describe students' language performance in numerical terms, more informal everyday assessment can be provided in a narrative. Worksheet 2 (see Appendix A) provides a place for the teacher to respond with a holistic narrative assessment of the student's productive pragmatic skills. Because teacher feedback is an integral part of assessment, this worksheet includes samples of learner production (in bold italics) and teacher response (in bold). Blank versions of all worksheets (those with sample responses) are available at http://www.tesolmedia.com/books/pragmatics.

In this type of assessment, the expression of learners' intentions and teacher feedback may end up being more extensive than learners' actual language production. Feedback can be given orally in a teacher–student conference or woven into a whole-class discussion. The section on learners' intentions may first appear complex but can be explained ahead of time and recycled so that learners know what is expected here (also see Worksheet 3, in Appendix A, for another way of eliciting learners' intentions).

Note that the use of written responses does not reflect the effect of tone of voice, intonation, facial expression, use of space, gestures, posture, and the like, which greatly affect the meaning constructed in interactive discourse. Paired role-plays (see Worksheet 4),[1] observation or reflection of role-plays (see Worksheet 5),[2] or even multiturn discourse completion tasks (see "Sample Scenario, Learner Language, and Teacher Assessment for Rubric 3" at http://www.tesol.com/books/pragmatics or in Ishihara & Cohen, 2010) may be more advantageous in stressing the importance of nonverbal features and the nature of spontaneous discourse often stretched over more than just a few turns.

---

[1] For more details on Worksheet 4, see the Peer- and Self-Assessment section.

[2] For more details on Worksheet 5, see the Peer- and Self-Assessment section.

Analytic Assessment

Unlike holistic assessment, which yields just one score or a set of descriptions for each instance of pragmatic language, analytic assessment evaluates various dimensions, providing more detailed feedback to learners on each area. Rubric 2 (see Appendix B) can be used for assessing pragmatics in learners' writing. The same scenario used in Worksheet 1 (see Appendix A) can be used with Rubric 2. Note that Rubric 2 weighs categories differently: the categories of semantic moves and directness, politeness, and formality are given 4 points, while the others are assigned 3 points. These categories can be collapsed, reorganized, or weighed differently according to the teacher's purposes. This type of detailed and comprehensive assessment may be more suitable for assessing extensive production (rather than a short single-turn response), such as first drafts for rewriting and completed versions for final grading.

Focused Assessment: Primary-Trait

Primary-trait assessment centers on one particular dimension of pragmatic language use. Therefore, it may be suitable for focused instruction and assessment, particularly for lower level or younger learners, or for instruction constrained by limited time. For example, assessment of learners' requests can center on the choice of grammatical structures (e.g., *would you mind —ing, I was wondering if you —ed*) or request softeners (e.g., "Can you hurry up *a little*?" "Can you *perhaps* buy this for me?"). The teacher's evaluation at the bottom of Worksheet 3 (see Appendix A) is a primary-trait assessment for the match between the learner's own goals and intentions and the hearer's interpretation.

Teachers' comments can touch on the sociocultural norms or general level of politeness that is likely to influence the hearer's interpretation. It is important that teachers highlight learners' awareness of the consequences of their own language use. Classroom discussion could cover how the dialogue might expand in authentic discourse.

Focused Assessment: Multitrait

Multitrait assessment allows teachers to focus on and assess several areas of pragmatic competence. Clearly, areas selected for assessment should align with the teacher's goals of instruction.

Multitrait Assessment of Productive Skills

In Rubric 3 (see Appendix B), four areas—the level of formality, semantic moves ("strategies of apologizing"), word choice, and tone—of a student's response are selected for assessment. See http://www.tesolmedia.com/books/pragmatics or Ishihara & Cohen (2010) for an additional worksheet "Sample Scenario, Learner Language, and Teacher Assessment for Rubric 3."

Multitrait Assessment of Receptive Skills

The majority of rubrics presented so far center on the assessment of learners' pragmatic production. In Worksheet 6 (see Appendix A), the focus shifts to receptive pragmatic skills. The sample teacher's assessment in Worksheet 6 focuses on the learner's analysis of (a) contextual factors in the situation, (b) hearer's interpretation, and (c) ways to improve pragmatic use of language.

Alternatively, the teacher might wish to suggest that learners take a closer look at the content of Michelle's explanation and offer of repair and think about their appropriateness in this situation. Learners could also consider what elements of her language make Michelle's apology more or less sincere. (See Ishihara, 2009, and Ishihara & Maeda, 2010, for activities focusing on student receptive skills through observation and journal writing of language used in the community.)

Multitrait Collaborative Assessment

A more-detailed collaborative assessment incorporating learner goals and intentions is provided in Worksheet 7 (see Appendix A). This worksheet—with sample learner response and teacher assessment—includes both a place for the student's response and a section for the teacher's comments. A detailed assessment such as that in Worksheet 7 may require metapragmatic awareness and linguistic ability that is already highly developed. In a foreign language context, some of the assessment and discussion could be done in the learners' first language.

Peer- and Self-Assessment

Given the complex and dynamic nature of pragmatic norms, it is neither possible nor desirable to teach learners pragmatic language use for every situation in every language variety and register that they may need or want to know. Instead, instruction and assessment can ultimately aim for pragmatic awareness raising. In this approach, teachers support learners in assessing their own language use, sometimes through their peers' eyes. The assessment may not necessarily be accurate or impartial, but the evaluative process itself can help enhance learners' pragmatic awareness, metapragmatic analysis, and reflective critical thinking. Peer- and self-assessment can be realized using any of the holistic, analytic, or focused assessment types previously discussed. The following sections introduce two multitrait assessments designed to be implemented by peers and learners themselves.

Peer-Assessment

To make peer-assessment an effective part of instruction, learners need varying levels of guidance in how to engage in systematic peer-evaluation. Learners can be given a set of prompts as in Worksheet 5 (see Appendix A) or a checklist (eliciting yes or no answers) to direct attention to important pragmatic features.

Self-Assessment

While engaging in self-assessment tasks, learners could draw on their knowledge of pragmatics or compare their work with a model dialogue to evaluate the key features. This approach might require substantial scaffolding or varying levels of guidance from the teacher according to the learners' characteristics and learning style preferences. Teachers might give learners individual comments or provide more collective feedback in a class-wide debriefing. Worksheet 4 (see Appendix A) provides an example of a multitrait assessment designed to facilitate self-evaluation of various key pragmatic aspects.

This chapter has included examples of holistic, analytic, primary-trait, and multitrait assessment specifically designed to assess learners' pragmatic competence. The examples in this section are primarily for illustrative purposes. Readers are invited to adapt these examples according to their needs and expand the collective repertoire of assessments by contributing their own to teachers' resources such as this one.

REFLECTIONS

Successful instruction of pragmatics cannot be complete without assessing learners' pragmatic competence. When classroom-based assessment is grounded in sound pedagogy, it can be a powerful tool for reflective thinking and independent learning. In reality, assessment of pragmatic competence is no simple task, as demonstrated in many of the examples in this chapter. Pragmatic norms are fluid and diverse, often used under the level of speakers' consciousness, and intertwined with learner subjectivity. A dilemma for language teachers may be simplifying what cannot readily be simplified; a challenge for learners may be the necessity of living with the complexity of pragmatic norms that allow a variety of possibly appropriate answers.

Classroom-based assessment is compatible with experiential learning and can be widely applied to various instructional contexts ranging from K–16 ESL to EFL. For young or lower level learners, the instructional language in this chapter may need to be simplified and the instructional foci narrowed. Scenarios should be appropriate for learners' age and communicative needs. For further resources, numerous books and websites on second language assessment in general are available. One of them is an assessment site by the Center for Advanced Research on Language Acquisition (http://www.carla.umn.edu/assessment/), which provides an abundance of background information, practical resources, and links related to the design of language assessment. Although it is beyond the scope of this chapter, it might be useful in the future to have a curriculum or at least some guidelines for a set of instructional and evaluative goals for various proficiency levels or instructional contexts (e.g., ESL, EFL, adult literacy, K–12, and university). It is hoped that the assessment attempts introduced in this chapter will be a springboard for further discussion and assist in the development of effective and culturally sensitive assessment practices in language education.

ACKNOWLEDGMENTS 

I would like to thank Andrew D. Cohen and Gloria Park for their valuable insights during the development of this chapter. An earlier version of this chapter was included in Ishihara and Cohen's (2010) teachers' guide, *Teaching and Learning Pragmatics: Where Language and Culture Meet* (Pearson Education). I am also grateful to the ESL and EFL learners for their collaboration and participation in the pilot testing.

---

*Noriko Ishihara is associate professor in EFL at Hosei University, Japan, and leads language teachers' professional development courses in Japan and in the United States. Her academic interests include pragmatics and identity, and teacher development. She has recently coauthored teachers' resources in instructional pragmatics (*Teaching and Learning Pragmatics, *with Andrew Cohen, Pearson/Longman;* Communication in Context, *with Magara Maeda, Routledge).*

APPENDIX A: WORKSHEETS 

Worksheet 1: Complaining

> Jack received a final grade of C from Professor Mill when he expected at least a B. Her class was hard but interesting, and Jack thinks he worked pretty hard on the projects and the final paper. He decides to write an e-mail to the professor so that she would reconsider his grade. Write an e-mail below, drafting what Jack would probably produce in this situation. Think of what Jack could say and couldn't say in this situation.

Note: Instructions might also be phrased as follows:

- What would most English speakers say in this situation?
- What would be a typical response in this situation?
- What could Jack say? What couldn't he say?

Worksheet 2: Responding to Compliments

1. Scenario: Your friend is giving you praise. Write your response as if you were talking to her.

    Kate: *I like your hat.*
    You: ***Keep liking.***

    Indicate your intention as a speaker.

    X I want to respond in a way most preferred in the community.

    __ I would want my response to sound a little more (formal/informal), (polite/impolite), or __________ than normal but still within the range of acceptable behavior.

    __ I want to communicate (or not communicate) my intention in my own way. In this situation, I choose not to behave like most people. (Specify what common behavior you decide against using and why you do not want to use it: ____________________________________.)

    __ Other (specify: ____________________________________.)

Teacher's comments:

- **Because you and Kate are friends, your level of formality is appropriate.**
- **Your response, *keep liking*, is uncommon in American English, but it will probably communicate your intention.**
- **Most fluent English speakers would say, "Thanks," or "(I'm) glad you like it."**

2. Scenario: Your friend is complimenting you on your class presentation. Write your response as if you were talking to him.

    Steve: *Nice job!*
    You: ***No, I didn't do well.***

Indicate your intention as a speaker.

__ I want to respond in a way most preferred in the community.

X I would want my response to sound a little more (formal/informal), (polite/ impolite), or (***humble***) than normal but still within the range of acceptable behavior.

__ I want to communicate (or not communicate) my intention in my own way. In this situation, I choose not to behave like most people. (Specify what common behavior you decide against using and why you do not want to use it: ____________________________________.)

__ Other (specify: ____________________________________.)

Teacher's comments:

- **Because you and Steve are friends, your level of formality is appropriate.**
- **Steve may understand your response if he knows you well, but other people might feel rejected because direct refusal of compliments can be taken as impolite.**
- **Most fluent English speakers express humility this way: "Do you really think so?" "Well, I didn't think so myself, but thanks," or "I think it could have been better."**

Note: This worksheet includes samples of learner production (in bold italics) and teacher response (in bold).

Worksheet 3: Making a Request of a Professor

Scenario: You are a university student and want to apply for jobs after graduation. To do so, you need letters of recommendation from one of your professors. You go to him or her after class and ask:

Learner 1: [learner writes]
You: ***When you have time, I would really appreciate if you could write letters of recommendation for me because I have started my job research.***

a) Your intention and goal as a speaker: How do you want to sound, and what do you want to achieve through your request? [learner writes]

Nice, polite, and not pushy to get a nice recommendation through this polite conversation.

b) Most probable hearer's interpretation: [teacher writes]
- **You made a fairly polite request using various strategies. However, the way you start with the request may sound a bit too forward.**
- **Your professor will probably ask you more questions about the job, the deadline and format of the letter, etc., and agree to write the letter.**
- **Your professor may expect more background information before the request.**

Match between a) and b): [teacher evaluates]

excellent (good) fair poor

Learner 2: [learner writes]
You: ***I have a favor of you. I'm going to apply for jobs after graduation. I'd like to ask you to write a recommendation letter for me.***

a) Your intention and goal as a speaker: How do you want to sound, and what do you want to achieve through your request? [learner writes]

My goal is to get the recommendation letter from him, so I will say it very eagerly, seriously to show him how much I need the letter from him.

b) Most probable hearer's interpretation: [teacher writes]
- **If this professor knows you well enough to write a supportive letter, he or she will probably do it for you.**
- **This seems a bit abrupt; you could add more strategies of politeness (e.g., *I'd like to ask you <u>if you could</u> write . . .*)**
- **A fluent English speaker might add something like, "You've known me for two years and I'd be honored if you would support me."**

c) Match between a) and b): [teacher evaluates]

excellent (good) fair poor

Note: This worksheet includes samples of learner production (in bold italics) and teacher response (in bold).

Worksheet 4: Assessing Your Own Refusal

Role-play the following situation with a partner (decide on your gender before you start). Switch your roles. Audio record your dialogue and replay it later for self-analysis as necessary.

> **Role A** (Chris, decide male or female): You are an owner of a large local restaurant. One day, you invite all your employees to a staff appreciation party. It is going to be fun and you heard that most employees will probably attend. However, Terry, an employee about 20 years younger than you, has not RSVP-ed to your e-mail invitation. You are not sure why, and decide to invite him or her personally.
>
> **Role B** (Terry, decide male or female): You've been working a part-time job at a large local restaurant for 6 months. One day, your boss and the store owner, Chris, who is about 20 years older than you, invites all the employees to a staff appreciation party. You hear that it is going to be fun and most of your coworkers will probably attend, but you are reluctant—you already have a date scheduled that night. You decide to skip the party and tell that to Chris as he or she talks to you.

1. Evaluation of the context: What are the relative social status, age, and level of familiarity with Terry and Chris, and the nature of Chris's invitation? Place an X on the line where you think it best characterizes the situation.

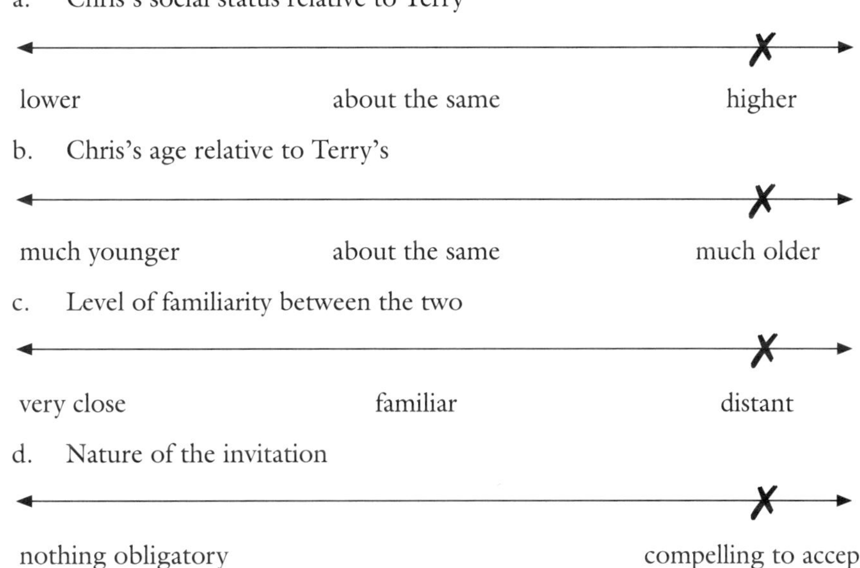

2. Evaluation of refusal strategies (when you played Role B)
   a. What refusal strategies did Terry use?
      give reason, apology, thanking, positive comment
   b. How appropriate was the choice of strategies, considering the context (refer to 1 [a–d] if necessary)? What makes you think so? (Also write any questions you have here.)

      ←——X————————————————→

      appropriate   somewhat appropriate   fair   inappropriate
   c. Given the context, how appropriate was each strategy used? What makes you think so?

      It was OK to say "I already have a plan to do that day" but it may be better to explain the reason more clearly. I wanted to say more clearly to promise that I'm going to attend later [late]. It's OK to say "sorry" to tell her not to go [that I can't go] to the party. I think I should not say "sorry" many times. It may sound a bit weird. I should tell him "thanks" to show appreciation to invite the party although I'm not going there.
3. Tone: How was Terry's tone of refusing? Why makes you think so?

   Terry's tone was very apologetic or hesitant. She said so [spoke that way] because appropriate words to refuse Chris's request didn't come up. She had tension when she say "no, I can't go" to her boss.

Teacher's evaluation:

	Language use in role-play	Self-analysis/awareness
Choice and use of refusal strategies	**Excellent use of positive comments (friendly and enthusiastic tone of voice!) and various other strategies. More details about your excuse would be desirable in order to sound more sincere (as you point out).**	**Great level of awareness of how the reason was used and how it can be improved. What could Terry actually say in this situation?**
Tone		

Note: This worksheet includes samples of learner production (in bold italics) and teacher response (in bold).

Worksheet 5: Assessing Each Other's Role-Plays

Find a partner and exchange your written (or orally recorded) role-play. Read (or listen to) your partner's work carefully and answer the following questions. Remember to be supportive and respectful rather than critical and evaluative in your review. Your review will be part of your grade.

- What makes your partner's language more appropriate for the context?
- What makes it less appropriate and why do you think so?
- What questions or suggestions do you have for your partner?
- What did you learn from this peer-review process?

Teacher Evaluation of Peer-Feedback		
Teacher comments on: • Analysis of appropriate and less appropriate language behavior • Tone of peer-feedback and engagement		Excellent
		Good
		Needs more work

Worksheet 6: Apologizing

Scenario: Michelle completely forgets a crucial meeting at the office with the boss at her new job. An hour later she shows up at his office to apologize. The problem is that this is the second time she's forgotten such a meeting in the short time she has been working at this job. Her boss is clearly annoyed when he asks, "What happened to you this time?"

1. Michelle: "So sorry, Mr. Peterson. I have sleeping problems and then I missed the bus. I can make it up to you."

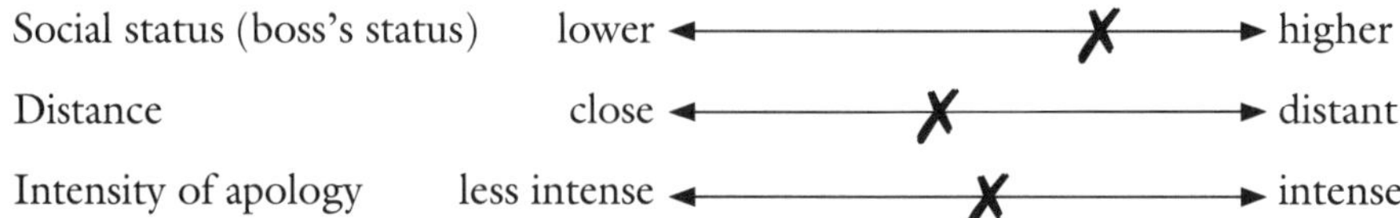

2. How would the boss interpret Michelle's utterance? [learner responds]

   They may feel her utterance simple, short but well explained. She didn't give her boss lots of detail about her mistake, but boss may be able to understand why Michelle was late.

3. Imagine that Michelle is your friend. What suggestions would you give her about the way she spoke? [learner responds]

   I'll say to her that she can say more excuse and apology to her boss. Michelle's utterance sounds little bit cold (too simple) so it will be better if she adds more expression into her utterance.

Teacher's evaluation:

	Excellent	Comments: • **Good point about the level of detail in Michelle's response; what would Michelle actually say?** • **Fluent English speakers would consider their boss at a much greater distance.** **Fluent speakers would make the apology more intense (I am really sorry . . .). Michelle could be put on observation or possibly fired if this happens frequently.**
	Good	
✓	Needs more work	

Note: This worksheet includes samples of learner production (in bold italics) and teacher response (in bold).

Worksheet 7: Making a Request of a Peer

Scenario: You are trying to do some homework but your roommate, Jenny, is watching a television comedy and has the volume up so loud that it is distracting you and making it hard to concentrate. Write what you would say to her, if you decide to speak to her about this.

a) What would most speakers say?

Jenny, would you mind turning the volume down a little bit? Thanks.

b) Your intention

__ (1) I want to make the request in a way most preferred in the community.

__ (2) I would want my response to sound a little more (formal/informal), (polite/impolite), or _______ than normal but still within the range of acceptable behavior.

X (3) I choose not to use common behavior because I want to communicate my intentions (or not communicate them at all) in my own way. Specify what community norms you decide not to use and why you don't want them:

They will mention that it's loud but I don't want her to take what I said as a criticism. So, I don't say anything but I will study somewhere else instead.

__ (4) Other (specify: _____)_________________________________.)

c) You say (if different from [a] above):

d) How does your roommate most likely interpret your behavior c)?

1. ***Don't notice about my action and continue watching with loud volume.***
2. ***Reading between the lines. It means she finds out I felt it was noisy.***
3. ***She takes that I'm very indifferent toward her or I'm cold. She feels it's a good sit-com and she wants me to watch it together.***

Teacher's evaluation:

1. Linguistic ability to use community norms (a and c)	4 very fluent	(3) proficient	2 fair	1 poor
2. Awareness of most probable hearer's interpretation (d)	(4) highly aware	3 aware	2 less aware	1 unaware
3. Match between (b) learner goal and intention and most probable hearer's interpretation	(4) excellent	3 good	2 fair	1 poor
Total Score	11/12			

Teacher's comments:

- **You made a nice analysis of how Jenny might interpret your action.**
- **About (a): your suggested request is polite.**
- **You decide not to say anything for now. What would you do if this situation continues?**

Note: This worksheet includes samples of learner production (in bold italics) and teacher response (in bold).

APPENDIX B: RUBRICS 

Rubric 1: Holistic Assessment Rubric—Quantitative and Descriptive

4: appropriate	Reflects a fine-tuned awareness of sociocultural norms and/or understanding of the cultural reasoning of the norms in the community; well-organized and coherent; appropriate in the levels of politeness, directness, and formality; contains an appropriate range of grammar structures, semantic moves, and word choice with minor errors (if any) that do not cause misinterpretation; carries a tone that is preferred in the community.
3: somewhat appropriate	Reflects some awareness of sociocultural norms and/or understanding of the cultural reasoning of the norms in the community; adequately organized and coherent; reasonably appropriate in the levels of politeness, directness, and formality; good or average use of grammar structures, semantic moves, and word choice with some errors that do not usually cause misinterpretation; carries a tone that is moderately appropriate in the community.
2: somewhat inappropriate	Reflects little awareness of sociocultural norms and/or understanding of the cultural reasoning of the norms in the community; some problems with organization and coherence; sometimes problematic in the levels of politeness, directness, and formality; fair use of grammar structures, semantic moves, and word choice with some major errors that can at times cause misinterpretation; carries a tone that may sometimes be perceived as inappropriate in the community.
1: inappropriate	Reflects very little awareness of sociocultural norms and/or understanding of the cultural reasoning of the norms in the community; lacks organization and coherence; inappropriate in the levels of politeness, directness, and formality; poor use of grammar structures, semantic moves, and word choice with some major errors that can often cause misinterpretation; carries a tone that can most likely be perceived as inappropriate in the community.

Note: This rubric was adapted from Tedick (2002).

Rubric 2: Analytic Assessment Rubric

1. Sociocultural norms: 3 total points		
Score	**Criteria**	**Comments**
	3 (Excellent): Shows fine-tuned awareness of sociocultural norms and/or well-developed understanding of the cultural reasoning of the norms in the community	
	2 (Good): Shows adequate awareness of sociocultural norms and/or good understanding of the cultural reasoning of the norms in the community	
	1 (Needs more work): Shows little awareness of sociocultural norms and/or poor understanding of the cultural reasoning of the norms in the community	

2. Organization: 3 total points		
Score	**Criteria**	**Comments**
	3 (Excellent): Well-organized and coherent; tightly connected and fluid; cohesive; excellent use of discourse markers (if any)	
	2 (Good): Mostly organized and somewhat coherent; loosely connected and somewhat fluid; somewhat cohesive; good use of discourse markers	
	1 (Needs more work): Poorly organized and lacks coherence; disconnected and confusing; lacks cohesion; little or no appropriate use of discourse markers	
3. Directness, politeness, and formality: 4 total points		
Score	**Criteria**	**Comments**
	4 (Excellent): Appropriate and effective in the level of directness, politeness, and formality; appropriate and effective register	
	3 (Good): Adequately appropriate in the level of directness, politeness, and formality; mostly appropriate and effective register	
	2 (Fair): Somewhat inappropriate in the level of directness, politeness, and formality; at times somewhat inappropriate and ineffective register	
	1 (Needs more work): Often inappropriate in the level of directness, politeness, and formality; often inappropriate and ineffective register	
4. Grammar strategies: 3 total points		
Score	**Criteria**	**Comments**
	3 (Excellent). Contains a great range of grammar structures; grammar used to communicate appropriately; minor errors (if any) that do not cause misinterpretation	
	2 (Good): Contains a range of grammar structures; grammar used to communicate appropriately; some errors that hardly cause misinterpretation	
	1 (Needs more work): Shows limited range of grammar structures; grammar used ineffectively or inappropriately; some major errors that can at times cause misinterpretation	

5. Semantic moves: 4 total points		
Score	**Criteria**	**Comments**
	4 (Excellent): Contains an excellent range of semantic moves used to communicate appropriately	
	3 (Good): Contains a range of semantic moves used to communicate mostly appropriately	
	2 (Fair): Contains a limited range of semantic moves used to communicate somewhat ineffectively or inappropriately	
	1 (Needs more work): Contains few (or no) semantic moves used to communicate ineffectively or inappropriately	
6. Word choice: 3 total points		
Score	**Criteria**	**Comments**
	3 (Excellent): Sophisticated and appropriate register; effectively and appropriately used; extensive variety of words	
	2 (Good): Not very sophisticated but appropriate register; mostly effective and appropriate; some variety in word choice	
	1 (Needs more work): Not sophisticated and often inappropriate register; at times ineffective or inappropriate; limited range of words	
7. Tone: 3 total points		
Score	**Criteria**	**Comments**
	3 (Excellent): Sophisticated and excellent range of verbal and nonverbal tone; appropriately and effectively used	
	2 (Good): Not very sophisticated but a range of verbal and nonverbal tone; mostly appropriately and effectively used	
	1 (Needs more work): Basic and very limited range of verbal and nonverbal tone; often inappropriately or ineffectively used	

Note: This rubric was adapted from Tedick (2002).

Rubric 3: Apologizing

Teacher's evaluation: 4—very appropriate; 3—somewhat appropriate; 2—less appropriate; 1—inappropriate				
1. Level of formality	4	3	2	1
2. Strategies of apologizing (e.g., expressing apology, acknowledging responsibility, giving explanation, offering repair, promising nonrecurrence)	4	3	2	1
3. Word choice	4	3	2	1
4. Tone (e.g., facial expression, tone of voice, gestures)	4	3	2	1
Teacher's comments:				

References

Alcón Soler, E. (2005). Does instruction work for learning pragmatics in the EFL context? *System, 33,* 417–435.

Altman, R. (1990). Giving and taking advice without offence. In R. Scarcella, E. Andersen, & S. Krashen (Eds.), *Developing communicative competence in a second language* (pp. 95–101). New York: Newbury House.

Archer, E. (2009a). *Invitation refusal videos* [Video file]. Retrieved January 22, 2010, from http://www.youtube.com/watch?v=6yJGVjlj27g

Archer, E. (2009b). *Refusal strategies* [Video file]. Retrieved January 22, 2010, from http://www.youtube.com/watch?v=2byjie-_E20

Audacity [Computer software]. (2006). Retrieved April 8, 2006, from http://audacity.sourceforge.net/

Austin, J. (1962). *How to do things with words.* Oxford: Clarendon.

Bardovi-Harlig, K. (2001). Evaluating the empirical evidence: Grounds for instruction in pragmatics? In K. Rose & G. Kasper (Eds.), *Pragmatics in language teaching* (pp. 13–32). Cambridge: Cambridge University Press.

Bardovi-Harlig, K., & Hartford, B. S. (1991). Saying "No": Native and nonnative rejections in English. In L. F. Bouton & Y. Kachru (Eds.), *Pragmatics and language learning* (Vol. 2, pp. 41–57). Urbana-Champaign: University of Illinois, Division of English as an International Language.

Bardovi-Harlig, K. & Hartford, B. S. (1993). Learning the rules of academic talk: A longitudinal study of pragmatic change. *Studies in Second Language Acquisition, 15,* 279–304.

Bardovi-Harlig, K., & Mahan-Taylor, R. (2003). *Teaching pragmatics.* Washington, DC: U.S. Department of State, Bureau of Educational and Cultural Affairs, Office of English Language Programs. Retrieved December 17, 2009, from http://exchanges.state.gov/englishteaching/resforteach/pragmatics.html

Beebe, L., & Takahashi, T. (1989). Sociolinguistic variation in face-threatening speech acts: Chastisement and disagreement. In M. Eisenstein (Ed.), *The dynamic interlanguage* (pp. 199–219). New York: Plenum Press.

Beebe, L., Takahashi, T., & Uliss-Weltz, R. (1990). Pragmatic transfer in ESL refusals. In R. Scarcella, E. Anderson, & S. Krashen (Eds.), *Developing communicative competence in a second language* (pp. 55–74). New York: Newbury House.

Beebe, L., & Waring, H. (2004). The linguistic encoding of pragmatic tone: Adverbials as words that work. In D. Boxer & A. Cohen (Eds.), *Studying speaking to inform second language learning* (pp. 228–249). Clevedon: Multilingual Matters.

Bloch, J. (2002). Student/teacher interaction via e-mail: The social context of Internet discourse. *Journal of Second Language Writing, 11,* 117–134.

Blum-Kulka, S. (1983). Interpreting and performing speech acts in a second language—A cross-cultural study of Hebrew and English. In N. Wolfson & E. Judd (Eds.), *Sociolinguistics and language acquisition* (pp. 36–54). Cambridge, MA: Newbury House.

Blum-Kulka, S. (1987). Indirectness and politeness in requests: Same or different? *Journal of Pragmatics, 11,* 131–146.

Blum-Kulka, S., Danet, B., & Gherson, R. (1985). The language of requesting in Israel society. In J. Forgas (Ed.), *Language and social situations* (pp. 113–139). New York: Springer-Verlag.

Blum-Kulka, S., House, J., & Kasper, G. (1989). *Cross-cultural pragmatics: Requests and apologies.* Norwood, NJ: Ablex.

Blum-Kulka, S., & Olshtain, E. (1984). Requests and apologies: A cross-cultural study of speech act realization patterns (CCSARP). *Applied Linguistics, 5,* 196–213.

Boxer, D. (1993a). *Complaining and commiserating: A speech act view of solidarity in spoken American English.* New York: Peter Lang.

Boxer, D. (1993b). Complaints as positive strategies: What the learner needs to know. *TESOL Quarterly, 27,* 277–299.

Boxer, D., & Pickering, L. (1995). Problems in the presentation of speech acts in ELT materials: The case of complaints. *ELT Journal, 49*(1), 44–58.

Brislin, R., Cushner, K., Cherrie, C., & Young, M. (1986). *Intercultural interactions: A practical guide.* Thousand Oaks, CA: Sage.

Brown, P., & Levinson, S. (1987). *Politeness: Some universals in language use.* Cambridge: Cambridge University Press.

Center for Advanced Research on Language Acquisition (CARLA). (n.d.). *Refusals.* Retrieved January 20, 2009, from http://www.carla.umn.edu/speechacts/refusals/index.html

Chen, X., Ye, L., & Zhang, Y. (1995). Refusing in Chinese. In G. Kasper (Ed.), *Pragmatics of Chinese as a native and target language* (pp. 119–163). Honolulu: University of Hawai'i Press.

Cohen, A. (2008, April). *Comprehensible pragmatics: Where input and output come together.* Paper presented at the Applied Linguistics Interest Section (ALIS) Academic Session at the 42nd Annual TESOL Convention, New York, NY.

Crystal, D. (1985). *A dictionary of linguistics and phonetics.* Oxford: Blackwell.

DeCapua, A., & Huber, L. (1995). "If I were you . . .": Advice in American English. *Multilingua, 14,* 117–132.

DuFon, M. (1995). [Review of the book *Complaining and commiserating*]. *Journal of Pragmatics, 23,* 693–707.

Félix-Brasdefer, J. C. (2004). Interlanguage refusals: Linguistic politeness and length of residence in the target community. *Language Learning, 4,* 587–653.

Félix-Brasdefer, J. C. (2006). Teaching the negotiation of multi-turn speech acts: Using conversation-analytic tools to teach pragmatics in the classroom. In K. Bardovi-Harlig, J. C. Félix-Brasdefer, & A. S. Omar (Eds.), *Pragmatics and language learning* (Vol. 11, pp. 165–197). Honolulu: University of Hawai'i at Manoa, Second Language Teaching and Curriculum Center.

Félix-Brasdefer, J. C. (2008). *Politeness in Mexico and the United States: A contrastive study of the realization and perception of refusals.* Amsterdam: John Benjamins.

Félix-Brasdefer, J. C. (2010a). *Listen to refusals.* Retrieved April 25, 2010, from http://www.indiana.edu/~discprag/spch_refusals.html

Félix-Brasdefer, J. C. (2010b). *Speech acts: Practice refusals.* Retrieved April 25, 2010, from http://www.indiana.edu/~discprag/practice_refusals.html

Fukushima, S. (1990). Offers and requests: Performance by Japanese learners of English. *World Englishes, 9*(3), 317–325.

Gass, S. M., & Houck, N. (1999). *Interlanguage refusals: A cross-cultural study of Japanese-English.* New York: Mouton de Gruyter.

Hatch, E. (1992). *Discourse and language education.* Cambridge: Cambridge University Press.

Hinkel, E. (1994, March). *Appropriateness of advice as L2 solidarity strategy.* Paper presented at the 28th Annual TESOL Convention, Baltimore, MD.

Holmes, J., & Stubbe, M. (2003). *Power and politeness in the workplace: A sociolinguistic analysis of talk at work.* London: Longman.

Houck, N., & Tatsuki, D. (in press). *Pragmatics: Teaching natural conversation.* Alexandria, VA: TESOL.

Iino, M. (1996). *"Excellent foreigner!" Gaijinization of Japanese language and culture in contact situations—An ethnographic study of dinner table conversations between Japanese host families and American students.* Unpublished doctoral dissertation, University of Pennsylvania, Philadelphia.

Ishihara, N. (2007). Web-based curriculum for pragmatics instruction in Japanese as a foreign language: An explicit awareness-raising approach. *Language Awareness, 16*(1), 21–40.

Ishihara, N. (2009). Teacher-based assessment for foreign language pragmatics. *TESOL Quarterly, 43,* 445–470.

Ishihara, N., & Cohen, A. (2010). *Teaching and learning pragmatics: Where language and culture meet.* Harlow, England: Pearson Education.

Ishihara, N., & Maeda, M. (2010). *Communication in context: Kotobato bunkano kousaten: Bunkade yomitoku nihongo.* London: Routledge.

Iwai, C., & Rinnert, C. (2001). Cross-cultural comparison of strategic realization of pragmatic competence: Implications for learning world Englishes. *Hiroshima Journal of International Studies, 7,* 157–181.

Iwai, C., & Rinnert, C. (2002). Strategic solution of sociopragmatic problems in using world Englishes. In M. Swanson, D. McMurray, & K. Lane (Eds.), *Proceedings of the 3rd Pan-Asian Conference at JALT 2001* (pp. 881–887). Tokyo: JALT.

Jeon, E. H., & Kaya, T. (2006). Effects of L2 instruction on interlanguage pragmatic development: A meta-analysis. In J. M. Norris & L. Ortega (Eds.), *Synthesizing research on language learning and teaching* (pp. 165–211). Amsterdam: John Benjamins.

Johnson, F. (2006). Agreement and disagreement: A cross-cultural comparison. *BISAL, 1,* 41–67.

Kasper, G. (1997). *Can pragmatic competence be taught?* (NetWork #6) [HTML document]. Honolulu: University of Hawai'i, Second Language Teaching & Curriculum Center. Retrieved December 17, 2009, from http://www.nflrc.hawaii.edu/NetWorks/NW06/

Kasper, G., & Rose, K. R. (2002). *Pragmatic development in a second language.* Malden, MA: Blackwell.

Katayama, A. (2007a). Japanese EFL students' preferences toward correction of classroom oral errors. *Asian EFL Journal, 9*(4), 289–305. Retrieved January 13, 2008, from http://asian-efl-journal.com/Dec_2007_ak.php

Katayama, A. (2007b). Students' perceptions of oral error correction. *Japanese Language and Literature, 41,* 61–92.

Kitao, K. (1990). A study of Japanese and American perceptions of politeness in requests. *Doshisha Studies, 50,* 178–210.

Kobayashi, H., & Rinnert, C. (2003). Coping with high imposition requests: High vs. low proficiency EFL students in Japan. In A. M. Flor, E. U. Juan, & A. F. Guerra (Eds.), *Pragmatic competence and foreign language teaching* (pp. 161–184). Castelló de la Plana: Publicacions de la Universitat Jaume I.

Levine, A., Oded, B., Connor, U., & Asons, I. (2002). Variation in EFL-ESL peer response. *TESL-EJ, 6*(3), 1–18. Retrieved April 3, 2010, from http://www.tesl-ej.org/wordpress/past-issues/volume6/ej23/ej23a1/

Liu, J., & Hansen, J. (2002). *Peer response in second language writing classrooms.* Ann Arbor: University of Michigan Press.

LoCastro, V. (1998, November). *Learner subjectivity and pragmatic competence development.* Paper presented at the Annual Conference of American Association for Applied Linguistics, Seattle, WA.

Mandala, S. (1999). Exiting advice. In L. Bouton (Ed.), *Pragmatics and language learning, 9* (pp. 89–111). Urbana-Champaign: University of Illinois.

Martinez-Flor, A., & Fukuya, Y. J. (2005). The effects of instruction on learners' production of appropriate and accurate suggestions. *System, 33,* 463–480.

Matsumoto, Y., Shimizu, T., Okano, H., & Kubo, M. (2004). Kizuki to sentaku [Notice and choice]. In *Gengogaku to nihongo kyouiku* [*Linguistics and Japanese language teaching*] (Vol. 3, pp. 41–58). Tokyo: Kuroshio.

Matsuura, H. (1998). Japanese EFL learners' perception of politeness in low imposition requests. *JALT Journal, 20,* 33–48.

McCarthy, M. (1990). *Vocabulary.* Oxford: Oxford University Press.

McNamara, T. F., & Roever, C. (2006). The social dimension of proficiency: How testable is it? In *Language testing: The social dimension* (pp. 43–79). Malden, MA: Blackwell.

Mendonca, C. O., & Johnson, K. E. (1994). Peer review negotiations: Revision activities in ESL writing instruction. *TESOL Quarterly, 28,* 745–769.

Morrow, C. (1995). *The pragmatic effects of instruction of ESL learners' production of complaint and refusal speech acts.* Unpublished doctoral dissertation, State University of New York at Buffalo.

Nelson, G., & Carson, J. (1998). ESL students' perceptions of effectiveness in peer response groups. *Journal of Second Language Writing, 7,* 113–131.

Netsu, M., & LoCastro, V. (1997). Opinion-giving and point of view in discussion tasks. *Proceedings of the 8th International University of Japan Conference on SLR,* 136–153.

Nguyen, M. (2005). *Criticizing and responding to criticism in a foreign language: A study of Vietnamese learners of English.* Unpublished doctoral dissertation, University of Auckland, New Zealand.

Nogami, Y. (2005). Learners' pragmatic awareness of softener use. In K. Bradford-Watts, C. Ikeguchi, & M. Swanson (Eds.), *JALT 2005 conference proceedings* (pp. 274–284). Tokyo: JALT.

Nogami, Y. (2006, May). *Complaining softly in Japanese and English.* Paper presented at the 2006 JALT PanSIG Conference, Tokai University, Tokyo.

O'Malley, J. M., & Valdez-Pierce, L. (1996). *Authentic assessment for English language learners: Practical approaches for teachers.* Reading, MA: Addison-Wesley.

Olshtain, E., & Cohen, A. D. (1989). Speech act behavior across languages. In H. W. Dechert & M. Raupach (Eds.), *Transfer in production* (pp. 53–67). Norwood, NJ: Ablex.

Pienemann, M., & Johnston, M. (1987). Factors influencing the development of language proficiency. In D. Nunan (Ed.), *Applying second language acquisition research* (pp. 45–141). Adelaide, Australia: National Curriculum Resource Center.

Richards, J. C., & Schmidt, R. W. (1983). *Language and communication.* Harlow, England: Longman.

Riddiford, N. (2007, April). *Raising awareness in L2 learning: Does instruction using authentic discourse make a difference?* Paper presented at the Social and Cognitive Aspects of Second Language Learning Conference, Auckland, New Zealand.

Rinnert, C. (1999). Appropriate requests in Japanese and English: A preliminary study. *Hiroshima Journal of International Studies, 5,* 163–176.

Rollinson, P. (2005). Using peer feedback in the ESL writing class. *ELT Journal, 59,* 23–30.

Rose, K. (1994). Pragmatic consciousness-raising in an EFL context. In L. F. Bouton (Ed.), *Pragmatics and language learning* (Vol. 5, pp. 52–63). Urbana-Champaign: University of Illinois.

Rose, K. (1997). Pragmatics in the classroom: Theoretical concerns and practical possibilities. In L. Bouton (Ed.), *Pragmatics and language learning, 8* (pp. 268–295). Urbana-Champaign: University of Illinois.

Rose, K. R. (2005). On the effects of instruction in second language pragmatics. *System, 33,* 385–399.

Ross, G. (Writer/Director). (1998). *Pleasantville* [Motion picture]. Los Angeles: New Line Cinema.

Saito-Stehberger, D. (2010). *Dan's ESL page.* Retrieved March, 14, 2010, from http://www.danasaito.de/pages/teachers.htm

Salsbury, T., & Bardovi-Harlig, K. (2000). Oppositional talk and the acquisition of modality in L2 English. In B. Swierzbin, F. Morris, M. E. Anderson, C. A. Klee, & E. Tarone (Eds.), *Social and cognitive factors in second language acquisition* (pp. 57–76). Somerville, MA: Cascadilla Press.

Schmidt, R. (1993). Conscious learning and interlanguage pragmatics. In G. Kasper & S. Blum-Kulka (Eds.), *Interlanguage pragmatics* (pp. 21–42). New York: Oxford University Press.

Schmidt, R. (2001). Attention. In P. Robinson (Ed.), *Cognition and second language instruction* (pp. 3–32). Cambridge: Cambridge University Press.

Searle, J. (1969). *Speech acts: An essay in the philosophy of language.* Cambridge: Cambridge University Press.

Siegal, M. (1996). The role of learner subjectivity in second language sociolinguistic competency: Western women learning Japanese. *Applied Linguistics, 17*(3), 356–382.

Soares, C. (1998, March). *Peer review methods for ESL writing improvement.* Paper presented at the 41st Annual TESOL Convention, Seattle, WA.

Springall, J. (2007). *Taking care—Trainer guide and DVD/CD pack.* Melbourne, Australia: Adult Migrant Education Services Victoria.

Swain, M. (1996). Three functions of output in second language learning. In G. Cook & B. Seidlhofer (Eds.), *Principle and practice in applied linguistics* (pp. 125–144). Oxford: Oxford University Press.

Takahashi, S. (2005). Noticing in task performance and learning outcomes: A qualitative analysis of instructional effects in interlanguage pragmatics. *System, 33*, 437–461.

Takahashi, T., & Beebe, L. M. (1993). Cross-linguistic influence in the speech act of correction. In G. Kasper & S. Blum-Kulka (Eds.), *Interlanguage pragmatics* (pp. 138–157). New York: Oxford University Press.

Takimoto, M. (2009). The effects of input-based tasks on the development of learners' pragmatic proficiency. *Applied Linguistics, 30,* 1–25.

Tateyama, Y., Kasper, G., Mui, L., Tay, H.-M., & Thananart, O. (1997). Explicit and implicit teaching of pragmatic routines. In L. Bouton (Ed.), *Pragmatics and language learning, 8* (pp. 163–177). Urbana-Champaign: University of Illinois.

Tatsuki, D., & Nishikawa, M. (2005). A comparison of compliments and compliment responses in television interviews, film and naturally occurring data. In D. Tatsuki (Ed.), *Pragmatics in language learning, theory and practice* (pp. 87–98). Tokyo: Japan Association for Language Teaching Pragmatics Special Interest Group.

Tedick, D. J. (2002). Proficiency-oriented language instruction and assessment: Standards, philosophies, and considerations for assessment. In D. J. Tedick (Ed.), *Proficiency-oriented language instruction and assessment: A curriculum handbook for teachers. CARLA working paper series* (pp. 9–48). Minneapolis: University of Minnesota, The Center for Advanced Research on Language Acquisition.

Trosborg, A. (1995). *Interlanguage pragmatics: Requests, complaints and apologies.* New York: Mouton de Gruyter.

Uso-Juan, E., & Martinez Flor, A. (2010). *Speech act performance: Theoretical, empirical, and methodological issues.* Amsterdam: John Benjamins.

Weiss, J. B. (Writer), & Danski, M. (Director). (2003). Colin the second [Television series episode]. In A. Ackerman (Producer), *Everwood.* Burbank, CA: Warner Bros. Television Network.

Weizman, E. (1989). Requestive hints. In S. Blum-Kulka, J. House, & G. Kasper (Eds.), *Cross-cultural pragmatics: Requests and apologies* (pp. 71–95). Norwood, NJ: Ablex.

Wierzbicka, A. (1991). *Cross-cultural pragmatics: The semantics of human interaction.* Berlin: Mouton de Gruyter.

Wigglesworth, G., & Yates, L. (2007). Mitigating difficult requests in the workplace: What learners and teachers need to know. *TESOL Quarterly, 41,* 791–803.

Yamanaka, E. (2003). Integrating language and content for acquisition of stress-handling factors of ICC. In S. Makino (Ed.), *The 11th Princeton Japanese Pedagogy Workshop Proceedings* (pp. 103–115). Princeton, NJ: Princeton University.

Yamanaka, E. (2004). *How to Talkpoint.* Retrieved January 23, 2010, from http://www.talkpoint.org/HowToTalkpoint.pdf

Yamashita, S. (1996). Six measures of JSL pragmatics. *Technical Report, 14.* Honolulu: University of Hawai'i .

Yates, L. (in press). Dinkas downunder: An evidence base for pragmatic instruction. *Pragmatics and Language Learning, 12.* Hawai'i: National Foreign Language Resource Center.

Yates, L., & Wigglesworth, G. (2005). Researching the effectiveness of professional development in pragmatics. In N. Bartels (Ed.), *Applied linguistics and language teacher education* (pp. 261–279). Amsterdam: Kluwer.

Index

Page numbers followed by *f* indicate figures.

A

C

L

M

N

S

T

U

W

Also Available From TESOL

TESOL Classroom Practice Series
Maria Dantas-Whitney, Sarah Rilling, and Lilia Savova, Series Editors

Authenticity in the Classroom and Beyond: Children and Adolescent Learners
Maria Dantas-Whitney and Sarah Rilling, Editors

Language Games: Innovative Activities for Teaching English
Maureen Snow Adrade, Editor

Authenticity in the Classroom and Beyond: Adult Learners
Sarah Rilling and Maria Dantas-Whitney, Editors

Adult Language Learners: Context and Innovation
Ann F. V. Smith and Gregory Strong, Editors

Applications of Task-Based Learning in TESOL
Ali Shehadeh and Christine Coombe, Editors

Explorations in Second Language Reading
Roger Cohen, Editor

Insights on Teaching Speaking in TESOL
Tim Stewart, Editor

Multilevel and Diverse Classrooms
Bradley Baurain and Phan Le Ha, Editors

Effective Second Language Writing
Susan Kasten, Editor

Integrating Language and Content
Jon Nordmeyer and Susan Barduhn

Using Textbooks Effectively
Lilia Savova, Editor

Classroom Management
Thomas S. C. Farrell, Editor

❋ ❋ ❋ ❋ ❋

Language Teacher Research Series
Thomas S. C. Farrell, Series Editor

Language Teacher Research in Africa
Leketi Makalela, Editor

Language Teacher Research in Asia
Thomas S. C. Farrell, Editor

Language Teacher Research in Europe
Simon Borg, Editor

Language Teacher Research in the Americas
Hedy McGarrell, Editor

Language Teacher Research in the Middle East
Christine Coombe and Lisa Barlow, Editors

Language Teacher Research in Australia and New Zealand
Jill Burton and Anne Burns, Editors

❋ ❋ ❋ ❋ ❋

Collaborative Partnerships Between ESL and Classroom Teachers Series
Debra Suarez, Series Editor

Helping English Language Learners Succeed in Pre-K–Elementary Schools
Jan Lacina, Linda New Levine, and Patience Sowa

Helping English Language Learners Succeed in Middle and High Schools
Faridah Pawan and Ginger Sietman, Editors

❋ ❋ ❋ ❋ ❋

CALL Environments: Research, Practice, and Critical Issues, 2nd ed.
Joy Egbert and Elizabeth Hanson-Smith, Editors

Learning Languages through Technology
Elizabeth Hanson-Smith and Sarah Rilling, Editors

Global English Teaching and Teacher Education: Praxis and Possibility
Seran Dogancay-Aktuna and Joel Hardman, Editors

Local phone: (240)646-7037
Fax: (301)206-9789
E-Mail: tesolpubs@brightkey.net
Toll-free: 1-888-891-0041
Mail Orders to TESOL, P.O. Box 79283, Baltimore, MD 21279-0283
ORDER ONLINE at www.tesol.org and click on "Bookstore"